FAMOUS MEN OF ROME AND GREECE

JOHN HAAREN

CONTENTS

FAMOUS MEN OF GREECE

FAMOUS MEN OF ROME

PREFACE

The study of history, like the study of a landscape, should begin with the most conspicuous features. Not until these have been fixed in memory will the lesser features fall into their appropriate places and assume their right proportions.

In order to attract and hold the child's attention, each conspicuous feature of history presented to him should have an individual for its center. The child identifies himself with the personage presented. It is not Romulus or Hercules or Cæsar or Alexander that the child has in mind when he reads, but himself, acting under the prescribed conditions.

Prominent educators, appreciating these truths, have long recognized the value of biography as a preparation for the study of history and have given it an important place in their scheme of studies.

The former practice in many elementary schools of beginning the detailed study of American history without any previous knowledge of general history limited the pupil's range of vision, restricted his sympathies, and left him without material for comparisons.

Moreover, it denied to him a knowledge of his inheritance from the Greek philosopher, the Roman lawgiver, the Teutonic lover of freedom. Hence the recommendation so strongly urged in the report of the Committee of Ten—and emphasized, also, in the report of the Committee of Fifteen—that the study of Greek, Roman and modern European history in the form of biography should precede the study of detailed American history in our elementary schools. The Committee of Ten recommends an eight years' course in history, beginning with the fifth year in school and continuing to the end of the high school course. The first two years of this course are given wholly to the study of biography and mythology. The Committee of Fifteen recommends that history be taught in all the grades of the elementary school and emphasizes the value of biography and of general history.

The series of historical stories to which this volume belongs was prepared in conformity with the foregoing recommendations and with the best practice of leading schools.

Teachers often find it impracticable to give to the study of mythology and biography a place of its own in an already overcrowded curriculum. In such cases they prefer to correlate history with reading and for this purpose the volumes of this series supply most desirable text-books. It has been the aim of the authors to make an interesting story of each man's life and to tell these stories in a style so simple that pupils in the lower grades will read them with pleasure, and so dignified that they may be used with profit as text-books for reading.

ROMULUS

I

Many, many years ago, in the pleasant land of Italy, there was a little city called Alba. It stood on the sunny side of a mountain, near the River Tiber and not far from the Mediterranean Sea. In this city and around the mountain lived a brave, intelligent people known as Latins. Several other tribes inhabited the adjacent mountains and plains.

The Latins were ruled by kings, and one of their kings in very early times was named Aeneas. He was a famous Trojan chief who had come over the seas to Italy and settled there with his family and friends after Troy was destroyed by the Greeks.

A great many years after the death of Aeneas one of his descendants named Procas was king of Alba. He ruled wisely and well for a long time, and his rather small kingdom on the mountain side, with its wheat-fields and vineyards, was very prosperous. He had two sons, one named Numitor, and the other Amulius. As Numitor was the elder he was heir to his father's throne, but when King Procas died Amulius seized the kingdom by force and made himself king.

Then Numitor, with his two children, a boy and a girl, left the king's palace at Alba and went to reside on a farm a short distance away.

II

Amulius was now king, but he did not feel quite happy. He was much troubled about Numitor's son and daughter. The son, he thought, might some day claim the right to be king as heir of his father, or the daughter might marry and have a son who could become king as grandchild of Numitor.

To prevent either of these things from happening Amulius had Numitor's son secretly put to death, and he appointed the daughter Sylvia to be a priestess, or an attendant, in the temple of the goddess Vesta. Only young girls were appointed attendants in this temple, and they had to take a vow that they would not marry for thirty years. They were called Vestal Virgins. It was their duty to keep a fire burning continually on the altar of the goddess. This was called the Sacred Fire, and it was believed that if it went out some great disaster would happen to the city.

Amulius now thought there was nothing to hinder him from being king of Alba all his life. But one day the god Mars came down to the city from his palace on a high mountain top and saw Sylvia as she went out of the temple to get water at a well. He fell deeply in love with her. She also fell in love with the god, for he had the appearance of a handsome young man. They were married secretly, and in course of time Sylvia had beautiful twin boys. When Amulius heard of this he gave orders that Sylvia should be put to death for breaking her vow and that the two infants should be thrown into the

6

Tiber. These wicked orders were carried out, for no one dared to disobey the king.

Fortunately, however, the babes had been placed in a stout basket, which floated along the Tiber until it was carried by the waters to the foot of a hill called Palatine Hill. Here the huge roots of a wild fig-tree upset the basket, and the little ones were thrown out upon the river bank.

At this moment a great she-wolf came strolling down the hill to drink at the river's edge. She heard the feeble cries of the infants and went to the place where they lay helpless on the wet sands. She touched them gently with her rough paws, turned them over and licked their faces and plump bodies. Perhaps she thought they were some of her own cubs. At any rate, she carried the babes up the hill to her cave under a large rock. There she fed them as she fed her own cubs and seemed pleased to have them near her. It is said that a woodpecker flew in and out of the cave many times a day, bringing berries for the boys to eat.

One morning, as Faustulus, the herdsman of King Amulius, was going over Palatine Hill looking for cattle that had gone astray he saw the boys playing with the wolf at the mouth of her cave. He frightened the wolf away and took the boys to his home. His wife pitied the little foundlings and cared for them as though they were her own children.

The herdsman named them Romulus and Remus. They grew up to be strong, handsome youths, brave and kind. Until they were twenty years old they lived with the herdsman and helped him in his work, and roamed over the hills light-hearted and free.

During all these years Numitor lived on his farm, and his brother Amulius remained king of Alba. Numitor did not know that his two grandsons had been saved from a watery grave and were liviing so near to him.

But one day Remus had a quarrel with some of the herdsmen of Numitor and they took him prisoner. They then brought him before Numitor, who was much impressed with the noble appearance of the youth and asked him who he was.

Remus told all he knew about himself and Romulus; how they had been found at the cave of the she-wolf and had been reared by the king's herdsman. Just then Faustulus and Romulus came searching for Remus, and were full of joy when they found that no harm had come to him. Numitor questioned the herdsman about the finding of the twins, and after hearing his story was convinced that Romulus and Remus were Sylvia's boys, who had been strangely saved from the wrath of their cruel uncle. He was very happy at finding his grandsons and he thanked the herdsman for his good care of them.

Romulus and Remus were also very happy at finding a grandfather and at the sudden change of their fortune. When they were told about Amulius and his wicked deeds, they resolved to punish him for the murder of their mother. So with a few followers they rushed to the palace at Alba and entered the king's chamber.

"Behold! we are Sylvia's sons whom you thought you had killed," they shouted to Amulius, as he started up in alarm at their entrance. "You killed our mother and you shall die for it."

Before he could utter a word they sprang on him with drawn swords and cut his head off. Then they brought Numitor to the palace, and the people welcomed him as the rightful king of Alba.

III

After a little time the two brothers thought they would build a city on Palatine Hill, where the she-wolf

8

had nursed them. So they went to the hill and selected a site. Then they began to talk of a name for their city.

"I will be king and give the new city my name," said Romulus.

"No," cried Remus. "I will be the king and name the city after myself. I have just as much right as you have."

So the brothers argued for a while, but at last they agreed to settle the matter in this way:

At midnight Romulus was to stand on Palatine Hill, and Remus was to stand on another hill a short distance off. Then they were to ask the gods to show them a sign of favor in the sky, and the first who should see anything very remarkable was to name the new city and be its king.

So they went to watch, but nothing appeared until sunrise of the second day, when Remus saw six great vultures flying across the sky from north to south. He ran swiftly to Palatine Hill and told Romulus of what he had seen. But just then twelve vultures, one after another, flew high over the head of Romulus in an almost unbroken line and were soon lost to view.

Then Romulus claimed that he had the favor of the gods, as more birds had appeared to him, but Remus claimed that the gods favored him, as the birds had appeared to him first. Romulus asked the opinion of some of his friends, and as they all agreed that he was right in his claim he paid no further attention to Remus, but began to lay out the new city. He gave it the name of Roma, or Rome, after himself. With a plow he marked out the space on Palatine Hill and along the banks of the Tiber, and he built a low wall round about to protect the city from invaders.

One day while the work was going on Remus came by in a very bitter mood. He was still angry with Romulus. He laughed scornfully at the little wall and said to his brother:

"Shall such a defence as this keep your city? It may

prevent children from getting in, but not men, for they can jump over it."

So saying, Remus put his hands on the wall and sprang over it, to show that his words were true. Romulus, in a sudden outburst of rage, struck him on the head with a spade and instantly killed him, at the same time crying out:

"So perish any one who shall hereafter attempt to leap over my wall."

Then Romulus continued his work. While he was building his wall he also built some houses. The first houses were nothing more than wood huts covered with mud and straw. But in course of time the Romans had houses of stone, and they built fine temples and theatres and streets and squares, and at last Rome became the greatest and grandest city in the whole world.

IV

Romulus founded Rome in the year 753 B.C. After he had built his city he had some difficulty in getting people to live in it. He had only a few followers and was not able to obtain any more. He decided, therefore, to make Rome a place of refuge, to which people who had got into trouble in other countries might come for safety.

And so when those who had committed crime in other places, and had to flee to escape punishment, found out that Romulus would give them a refuge, they came in large numbers to his city. People also came who had been driven from home by enemies, or had run away for one reason or another. It was not long, therefore, until Rome was full of men. There were men from many different tribes and countries. Thus the Roman nation began, and for years it steadily grew and prospered.

But the Romans were much troubled about one

thing. A great many of them had no wives, and they could not get any, because the women of the neighboring tribes would not marry them, for the Romans had a bad name. Romulus was very anxious that his people should have good wives, but how they should get them greatly puzzled him for a long time. At last he hit upon a plan and began at once to carry it out.

He sent messengers to the cities all around to announce that on a certain day a great festival in honor of the god Jupiter would be held on the plain in front of Rome. There were to be games, combats, horse-racing, and other sports. The people were invited to attend the festival and also to take part in the contests for the prizes.

When the festival day came a multitude of men and women from far and near assembled before the walls of Rome. Hundreds of pretty girls were there in fine dresses. A great many came from the Sabine tribe. This was a tribe of warriors that lived on a mountain near Rome.

Suddenly Romulus blew a loud blast upon a horn. Then, quick as a flash, the Romans seized the girls and bore them off to Rome.

The Sabines were greatly enraged at this, and their king, Titus Tatius, raised a large army and at once began a war against the Romans. The war went on for three years, but the Sabines were so strong that Romulus could not defeat them in the field. He therefore withdrew his army into the city. King Tatius quickly marched after him, resolved to take Rome or perish in the attempt.

Now Romulus had erected a strong fortress on a hill near the Palatine, to keep invaders from Rome. The hill was called the Saturnian Hill, and the fortress was in charge of a brave Roman captain, who had a daughter named Tarpeia.

When the Sabines reached this fortress they could go

no further. They marched up and down seeking for a spot where they might force an entrance, but they could find none. There was a small, barred gate in the fortress, and through this gate Tarpeia came out to get water. King Tatius saw her. He at once stepped forward and said:

"Fair maiden, open the gate and let us in. If you do you shall have for your reward anything you ask."

Tarpeia was gazing with admiration at the bracelets of gold which the Sabines wore on their arms.

"I will open the gate," said she, "if you will give me some of those things which your soldiers wear upon their arms."

King Tatius agreed, and Tarpeia opened the gate. As the Sabines strode past the silly maiden each threw at her, not his bracelet, but his shield.

The shield then used was round or oblong and made of bronze, or of wicker-work or ox-hide covered with metal plates. It had two handles at the back, and the soldier held it with his left hand and arm so that he could move it up or down to save his head or breast from blows.

Tarpeia stood in amazement as the heavy shields began to pile up around her. One struck her, and then another and another. At last she fell to the ground and was soon crushed to death.

When the soldiers saw that Tarpeia was dead, they took up the shields they had thrown at her. Then they hurled her body from the top of a great rock that was near the gate she had opened. The rock was afterwards known as the Tarpeian Rock, and for hundreds of years the punishment for traitors in Rome was to be thrown from this rock.

As soon as they passed the fortress the Sabines ran down the Saturnian Hill to make an attack on Rome. But Romulus and his band of warriors bravely came out of the city to drive back the enemy. The two forces met in the valley, and then a fierce battle began.

But while they were fighting a crowd of excited women came running from the city. They were the Sabine women whom the Romans had carried off. Some of them had their infants in their arms and they rushed between the lines of soldiers and begged that the fight should stop.

"Do not fight any more for us," they said to their fathers and brothers. "We love the Romans we have married. They have been good to us, and we do not wish to leave them."

Of course, this settled the matter. Romulus had a talk with King Tatius, and they agreed not to fight any more. They also agreed that the two nations should be as one. They joined their governments and their armies, and each of the kings had equal power.

Soon afterwards King Tatius died. Then Romulus ruled alone for nearly forty years. He was a wise and just king, and did a great deal of good for his people. He established a body called the Senate, to help him in important affairs of government. It was called the Senate from *senex*, the Latin word for an *old man*. It was formed of the chiefs or *old men* of the earliest settlers in Rome. The descendants of those settlers were called *patricians*, or fathers, from the Latin word *pater*, a father. They were the nobles, or upper class, in Rome. The ordinary citizens were called *plebeians*, from *plebs*, the Latin word for the *common people*.

Romulus took care to train up the young Romans to be good soldiers. Outside the city, along the bank of the Tiber, there was a great plain which in later times was called Campus Martius, or Field of Mars. Here the Roman soldiers were drilled. They were taught how to use the spear and the javelin and the sword and the shield. They were also exercised in running and jumping, and wrestling and swimming, and carrying heavy loads. Thus the young men were made fit to bear the hardships of war and to fight and win battles for their country.

It is related that in his old age Romulus suddenly disappeared from the earth. He called his people together on a great field one day, and while he was speaking to them a violent storm came on. The rain fell in torrents, and the lightning and thunder were so terrible that the people fled to their homes.

When the storm was over the people went back to the field, but Romulus was nowhere to be found. Then it was said that his father, the god Mars, had taken him up to the clouds in a golden chariot.

Next morning at early dawn a Roman citizen named Julius saw a figure descending from the heavens. It had the appearance of Romulus, and it approached Julius and said:

"Go and tell my people that it is the will of the gods that Rome shall be the greatest city of the world. Let them be brave and warlike, and no human power shall be able to conquer them."

Afterwards the Romans worshiped Romulus as a god. They worshiped him under the name Quirinus, which was one of the names of the god Mars, and they built a temple to him on a hill which was called the Quirinal Hill.

NUMA POMPILIUS

I

For a year after the disappearance of Romulus there was no king of Rome. The city was ruled by the Senate. But the people were not satisfied. They preferred to be ruled by one man, and, though they had the right to elect a king themselves they left the choice to the Senate. The Senate chose Numa Pompilius, a very good and wise man, who belonged to the nation of the Sabines.

The first thing that Numa did after learning that he had been chosen king was to consult the augurs, to find out if it was the will of the gods that he should be the ruler of Rome.

The augurs were what we should call fortune-tellers. A number of them lived in Rome. They were much respected and occupied a large temple at the expense of the public. They pretended that by watching the sky and observing how birds and animals acted they could tell what would happen to people and to nations. Then when they were alone they would have a great deal of fun over the tricks they played upon the foolish people.

Numa made many important changes at the very beginning of his rule. Before he came to the throne Roman young men were brought up to no business but war. It was considered disgraceful for a Roman citizen, whether rich or poor, to work at any trade or manufacture. The slaves, who were persons taken prisoners in wars, did all the hard work. They made all the clothing, tools, arms, and household articles. They cooked and served the meals, and were general servants for the Roman families. Roman citizens might, however, without being degraded work on farms and vineyards, and many of them made their living in this way.

Shortly after King Numa began his reign he divided some of the public lands into small farms and gave one of these farms to every poor Roman. The public lands were lands that belonged to the nation and not to private persons.

It was rather hard at first for the new-made farmers to be contented on their farms and to do good work. They were mostly soldiers and had very little knowledge of anything except marching and fighting. But it was not long before they began to understand what a blessing it is to be self-supporting and independent. Their little farms were pleasant homes. They began to love their new life and soon were able to raise enough for the support of themselves and their families, with something to spare.

II

King Numa made many good laws. These laws were engraved on tablets of brass and at certain times were read and explained to the people by lawyers.

Numa was very friendly with the people of the countries surrounding Rome. He gave them help in times of trouble, and would never listen to any talk of war with them. During the many years that he was king Rome had no enemies and no wars.

In a sacred grove, just outside the walls of Rome, there lived in a handsome grotto, or cavern, a beautiful woman named Egeria. Some persons called her a goddess, while others thought she was a fairy. She seemed to have a great knowledge of magic and could do wonderful things. Whenever she called to the song-birds they would come flying around her. They would also perch on her head and shoulders and hands, and sing their sweetest songs. Even the fierce animals of the woods were her friends, and great bears and wolves would lie at her feet for hours and purr like cats.

This mysterious woman-goddess, or fairy, or whatever she was, greatly loved and honored good King Numa, and at last they were married. Then she taught him many of the magical secrets she possessed. He carefully studied the lessons she gave him, and in time he was able to do wonderful things himself.

III

The Romans were earnest worshipers of the gods and goddesses. They believed that there were many such beings, and they had many grand temples for religious service.

King Numa always paid great attention to religion. He appointed a large number of officials to take care of the temples, and to see that all the sacred ceremonies were properly carried out. He was constant and faithful in his own worship and thus, by his example, gradually induced the whole Roman people to become attentive to their religion.

The greatest of the gods that the Romans believed in was the god Jupiter. He was supposed to rule both the sky and the earth. He was so powerful that he could send thunderbolts from the heavens, and make the earth tremble by his nod. He had a wife named Juno who had a great deal to do with managing the affairs of the earth. It was at one time believed that Jupiter resided with many other gods on the top of a high mountain in Greece. This mountain was so thickly covered by clouds that the gods could not be seen. But they could see everything that took place on the earth.

Jupiter had two brothers named Neptune and Pluto. Neptune was the god of the sea. He lived in a grand, golden palace at the bottom of the Mediterranean. He ruled everything under and upon the waters of the world. Now and then he sailed over the ocean in a grand chariot drawn by large fish called dolphins. When he was angry he caused the sea to rise in huge waves.

Pluto, the other brother of Jupiter, was the god of Hades, or the land of the dead. His home was far down in the earth, where all was dark and gloomy. The Romans believed that when people died they were borne away to the gloomy kingdom of Pluto.

The other principal gods were Mars, Mercury, Vulcan, Apollo, and Janus.

Mars was the god of war, and was especially honored in Rome because it was believed that he was the father of Romulus. Certain days of the year were made festival days in his honor, and tben there were splendid processions, songs of praise, and religious dances.

Mercury, the son of Jupiter, was the god of eloquence and commerce. He was also the messenger of the other gods. He was generally represented as flying swiftly through the air, carrying messages from place to place. On his head and feet were small wings, and in his hand he bore a golden staff with serpents twined around it.

Vulcan was a skillful worker in metals. He had a great forge in the heart of a burning mountain, where he made wonderful things of iron, copper, and gold. He looked after the welfare of blacksmiths, coppersmiths, and goldsmiths, and was their special god.

Apollo, also called Phoebus, which meant the sun, was the god of day. He gave light and heat to the world. He was also the god of music, archery, and medicine. His sister Diana was the moon goddess or goddess of the night. She was also the goddess of hunting. In pictures she is sometimes represented with a quiver of arrows over her shoulder and holding a stag by the horns.

The god Janus was very much honored by the Romans. It was believed that this god presided over the beginning of every undertaking, and so when the Romans began any important work or business they prayed first to Janus. For this reason the first month or beginning of the year was called the month of Janus, or *January*. Janus was also the god of gates and doors. In statuary and pictures he is often shown with two faces looking in opposite directions, because every door faces two ways—outward and inward.

Numa Pompilius built a temple in honor of Janus. The door of this temple was always open in time of war, as a sign that the god had gone out to help the Romans. In time of peace the door was shut.

The Romans also believed in Venus, the goddess of love; Minerva, the goddess of wisdom; Flora, the goddess of flowers, and many others.

The Romans had no special day, such as our Sunday, for religious service, but their temples (except the temple of Janus) were open every day. They had prayers and songs, and sometimes what they called sacred dances. They also made offerings to the gods, such as fruits or vegetables, and oxen, lambs, or goats. The offerings went finally into the hands of the priests of the temples.

Numa Pompilius reigned for nearly half a century, and under him the Romans were a peaceful, prosperous, and happy people.

THE HORATII AND THE CURIATII

I

The third king of Rome was Tullus Hostilius. In his reign a remarkable combat took place between three Roman brothers and three Latin brothers. The combat came about in this way:

For years the people of Rome and the people of Alba, also called Latins, as has been already said, were continually quarreling. They would invade and plunder each other's lands. At last, after many petty contests, war was declared between the two nations.

King Tullus marched the Roman army to the border of Alba, but here his progress was stopped by a great force of Latins, under the command of Mettius, the Alban king.

Tullus looked at the strong lines of Latin soldiers, standing firm and resolute to resist the advance of the Romans, and thought that it might be well to have a talk with Mettius to see whether they could not agree on some way of settling the quarrel without a fight between the two armies. So he sent for Mettius and they talked the matter over. Mettius also wished very much to avoid a battle, and he said to Tullus:

"Would it not be well to fight in such a way that only a few of our soldiers would be killed instead of many? My plan is this: You shall select three of the best fighting men in the Roman army, and I will select the best three in the army of Alba. The six men shall fight in the presence of the two armies. If the Romans win Alba will submit to Rome; but if the Latins win then Rome must submit to Alba. What say you to the plan?"

"It is a good one," said King Tullus, "and I agree to it. May the best men win!"

With these words they separated, and went to prepare for the combat on which was to depend the fate of the two nations.

II

The Romans selected as their champions three brothers belonging to a family known as the Horatius family. The brothers were called the Horatii because this word is the plural form of Horatius. The Horatii brothers were tall, handsome men, with wonderful strength, endurance, and courage.

The Albans also selected three brothers as their champions. They were called the Curiatii. They were bold, skillful soldiers, famous for manly beauty and strength, and were champions well worthy to fight for a nation.

When all was ready the Horatii and the Curiatii advanced to the centre of a large field and took their places. They carried short, thick swords and large, round shields made of stout leather and metal. The two armies gathered around the six champions, but at a distance, so as to leave them plenty of room to fight.

There was silence for a few moments, and then the shrill notes of a trumpet rang out as a signal for the battle. Clash! clang! went the swords upon the shields, and the fight began.

Quick, skillful blows were given for a short time, but no one was seriously hurt. Suddenly the Latins shouted in intense excitement. Lo! one of the Horatii, after a fierce struggle with one of the Curiatii, was stricken down dead! The Romans groaned, hung their heads, and looked in anxious doubt at their remaining two champions.

Bravely the Horatii stood—two to three—and fought with all their might. Step by step they drove the Curiatii back across the field. Cheers rang out from the Romans at this heroic effort. The victory might yet be theirs!

But alas! one of the Curiatii, with a swift, sly sword-thrust, killed another of the Horatii. Then the Latins shouted:

"We have won! We have won! We have won! Hail to the brave Curiatii!"

The Romans were wild with grief and rage. They had now but one champion left—Horatius, the last of the heroic Horatii—and he was running from the field, as if he had given up the fight. He was followed by the Curiatii, though they were all wounded. One of them, running ahead of the others, came up to Horatius and was raising his sword when the Roman turned upon him quickly and slew him.

The cries of the two armies were now hushed, as if by magic. All eyes were upon the champions, and there was a painful silence.

Another of the Curiatii now came up and began to fight Horatius. But the Roman met the attack with great coolness and skill, and soon killed the second Latin. Thus, under the pretence of running away, Horatius separated the Curiatii and slew two of them. Then he advanced in a furious manner on the other Latin and began a desperate fight with him. Soon he struck him down with a deadly blow. Rome was victorious! From the whole Roman army now came the cry, as if from one man:

"Hail to the brave Horatius! Hail to the champion and savior of his country!"

Then they seized Horatius in their arms and bore him in triumph to King Tullus, who placed on his head the laurel wreath of victory. This was one of the ways by which the Romans honored any of their soldiers who had been very brave in battle. But they also honored Horatius by erecting a statue of him in one of the temples of the city.

III

With songs of joy the army marched back to Rome. Horatius walked by the side of the king. A throng of women came forth from the gates of the city, eager to greet the soldiers and to rejoice with them over the great victory. The sister of Horatius was in the throng. She had been secretly engaged to be married to one of the Curiatii, for the Romans and Albans were near neighbors and frequently visited one another in times of peace. When she learned that her brother had slain her lover she began to weep bitterly. Then pointing at Horatius she cried out:

"You have killed my lover. Do not come near me. I hate and curse you."

Horatius, in a fit of anger, suddenly drew his sword and stabbed her to the heart. As she fell dead at his feet he cried in a loud voice:

"So perish the Roman maiden who weeps for her country's enemy!"

For this shocking murder Horatius was tried and sentenced to death. But the people would not allow the sentence to be carried out. He was made to do a certain penance for the crime and afterwards was set free.

THE TARQUINS

I

The next king of Rome was Ancus Marcius. He was a grandson of Numa Pompilius, and a very good king. He thought that it would be an advantage to Rome to have a sea harbor for ships. So he founded a city at one of the mouths of the Tiber, on the coast of the Mediterranean, about fifteen miles from Rome. The city was called Ostia, which is a Latin word meaning *mouths*. Latin was the language spoken by the Roman people.

During the reign of Ancus Marcius, a rich man named Lucumo came to live in Rome. He came from Tarquinii, a town some miles distant from Rome, in a district or country called Etruria, so the Romans called him Tarquinius, which in English is Tarquin.

A very wonderful thing happened to Tarquin while he was on his way to Rome. He drove in a chariot, with his wife Tanaquil seated beside him, and their servants following behind. As they were approaching the city an eagle which appeared in the sky above them came gently down and snatched the cap from Tarquin's head with its beak. After hovering around for a few moments the eagle replaced the cap and with loud screams flew away.

Tarquin was much surprised at this strange event. He did not know what to think of it. But Tanaquil was much pleased. She said to her husband that it was a sign sent by the gods and meant that he was to be a great man—perhaps a king.

Tarquin was not long in Rome before he became a favorite with everybody. The people liked him because he spent a great deal of money in doing good. The king also liked him and often asked his advice in affairs of government, for Tarquin was a man of great knowledge and wisdom. And when King Ancus became old and felt that his death was near, he appointed Tarquin the guardian of his two sons who were then but boys.

Soon afterwards Ancus died, and the people elected Tarquin king. He reigned for nearly forty years and did a great deal for the good of the city.

II

It was King Tarquin who began the building of the famous temple of Jupiter on the Saturnian Hill—the same hill on which stood the fortress that Romulus built. While the workmen were digging for the foundations of the temple they found a man's head so well preserved that it looked as if it had been buried quite recently. This was so strange a thing that the augurs were asked about it, and they said it was a sign that Rome would become the *head* or chief city of the world. So the new building was called the Capitol, from *caput,* the Latin word for *head,* and the hill was called the Capitoline Hill. This has given our language a word. We call the building in which our Congress meets—as well as that in which a state legislature meets—the Capitol.

It took a long time to finish the Capitol, but when finished it was a great and beautiful building. It covered more than eight acres. Its gates or doors were of solid brass, thickly plated with gold. The walls inside were all marble, ornamented with beautiful figures engraved in silver.

Tarquin also began several other works in Rome, which were too great and costly to be finished in a lifetime. One of them was a wall round the city. The wall that Romulus made was only round Palatine Hill. But since then the city had been much enlarged. In course of time it covered seven hills. This is why Rome is often called the seven-hilled city. The seven hills were the Palatine, the Capitoline, the Cælian, the Quirinal, the Esquiline, the Viminal, and the Aventine.

One of the other things Tarquin did was to establish a kind of police called *lictors*. These were officers who always walked before the king whenever he appeared in public. Each lictor bore upon his shoulder an ax enclosed in a bundle of rods tied with a red strap. This was called the *fasces* . It was a mark of the power of the king. The ax meant that the king might order criminals to be beheaded, and the rods meant that he might punish offenders by flogging.

Another work of Tarquin was the Circus, afterwards called the Circus Maximus (*great circus*). This was a place where horse-races and games and shows of various kinds were held. The Romans were very fond of such amusements. Great numbers of them always went to the shows, but it was easy for them to go, for they did not have to pay for admission. The cost of the shows was paid often by rich Romans who wanted to gain the favor of the people, and often by the government.

The circus had no roof, but there were a great many

seats all round and in the middle was a large open space for the performers. This space was covered with sand, and was called the *arena*, a word which is Latin for *sand*.

As so many people attended the circus it had to be very large. In the time when Rome was an empire, about which you will read later on in this book, the Circus Maximus was so large that it contained seats for 250,000 people. From the circus and arena of the Romans these words have come into use in our own language.

III

Besides building a circus, King Tarquin also greatly improved the Forum by making covered walks or porticoes all round it. The Forum was a large open space at the foot of the Capitoline Hill, where public meetings were held, and where people came to hear the news or talk about politics. It was also used as a market-place, and merchants showed their goods in shops or stores along the porticoes. In course of time great buildings were erected round the Forum. There were courts of justice and temples and statues and monuments of various kinds. The Senate House, where the Senate held its meetings, was also in the Forum. From the end of the Forum next the Capitoline Hill there was a passage leading up to the Capitol.

But the most useful thing King Tarquin did was the building of a great sewer through the city and into the Tiber. Before his time there were no sewers in Rome, though the places between the hills were swampy and wet. This made many parts of the city very unhealthy. Tarquin's sewer drained the swamps and carried the water into the river. It crossed the entire city. It was so high and wide that men could sail into it in boats, and it was so strongly built that it has lasted to the present time. The great sewer is still in use.

Tarquin wanted very much to change one of the laws about the army, but an augur named Attius Navius told him such a thing could not be done without a sign from the gods. This made the king angry, and he thought he would try to show that the augurs had not the power or knowledge they were supposed to have, so he said to Attius:

"Come, now, I will give you a question. I am thinking whether a certain thing I have in my mind can be done or not. Go and find out from your signs if it can be done."

Navius went away, and shortly afterwards returned and told the king that the thing could be done. Then Tarquin said:

"Well, I was thinking whether or not you could cut this stone in two with this razor. As you say it can be done, do it."

Navius took the razor and immediately cut the stone in two with the greatest ease. The king never again doubted the power of the augurs.

IV

On the death of Tarquin his son-in-law Servius Tullius was made king. Tarquin had two young sons, and the sons of Ancus Marcius were also living; but the people preferred to have Servius Tullius for their king.

Servius was a very good king. He had many good laws made and, like King Numa Pompilius, he divided some of the public lands among the poor people of the city.

One of the important things Servius did was to finish the wall round the city which Tarquin had begun. This wall was very high. It was made of stone and earth, and on the outside there was a ditch a hundred feet wide and thirty feet deep. There were several gates in the wall, but they were all well guarded night and day by soldiers, so that no enemy could enter.

King Servius was the first to have a census taken in Rome. He made a rule or law that once every five years all the people should assemble in the Campus Martius to be counted. The word *census* is a Latin word, meaning a *counting* or reckoning, and so we use it in our own country for the counting of the people which takes place every ten years.

Servius Tullius was killed by King Tarquin's son, who was also called Tarquin but got the name of Superbus, or Proud, because he was a very haughty and cruel man. The dead body of Servius was left lying on the street where he had been killed, and Tullia, wife of the wicked Tarquin and daughter of the murdered king, drove her chariot over it.

Tarquin the Proud now became king. It was during his reign that the Sibylline Books were brought to Rome. These books were not like our books. They were merely three bundles of loose pieces of parchment, having moral sentences on them written in the Greek language. This is the story of how the books were obtained:

One morning an old woman came to King Tarquin, carrying nine books in her hands. She offered to sell them to the king, but when she named a large sum as the price he laughed at her and ordered her away. The next day the woman came again, but with only six books. She had burned the other three. She offered to sell the six, but she asked the same price that she had asked the day before for the whole nine. The king again laughed at her and drove her away.

The same day Tarquin went to visit the augurs in their temple, and he told them about the old woman and her books. The augurs declared that she was certainly a sibyl and that her books doubtless contained important predictions about Rome.

The sibyls were women who pretended to be able to foretell events. There were sibyls in many countries, but the most famous of them all was the Sibyl of Cumæ, a town in the south of Italy. This was the sibyl who brought the books to Tarquin.

Tarquin was now sorry he had not taken the books, and he hoped the woman would come again. She did come on the following day, but she had only three books instead of six. She had burned the other three the day before. The king was very glad to see her, and he bought the remaining three books, but he had to pay just as much for them as the old woman had asked at first for the nine. Then the Sibyl disappeared, and was never seen again.

The ordinary books the Romans had were not like the Sibylline Books. They had no printed books, for printing was not known for many centuries after. Their books were written with pens made of reeds. Their paper was made of the pith of a plant called the *papyrus*, and from this name the word *paper* is derived. To make a book they cut the paper into leaves or pages, and after writing on them they pasted the pages one to another sidewise until all the pages of one book were put together. This long strip was made into a cylindrical roll, and was called a *volume*, from the Latin word *volumen*, a roll. When the volume was being read it was held in both hands, the reader unrolling it with one hand and rolling it with the other.

The Sibylline Books were put in the temple of Jupiter on the Capitoline Hill. Two officers were appointed to keep watch over them. Whenever the Romans were going to war, or had any serious trouble, they would consult the books. The way they did it was this: one of the officers would open the stone chest where the books were kept and take out the first piece of parchment he laid his hand on. Then the Greek sentence found on the piece would be translated into Latin. It was sometimes very hard to tell what the sentence really meant. Often they had to guess. When they made sense out of it they said that it was a prophecy of the Sibyl and would surely come to pass.

JUNIUS BRUTUS

I

Tarquin the Proud had a nephew named Junius Brutus. He seemed to be a simpleton, but he was really a very wise man. His brother had been murdered by the king, and he feared the same fate himself, so he pretended to be half-witted and went about saying and doing silly things. Tarquin therefore did him no harm, but rather pitied him.

Two sons of Tarquin once went to a noted fortune-teller, taking Brutus with them. The young men asked several questions. One was:

"Who shall rule Rome after Tarquin?"

The fortune-teller gave this answer:

"Young men, whichever of you shall first kiss your mother shall be the next ruler of Rome."

The king's sons at once started for home, each eager to be the first to kiss his mother. But Brutus thought that something else was really meant by the answer. So after they had left the fortune-teller he managed to stumble and fall on his face. Then he kissed the ground, saying,

"The earth is the true mother of us all." And as we shall see, Brutus became the next ruler of Rome.

II

The eldest son of Tarquin was named Sextus. He was a very bad man. He deeply injured a beautiful woman named Lucretia, the wife of Collatinus, his cousin. Lucretia told her husband and father and Junius Brutus of what Sextus had done and called upon them to punish him for his wicked deed. Then she plunged a dagger into her breast and fell dead. Brutus drew the dagger from her bleeding body and, holding it up before his horrified companions, exclaimed:

"I vow before the gods to avenge the wronged Lucretia. Not one of the Tarquins shall ever again be king in Rome. Rome shall have no more kings."

They all vowed with Brutus that Lucretia should be avenged and that there should be no more kings in Rome. Then they took up her body and carried it to the Forum. There they showed it to the people, who gathered around in horror at the sight. Brutus no longer appeared dull and simple, but stood with head erect and flashing eyes and spoke to the crowd in eloquent, stirring words.

"See what has come from the evil deeds of the Tarquins!" he shouted, pointing to the dead woman. "Let us free ourselves from the rule of these wicked men. Down with Tarquin the tyrant! No more kings in Rome!"

The people were much excited by his speech, and they made the Forum ring with their cries: "Down with Tarquin! Down with Tarquin! No more kings! No more kings!"

Then they resolved to take the power of king away from Tarquin and to banish him and his family from Rome. They also decided to adopt the good laws which had been made years before by King Servius Tullius, and to choose two men each year to govern the nation, instead of a king. The men were to be called consuls and were to rule in turn—one for one month, the other for the next, and so on for twelve months. At the end of the year two new consuls were to be elected.

Meanwhile news of the revolt reached King Tarquin, who was at the time in camp with his army some distance from Rome. He instantly mounted his horse and rode in haste to the city. When he reached the gates he found them shut against him. As he stood impatiently demanding to be admitted, a Roman officer appeared on the wall and told him of the sentence of banishment. Tarquin rode away, and Rome was rid of him forever (510 B.C.).

III

The people elected Junius Brutus and Lucius Collatinus, the husband of Lucretia, to be their first consuls; but after a short time Collatinus resigned, because he was himself a Tarquin. Publius Valerius was elected in his stead.

Tarquin now sent messengers for his household goods and other things belonging to him which were in Rome. The messengers while in the city had secret meetings with a number of young men of noble families, and a plot was formed to restore Tarquin to the throne.

The young nobles vowed that they would destroy the new republic and bring back the king, for they did not like government by the common people. But while they were making their plans an intelligent slave overheard what they were saying. This slave went to Brutus and told him of the plot. All engaged in it were at once arrested and put in prison. Two sons of Brutus himself, Titus and Tiberius, were found among the plotters.

When Brutus learned that his own children were

traitors he was overcome with sorrow. For several days he shut himself up in his house and would see no one. But when the day for the trial came he did his duty sternly as judge—the consuls being judges as well as rulers. Titus and Tiberius were proved guilty of treason, together with the others, and Brutus sentenced them to be whipped with rods and then beheaded. He even was a witness of the execution of the sentence, and we are told that he sat unmoved in his chair and did not turn away his eyes while his two sons were put to death. It was his duty to punish traitors, and he did his duty without sparing his own flesh and blood.

After the loss of his sons Brutus became dull and melancholy and appeared to care very little for life. Tarquin made an attempt to take Rome, with the aid of the people of two cities of Etruria, and Brutus led the Romans to the field to fight against their former king. During the first part of the battle, a son of Tarquin rode furiously at Brutus to kill him. Brutus saw him and advanced rapidly on his horse to meet the attack. When they came together each ran his spear through the body of the other, and both were killed.

The death of Brutus maddened the Romans, and they fought fiercely until dark. Then the armies went to their camps, and no one knew which side had won. But in the middle of the night a loud voice came from a wood close by the camp of the Etruscans, as the people of Etruria were called. The voice said:

"One man more has fallen on the side of the Etruscans than on the side of the Romans; the Romans will conquer in this war."

The Etruscans believed that this was the voice of the god Jupiter, and they were so frightened that they broke up their camp and quickly marched back to their own land.

HORATIUS

For a time Rome was ruled by Publius Valerius. He was a good man. He caused laws to be passed for the benefit of the people and was therefore called Publicola, which means the people's friend. He had to fight Tarquin frequently. The banished king was constantly trying to capture Rome and get back his throne. He got help from various nations and fought very hard, but was never successful in his efforts. At one time he was aided by Lars Porsena, king of Clusium, a city of Etruria, who gathered a large army and set out to attack Rome.

But Porsena could not enter the city without crossing the Tiber, and there was only one bridge. This was called the Sublician Bridge. It was so called from the Latin word *sublicæ*, which means wooden beams. When the Romans saw the great army of Etruscans in the distance, they were much alarmed. They were not prepared to fight so powerful a force. The consul thought for a while, and then he resolved to cut down the bridge as the only means of saving Rome. So a number of men were at once set to work with axes and hammers.

It was hard work, for the bridge was very strongly built. Before the beams supporting it were all cut away the army of Porsena was seen approaching the river. What was to be done? It would take a few minutes more to finish the work, and if the farther end of the bridge could be held against the Etruscans for those few minutes all would be well for Rome. But how was it to be held, and who would hold it? Suddenly from the ranks of the Roman soldiers the brave Horatius Cocles stepped out and cried to the consul:

"Give me two good men to help me, and I will hold the bridge and stop the enemy from coming over."

Immediately two brave men, Spurius Lartius and Titus Herminius, ran to his side. Then the three hurried over to the other end of the bridge, and stood ready to keep off the enemy.

When the army of Etruscans saw the three men standing to keep them back a shout of laughter went up among them. Three men to keep back thousands! How ridiculous! There the three brave Romans stood, however, at the entrance of the bridge, with determined faces and fearless eyes.

Very quickly three Etruscans—stout, able fighters— came forth from the army to give battle to the three Romans. After a sharp combat the Etruscans were killed. Three more came out and continued the fight, but they too were beaten by Horatius and his companions.

But now the bridge began to shake and crack. Horatius felt that it was about to fall, and he cried to Spurius and Titus to run back to the other side. While they did so he stood alone and defied the whole Etruscan army, which was now rushing upon him. A whole army against one man! Javelins were hurled at him, but he skillfully warded them off with his shield.

Just as the Etruscans reached him the last beam was

cut away, and the bridge fell with a tremendous crash. As it was falling Horatius plunged into the Tiber, and praying to the gods for help, he swam to the other side in safety. The Romans received him with shouts of joy, and even the Etruscans could not help raising a cheer in admiration of his bravery.

The three Romans were well rewarded. A fine statue of Horatius was built in one of the squares of the city. On the base of the statue was placed a brass tablet, with an account of the heroic deed engraved on it. The Senate also gave Horatius as much land as he could plow around in a day.

MUCIUS THE LEFT-HANDED

But Porsena still remained with his army on the other side of the river. He thought that by preventing food from being sent into the city he could force the inhabitants to surrender. So he got ships and stationed them on the Tiber to drive away or seize any vessels that should attempt to come to Rome with food.

Now there was in Rome at this time a very brave young man named Caius Mucius, and he thought of a plan to save the city. His plan was to march boldly into the enemy's camp and kill King Porsena. So he concealed a sword under his tunic and went across the river to the Etruscan camp. Then he made his way to the place where the king was sitting.

It happened that it was pay day in the army and the soldiers were getting their money. A secretary, who sat beside the king and was dressed very much like him, was talking to the men and giving them orders. Mucius mistook the secretary for Porsena and rushed forward and stabbed him to death. Instantly the daring Roman was seized by the guards. He heard the soldiers crying out that the secretary was killed. Then he knew what a mistake he had made.

Porsena was greatly enraged at seeing his secretary killed, and in a loud and angry voice he commanded Mucius to tell who he was and why he had committed such a deed. Without showing any sign of fear the bold Mucius answered:

"I am a Roman citizen. I came here to kill you, because you are an enemy of my country. I have failed, but there are others to come after me who will not fail. Your life will be constantly in danger, and you will be killed when you least expect it."

On hearing these words Porsena jumped from his seat in a great fury and threatened to burn Mucius to death if he did not at once tell all about the others who were coming to kill him. But Mucius was not frightened, and to show how little he cared about the king's threat he thrust his right hand into the flame of a fire which had been lighted close by and held it there without flinching. At the same time he cried out to the king:

"Behold how little we Romans care for pain when it is to defend our country."

Porsena was astonished at this sight, and he so much admired the courage and patriotism of the Roman that he ordered the guards to set him free. Then Mucius said to the king:

"In return for your kindness I now tell you of my own free will what I would not tell you when you threatened me with punishment. Know then that three hundred Roman youths have bound themselves by oath to kill you, each to make the attempt in his turn. The lot fell first on me. I have failed, but the attempt will be made again and again until some one succeeds."

King Porsena was so terrified on hearing this that he resolved to make peace at once with Rome. So he immediately sent messengers to the Senate, and terms of peace were quickly agreed upon.

The Senate rewarded Mucius by giving him a tract of land on the banks of the Tiber. This land was afterwards called the Mucian Meadows. Mucius himself got the name of Scævola, a Latin word which means *left-handed*. He had lost the use of his right hand by burning it in the fire.

CORIOLANUS

I

One of the great men of Rome not long after the banishment of the Tarquins was Caius Marcius. He was a member of a noble family, and from his youth he had been noted for his bravery.

In his time there was a war between the Romans and the Volscians, a people of a district in Latium. The Romans made an attack on Corioli, the capital city of the Volscians, but were defeated and driven back. Caius Marcius reproached the Roman soldiers for running from the enemy. His words made them ashamed and they turned again to the fight. With Caius at their head they sent the Volscians flying back into the city. Caius followed the enemy to the gates, which were partly open. When he saw this he shouted to the Romans:

"The gates are open for us; let us not be afraid to enter!"

Caius himself sprang in and kept the gates open for the Romans. After a short fight the city was taken.

Then everybody said that it was Caius who had taken Corioli, and that he should be called after the name of the city he had won. So ever afterward he was known as Coriolanus.

II

But though Coriolanus was a brave soldier and always ready to fight for Rome, he had some qualities that were not so good. He had great contempt for the common people, and he took part with those who tried to oppress them.

Only a little while before the taking of Corioli, there was a serious trouble between the people and the patricians. A great many of the people earned their living by farming. But when there was a war the strong men had to become soldiers, and as Rome was almost constantly at war the men were nearly always away from their farms. Very often, therefore, they had to borrow money to support their families while they themselves were away fighting, for at this time Roman soldiers got no regular pay.

Now it was the rich patricians who loaned the money, and if it was not paid back at the time agreed upon they could put the people who owed it in jail, or they could sell their wives and children as slaves.

In this way the plebeians often suffered much hardship. At last a great number of them resolved to leave Rome and make a settlement for themselves somewhere else in Italy. The patricians did not like this very much, for if the common people went away there would be a scarcity of soldiers for the army. So the Senate, after thinking the matter over, proposed that the plebeians should elect officers of their own, to be called tribunes, who should have power to veto laws they did not like, that is, prevent them from being passed. The word *veto*, which is Latin for *I forbid*, is used in the same way in our own country. The President of the United States and the governors of some states have, within certain limits, power to prevent the passing of laws they do not approve. This is called the veto power.

The plebeians were pleased with the proposal that they were to have tribunes, so they returned to Rome, and for a time there was peace between them and the patricians.

But Coriolanus and other patricians were opposed to the election of tribunes, because they thought it gave the common people too much power. Once when there was a famine in Rome, and the poor were suffering greatly from want of food, the Greeks living in Sicily sent several ships laden with corn to Rome to relieve the people in distress. When the corn arrived the Senate was about to order that it should be divided among the people who needed it, but Coriolanus interfered.

"No, no," he said, "if the people want corn let them first give up their tribunes. It must be either no corn or no tribunes."

The people were so angry when they heard of this speech that they talked about killing Coriolanus. And they would have done so but for the wise advice of the tribunes.

"No, no," said the tribunes, "you must not kill him; that would be against the law. But you can have him tried for treason against the people and we will be his accusers."

Coriolanus was then ordered to appear before the assembly of the people to be tried, for the people had power to try in their assemblies persons charged with such offences. But Coriolanus was afraid the assembly would condemn him, so he secretly fled from the city, leaving his family behind, and went to a town of the Volscians.

The chief of the Volscians received Coriolanus in a

friendly manner. Coriolanus then told him why he had left Rome. The Volscian chief was glad to hear it. He had long wanted to fight the Romans, but had been afraid to make the attempt. With the aid of such a soldier as Coriolanus, however, he was sure that Rome might be taken. So he raised a large army and put it under the command of the great Roman.

III

The Volscian army, led by Coriolanus, captured many cities belonging to the Roman Republic. At last Coriolanus resolved to attack Rome itself, and he marched his army towards the city. The Romans just then were not very well prepared for a battle, so the Senate decided to send messengers to Coriolanus to beg him to spare his native city and make terms of peace.

The messengers chosen were five of the leading nobles, and they at once set out for the Volscian camp. Coriolanus received them cordially, for they were old friends; but he said that he would not spare Rome unless the Romans would give up all the lands and cities which they had taken from the Volscians in former wars.

To this the Senate would not agree, and Coriolanus refused to listen to any other terms. The Romans then began to prepare for battle, though they feared very much that they would be defeated.

But while the men were thus in fear and doubt, the women of Rome saved the city! Valeria, a noble Roman lady, remembered that Coriolanus had always dearly loved his mother.

"Perhaps," thought she, "he may listen to her though he will hear no one else."

So Valeria, with a large number of noble ladies, went to the house of Veturia, the mother of Coriolanus, and said to her:

"The gods have put it into our hearts to come and ask you to join with us to save our country from ruin. Come then with us to the camp of your son and pray him to show mercy."

The aged mother at once agreed to go, so she got ready immediately and set out for the camp of the Volscians, accompanied by a great number of ladies and her son's wife and little children. It was a strange sight, this long line of Roman ladies, all dressed in mourning, and even the Volscian soldiers showed them respect as they passed along.

Coriolanus happened to be sitting in front of his tent in the Volscian camp with a number of officers around him as the procession came in view. "Who are these women?" he asked. Before an answer could be given he saw that among them were his mother and wife and children, and he stood up and hastened forward to meet them. They fell on their knees and begged him to spare his native city.

Coriolanus seemed deeply distressed. He made no answer, but bent his head, pressed his hand to his breast and gazed down upon the dear ones who knelt at his feet. Then his mother said:

"If I had no son Rome would not be in this danger. I am too old to bear much longer your shame and my own misery. Look to your wife and children; if you continue in your present course you will send them to an early death."

Coriolanus was so grieved that for some minutes he could not speak. At last he cried out:

"Oh, mother, what have you done to me? You have saved Rome, but you have ruined your son."

Then he embraced his mother and looked at her sadly for a moment. He also embraced and kissed his wife and children and told them to go back to Rome, for they would be safe there. The women then returned to the city and Coriolanus marched away with the Volscian army. Rome was saved!

Coriolanus lived the rest of his life with the Volscians, but he never again made war against his native city. It is supposed that he died about the middle of the fifth century before Christ.

THE FABII

At about the time in which Coriolanus lived the family of the Fabii were very powerful in Rome. Among the leaders or chief men of the family at that period were Quintus Fabius, Marcus Fabius, and Cæso Fabius.

In those times the Roman nobles were very rich and powerful. They held all the high offices of government and cared very little about the welfare of the plebeians. Often they treated them very harshly.

The Fabii also treated the plebeians harshly. Once when Quintus Fabius defeated the Volscians in a battle, he sold all the valuable things he took from the enemy and put the money into the public treasury. Such things were called spoils. The Roman generals usually divided the spoils among the soldiers. This was the way the soldiers were paid in those days. But Quintus Fabius would not divide the spoils. So the soldiers were very bitter against him.

But some time afterwards Marcus Fabius was elected consul, and once after a great battle with the Veientians, a people of Etruria, he took the entire care of the poor wounded soldiers and supplied all their wants at his own expense.

The next year his brother Cæso Fabius was consul, and he tried to get the Senate to divide among the poor citizens the lands that had been taken from the Veientians and other people whom the Romans had defeated in war. Often afterwards in the Senate the voice of a Fabius was heard speaking for justice to the plebeians. The common people, therefore, soon loved the whole family of the Fabii instead of hating them as they had before.

The nobles were very angry because the Fabii took the side of the plebeians, and they threatened to do all they could against them. Now the Fabii saw clearly that it would be useless to attempt to fight the nobles, because the nobles had a great deal of power and could do almost whatever they pleased in Rome. Therefore, the Fabii thought that it would be better for them to remove from the city and make a new home for themselves somewhere else. So they resolved to do this, and the place they selected was on the banks of the River Cremera, a few miles from Rome.

At this time the Romans were again at war with the Veientians. These people lived in Veii, a city on the Cremera River. One day, when there was a discussion in the Roman Senate about this war, Cæso Fabius said:

"As you know, we of the house of the Fabii are going to leave Rome and settle on the borders of the country of the Veientians. If you give us permission we will fight those people and try to defeat them for the honor of Rome and the glory of our house. We will ask neither money nor men from the Senate. We will carry on the war with our own men and at our own cost."

The senators were glad of the chance to get rid of the Fabii, and so they at once gave them the permission they asked for. The Fabii then began to make preparations for their departure. There were over three hundred men in addition to women-folk, children, and servants, and when all were ready they marched out of the city to their new home with Cæso Fabius at their head.

At first the Fabii had only a camp on the Cremera River, but afterwards they built a small city, with a strong fortress. Many good Roman soldiers came and joined them, and soon they had a fine army of earnest, devoted men.

The Veientians were soon conquered. Fabius and his brave men defeated them in several battles, and at last the Veientians made up their minds that they had got enough of war. Then they returned to their own city of Veii and remained quiet for a long time. But they declared that they would destroy the Fabii whenever they could get the chance.

Now it was an old custom of the Fabii to have a special worship of the gods on a certain day of every year. Early in the morning of that day all the men of the family would go in a body to a famous temple on a hill near Rome and have religious services for several hours. The men took no arms with them, as it was thought improper to go armed to religious worship.

The Veientians heard of this annual religious service of the Fabii and saw in it a chance for revenge. So they resolved to kill the Fabii the next time they went to the temple for their special service. When the day came the Fabii set out as usual. On their way to the temple they had to go over a road which had high, steep rocks on each side. There a large number of Veientian soldiers hid themselves, and when the unsuspecting Fabii came along a furious attack was made on them from front and rear. Without arms they could not fight very well. They made the best defence they could, but it was useless. They were all killed except one young man who escaped to Rome. Thus the cowardly Veientians had their revenge.

CINCINNATUS

I

In the mountains east of Latium there lived a rather wild people called Æquians, who were very often at war with Rome. After some time of peace and good conduct these people suddenly began to plunder the rich farms of the Romans. This was about four hundred and fifty years before the birth of Christ and not long after the Veientians had destroyed the Fabian family. As soon as the Roman Senate heard what the Æquians were doing it sent messengers to the Æquian king to complain of the wrong. The messengers found the king in his camp, sitting near a huge oak tree. But when they spoke to him he answered them rudely, saying:

"I am too busy now with other matters. Go tell your message to the oak yonder!"

This made the messengers very angry, and one of the them said:

"We shall tell it to the oak, but we shall tell it also to

the gods and call them to witness how you have broken the peace! And they shall be on our side when we come to punish you and your people for the crimes you have committed against us."

And it is said that the angry messengers did tell the message to the oak, and to all the other trees around, and boldly shouted that war would come from this insult to Rome.

Then the messengers returned to Rome and told the Senate how they had been insulted by the Æquian king. The Senate at once declared war against the Æquians and ordered the Consul Minucius to lead an army against them.

The Romans easily won a few battles at first. Then the Æquians began to retreat as if they did not mean to fight any more. The Romans followed swiftly, until they were drawn into a narrow valley on each side of which were high, rocky hills. It was a trap, and the Romans knew it before they had marched very far from the entrance.

The Æquian king then closed up the valley with strong barricades and placed his troops at the entrance and along the hills, so that the Romans could not get out.

In the valley there was very little grass for the horses and no food for the men, so that if the Romans were not soon relieved both they and their horses would die of hunger.

II

But luckily for the Romans a few of their horsemen had managed to get out of the valley before the Æquians closed it. These horsemen rode as fast as they could to Rome and told the Senate how Minucius and his soldiers were placed. What was to be done? No one seemed to know at first, but after a good deal of discussion, a senator said:

"Let us make Lucius Quinctius dictator. He is the only man who can save us."

The Senate agreed to this, and so Lucius Quinctius was chosen dictator. A dictator had more power than the Senate or the consuls. All his commands had to be obeyed just as if he were a king. But there was not a dictator always. A dictator was appointed only when there was some great danger, and he held office only for six months.

Lucius Quinctius belonged to a noble family. He was a great soldier and had won many battles for his country. He had such beautiful, long, curly hair that the people called him *Cincinnatus,* which means curly-haired, and this is the name by which he is known in history.

At the time Cincinnatus was appointed dictator he lived on a small farm outside of Rome. He worked on the farm himself, and when the messengers from the Senate came to tell him that he had been chosen dictator they found him ploughing in one of his fields. He left his plough where it stood and hastened to Rome, where he was welcomed by all the people.

The first thing he did was to raise a new army. He gave orders that every man of suitable age should buckle on his sword and be ready in a few hours to march to the help of Minucius and his soldiers.

Before evening Cincinnatus and his army marched out of the city for the Alban Hills, where the Romans were shut up. They reached the place in the early morning and formed in a line all around the hills. The Æquians then found themselves hemmed in on every side between two Roman armies—the army of Minucius and the army of Cincinnatus. They fought as well as they could, but they were quickly overpowered, so that they could do nothing but cry to the Roman commander to spare their lives.

Cincinnatus spared their lives, but he made them *pass under the yoke*. The yoke was formed of two spears, fixed upright in the ground, and a third fastened across near the top from one to the other. Cincinnatus made the Æquians lay down their arms and pass out, every man of them, under the yoke of spears. They had to bend their heads as they did so, for the spears were not very long, and the one on the top was only a few feet from the ground. The yoke was set up between two lines of Roman soldiers, and as the Æquians passed under it the Romans jeered at them and taunted them.

Having to pass under the yoke was regarded as the greatest disgrace that could happen to soldiers. Many much preferred to suffer death. The practice has given to our language the word *subjugate*, meaning to subdue or conquer, from the Latin words *sub*, under, and *jugum*, a yoke.

When the soldiers of Consul Minucius came out of the valley they shouted for joy and crowded around Cincinnatus, thanking him as their deliverer and protector. "Let us give Cincinnatus a golden crown!" they cried; but the great general only smiled, shook his head, and gave the order for the homeward march.

Great was the rejoicing in Rome when the news of the victory was received. The Senate ordered that there should be a general holiday and a grand parade through the city. And so the victorious army marched into Rome amid the shouts and cheers of the people.

Cincinnatus rode in a splendid chariot drawn by six handsome black horses. He wore the dress of dictator of Rome, and on his head was a laurel wreath. Behind his chariot the Æquian king and his chiefs walked, looking very humble and forlorn. Following them were slaves laden with the arms and other valuable things taken from the enemy's camp. With bugles and trumpets gayly sounding, the parade went through the city. The chariot of Cincinnatus was followed by a throng of people cheering and crying, "Hail to the Dictator! Hail to the Conqueror!" Flowers were showered upon him and thrown before his chariot wheels.

A few days afterward Cincinnatus gave up the office of dictator and went back to his little farm.

CAMILLUS

I

About three hundred and eighty years before the birth of Christ the Romans had another war with the Veientians. During this war they tried to take the rich city of Veii, which was about twelve miles from Rome. But there was a great wall of stone all around the city, and the gates, which were of brass, were very high and very strong. So the Romans, though they tried as hard as they could for seven years, were not able to take Veii.

And to make matters worse for them it was reported that twelve Etruscan cities were going to send armies to help the Veientians. It was also said that as soon as the twelve armies had driven the Romans away from the walls of Veii, they would march to Rome and destroy the city.

The Romans were much alarmed by these reports, and they resolved that there should be a dictator. So the Senate appointed a dictator, and the man appointed was Marcus Furius Camillus.

Camillus was one of the greatest men of Rome. He belonged to a very rich and powerful family, and he was a great soldier. When he was made dictator he raised a large army and marched at once to Veii. He tried a long time to break down the walls or gates, but he could not do it. Then he thought of the plan of digging a tunnel under the walls.

This seemed a good idea, so Camillus set a great number of his men to work. Soon they had a tunnel dug under the walls and so far under the city that they thought they were as far as the great temple of Juno, which was in the fort or strongest part of Veii. Here they stopped to consider what next to do. Suddenly the sound of voices, as of people talking in the temple above them, reached their ears. So they sent for Camillus, and when he came he listened to the voices.

Now it happened that at that moment the king of Veii was in the temple preparing to offer an ox as a sacrifice to Juno and praying to the goddess to save the city from the Romans. The ox was killed and its carcass was ready to be laid on the altar. After the king had prayed one of the priests, pretending that he had received an answer from Juno, cried out:

"The goddess declares she will give victory to him who offers this as a sacrifice upon the altar."

As soon as Camillus, who was listening all the time, heard these words of the priest, he ordered his men to break an opening in the earth over their heads. This was quickly done, and the Romans sprang through into the midst of the worshipers. They at once seized the carcass of the ox, and Camillus himself offered it upon the altar to Juno. Then he and his companions rushed out of the temple and opened the gates of the city before the astonished and frightened people knew what was being done.

As soon as the gates were opened the Roman soldiers poured in by thousands. The Veientians fought bravely, but they were quickly defeated, and their great and rich city was at last in the hands of the Romans.

In those times, as has already been said, it was the custom to divide among the victorious soldiers the valuable things taken from a defeated enemy. The riches of Veii were, therefore, divided among the Roman soldiers, and there were so many precious things—gold and silver and jewelry—that the men were quite rich when each got his share.

II

Some time after the taking of Veii the Romans were at war with the Faliscians, another people of Etruria, and Camillus went with an army to besiege their chief town, which was called Falerii. He made his camp in front of the walls, stationed soldiers all round and tried hard to take the town. But the Faliscians were very strong and brave, and they defended their town so well that Camillus began to be afraid he would not be able to take it at all.

Now there was at that time in Falerii a schoolmaster who taught the sons of the chief citizens of the town. This schoolmaster used to take his boys every day for a walk outside the walls. One day he led them within the lines of the Roman army and brought them into the camp of Camillus.

Camillus was surprised at seeing the boys. He asked the schoolmaster who they were and why he had brought them there. The schoolmaster told who the boys were and then said:

"I bring them here to give them up to you. In doing this I give you up the city, for their fathers will surrender the city to you in order to get back their children."

Camillus stood for a moment in silence, gazing at

the traitor with a look of disgust. Then in an angry voice he cried out:

"Villain, we Romans are not so base as you are. We do not make war upon children, but upon men who do us wrong."

He then ordered some of his soldiers to tie the schoolmaster's hands behind his back and to give each of the boys a rod, telling them to scourge the traitor before them into the city. This the boys did with a hearty good-will. They whipped the unworthy schoolmaster into Falerii, and when the people saw the sight and heard of the noble conduct of Camillus, they resolved not to fight any more against so good a man. So they sent ambassadors to Rome to make peace, and the Romans and Faliscians became good friends.

III

Not long after this time one of the tribunes brought a charge against Camillus that he had kept for his own use more than his fair share of the spoils of Veii. Some valuable things were noticed in his house, and it was said that he had not got them as part of his share. It was believed, therefore, that he had taken them secretly from Veii.

The Romans were very particular upon this point. They had strict laws for the division of spoils obtained in war, and no one was permitted to take more than he was entitled to, according to his rank in the army.

Camillus was summoned to appear in the people's court to answer the charge made against him. But he would not humble himself so much as to go before the plebeians to be tried. He preferred rather to leave Rome forever. So the great Camillus departed from his native city, intending never to return. As he passed out of the gates he prayed to the gods that some dreadful thing might happen to the Romans, so that they would be forced to call him back again to Rome to save the city.

And very soon something did happen which compelled the Romans to ask for the help of Camillus. For a long time a people called the Gauls had been doing a great deal of mischief in some parts of Italy. These people came from the country now known as France, which in ancient times was called Gaul. Thousands of them made their way across the high mountains called the Alps and settled on the plains of northern Italy. For many years they lived in this region. Then they heard that further south the country was very beautiful and was rich in corn and cattle, so they started out in great numbers to conquer it.

They were a strange, savage people, very different from the Romans or the Etruscans. They were very tall and strong and had long, shaggy black hair and dark, fierce faces, so that they appeared very terrible to the Italians. In battle they showed all their savage nature. They rushed furiously at their enemies, yelling at the top of their voices, flourishing enormous swords, and blowing trumpets.

The chief or king of the Gauls at this time was called Brennus. He was a man of great strength and size. He wore a golden collar around his neck, and on his arms, which were bare, he sometimes wore bracelets of gold.

The Gauls found the southern lands very much to their liking. They robbed farms, attacked some of the Etruscan cities, and then, after a short time, they marched for Rome. A great Roman army went out to fight them, and the two armies met on the banks of a river called the Allia.

The Roman soldiers had never before seen the dreadful Gauls. They were, therefore, greatly terrified when the tall, fierce-looking savages came running over the plains in vast numbers, shouting furiously and blowing their trumpets. And though the Roman general, Marcus Manlius, tried to make his men go forward bravely to meet the Gauls it was useless. They fought badly and were killed by thousands. At last they ran from the field and fled toward Rome.

IV

When the defeated soldiers reached Rome and told what had happened, there was great terror in the city. Most of the people bundled up their household goods and fled to hiding-places in the mountains close by, where they thought they would be safe from the Gauls.

But many of the senators and other brave men, both nobles and plebeians, instead of running away from the city went up to the Capitol, fastened the gates, and made ready for a siege. The Capitol was the most sacred part of the city. It contained splendid statues of Jupiter, Juno, and Minerva, and, as you know, the famous Sibylline Books.

Some old men who had been consuls resolved to remain in the city and wait for the Gauls to come. They thought that if the Gauls should kill them they would then be satisfied and would spare the city. So the patriotic old men dressed themselves in their finest robes and sat in chairs in the Forum, each with an ivory staff in his right hand.

When the Gauls reached the city there was no one to oppose them. They marched on to the Forum and found the old men, with long white beards, sitting in their chairs, so still that they looked like statues. A Gaul went up to one of them and pulled his beard to see if he were a living person. Instantly the old man raised his staff and struck the barbarian in the face. The Gauls then fell upon the patriots and killed them. Then they began to plunder.

After destroying the greater part of the city the

Gauls turned their attention to the Capitol. The rock on which it was built was high and steep.

Brennus led his soldiers up the hill, but the Romans in the Capitol rushed down the narrow road and after a few minutes of brave fighting drove them back. The Gauls made another attempt, but it was no more successful than the first.

Brennus saw that the Romans could not be driven from the Capitol. He therefore decided to starve them out. He put a strong guard at the entrance, so that the Romans could not come out to get food. For weeks the Capitol was thus besieged, but its faithful defenders held out manfully.

Meanwhile the people who had fled from Rome took courage again. They gathered at the city of Veii and organized a strong army to fight the Gauls. But they wanted a commander, and then they thought of Camillus. All agreed that he would be the right man to be their general. So they resolved to send for him, but first they thought they must have the approval of the Senate. Here was a difficulty. How could a messenger get to the Senate while the Gauls were around the Capitol? This puzzled them for a good while, but at last a young man named Pontius Cominius volunteered to carry a message to the Capitol.

So on a very dark night Pontius left Veii and swam down the Tiber until he reached the Capitoline Hill. Then he went on shore and crept up the hill as far as the great rock. The Gauls had put no guard there, for they thought no one could climb the rock because it was so steep.

By great efforts Pontius managed to climb up. Several times he was near falling. But by clinging to the vines and bushes that grew on the rock he came to the top at last. His countrymen in the Capitol were delighted to see him. They were also very glad when they heard about the army at Veii, and the Senate at once approved of the proposal about Camillus. It was agreed not only to make him general, but to make him dictator. Then Cominius went down the rock and the hill by the way he had come up and hastened off to Veii.

V

The next day some of the Gauls, while walking along this side of the hill, noticed footmarks in the soil. They also noticed that bushes, growing high up on the rock, were crushed and torn. Then they knew that some one had gone up or come down the cliff, and they resolved to try to go up themselves that night.

So shortly after midnight, when they thought that the Romans would be fast asleep, a party of Gauls began cautiously and silently to clamber up the steep rock. Some placed their shields across their shoulders for others to stand upon, and in this way they supported one another, until at last some of them made their way very near to the top and one got just to the edge of a balcony of the Capitol. No one within the building heard them, not even the watch-dogs.

But at that moment there was a loud cackling of geese. These birds were thought to be favorite birds of the goddess Juno. Many were kept in the Capitol, and some of them happened just then to be at the side the Gauls were climbing up. The movements of the climbers, quiet though they were, disturbed the geese and they began to cackle and flap their wings.

The noise aroused Marcus Manlius from his sleep. He sprang from his bed, seized his sword and shield, and ran to the balcony. There he saw a Gaul climbing on to the parapet and others scrambling up behind. Marcus rushed upon him, struck him in the face with his shield, and tumbled him headlong down the rock.

As the Gaul fell he knocked down some of his companions who were climbing behind him. The geese still

63

kept up their loud cackling, and soon all the Romans were awakened and came quickly to the assistance of Marcus. The Gauls were hurled back as they mounted the rock, and in a few minutes all who had come up were dashed down the steep cliff and killed. Thus the Capitol was saved by the cackling of geese. For his brave action on this occasion Marcus Manlius was honored by being called Marcus *Capitolinus*.

VI

Brennus now saw that he could not take the Capitol, so he thought it would be useless to remain any longer in Rome. He therefore offered to go away if the Senate would give him a thousand pounds of gold. The Senate thought it better to do this. Food was very scarce in the Capitol and in a few days the brave men there would have none at all. They had heard nothing further from the army at Veii and they were not sure that help could come in time to save them.

So the Senate resolved to give the thousand pounds of gold to the Gauls, and an officer named Quintus Sulpitius was sent with some lictors to deliver it to Brennus. But the gold had to be weighed and the Gauls attempted to cheat the Romans by using false weights. When Sulpitius complained of this, Brennus took off his sword and threw it, belt and all, into one of the scales, and when Sulpitius asked what that meant Brennus answered:

"What should it mean but woe to the conquered?"

At that moment Camillus appeared at the gates with his army. He soon learned what was going on. Quickly he marched to the spot and ordered the lictors to take the gold out of the scale and carry it back to the Roman treasury. Then he turned to Brennus and addressing him in a stern voice said:

"We Romans defend our country, not with gold, but with steel."

Immediately there was a battle, and the Gauls were defeated and driven out of the city. Next day there was another battle a few miles from Rome, and the Gauls were again defeated and thousands of them slain.

Camillus then returned to Rome at the head of his victorious army. The people received him with shouts of joy and for several days they had celebrations in his honor. They called him the second Romulus, meaning that he was the second founder of the city. They also called him the FATHER OF HIS COUNTRY.

VII

It was in the time of Camillus that a great hole or chasm, caused perhaps by an earthquake, suddenly appeared in the ground in the middle of the Forum. Workmen were sent to fill it up, but no matter how much earth they threw into it the hole seemed to be as large and deep as before. The Senate then consulted the augurs and they said the hole could not be filled up until what was most valuable in Rome was cast into it. Then the people began to throw in gold and silver and jewelry, but still the hole was as deep as ever. At last a young man named Curtius said that the most valuable things the Romans had were their arms and their courage. Then he put on his armor and his sword and mounting his horse rode into the Forum and leaped into the great hole. Immediately it closed up behind him, and neither he nor his horse was ever seen again.

In the old Roman stories Curtius is much praised as a patriot and hero. The people thought he had saved his country from some great evil, which they believed would have happened to it if the hole in the Forum had not been closed up.

65

MANLIUS TORQUATUS

Marcus Manlius, who commanded the Roman army at the battle of Allia and who so well defended the Capitol against the Gauls, belonged to a family known as the Manlii. This family gave many brave generals to the Republic. One of them was named Titus Manlius.

Some years after the siege of the Capitol Titus had a remarkable fight with a huge Gaul. The Gauls had come back to make war again upon Rome. Their army was encamped near a bridge on the Anio, a small river a few miles from the city, and the Roman army sent to oppose them was on the other side of the river, waiting for a good opportunity for battle.

Every day a Gaul of gigantic size, who wore round his neck a collar or chain of twisted gold threads, used to come to the bridge to insult the Romans. He would call them cowards who were afraid to fight. One day he dared them to send some one out to fight with him. Manlius at once accepted the challenge, and the two immediately took their places in an open space within sight of both armies.

The Gaul was so tall and strong that the Roman appeared like a boy beside him, and everybody thought the big warrior would have an easy victory. But Titus was very quick in his movements. For a few moments after the fight began he skillfully dodged the furious blows of his opponent. Then he suddenly ran close up to him, sprang under his great shield and plunged his sword deep into the Gaul's body.

The Gaul fell to the ground dead. Then Titus took the golden collar from the dead man's neck and put it on his own. So afterwards he was called Manlius Torquatus, from the word *torques*, which is Latin for a *twisted collar*.

Manlius Torquatus became consul, but he was not much liked by the people, for he was a very stern and severe ruler. During a war which the Romans had with the Latins and some tribes of South Italy, Manlius was in command of the Roman army. He marched to meet the enemy, who were assembled in force at the foot of Mount Vesuvius.

While the two armies were encamped opposite to each other, Manlius ordered that none of his men should fight with any of the Latins until the word for battle was given. Soon after a Latin officer met young Manlius, the consul's son, riding in front of the lines with a troop of his comrades. They entered into conversation about the coming battle, and each boasted of the valor of the soldiers on his own side. At last the Latin officer challenged the young Roman to single combat.

"Wilt thou," he cried, "measure thy strength with mine? It will then be seen how much the Latin horseman excels the Roman."

Manlius accepted the challenge, and in the fight which immediately took place he was the victor. He killed the Latin and, according to the custom of those times, stripped him of his armor and carried it to the

Roman camp. Then he went to tell his father what he had done.

"Father," said he, "I present you this armor, which I have taken from the enemy. I hope you will accept it as a proof that I am ready and able to do my duty as a Roman soldier."

Torquatus looked at his son sadly and then said:

"My son, you say you are willing to do your duty as a soldier. But the first duty of a soldier is obedience. This duty you have not performed, for you have just now disobeyed me, your commander. You have fought with the enemy without receiving orders to do so. But you shall not escape punishment because you are my son."

Then turning to his lictors he said:

"Go, bind him to a stake and cut off his head."

At this cruel order loud cries of horror came from the soldiers. Young Manlius threw himself at his father's feet and begged for mercy. But the stern consul turned away from him and ordered the lictors to perform their duty. So the brave young Manlius was led to a stake and bound, and with one stroke of the lictor's axe his head was cut from his body.

Soon afterwards there was a battle between the two armies, and the Romans gained a great victory. But the war continued for some time longer. It ended, however, in the defeat of the Latins. Manlius took possession of one of their towns—the town of Antium, on the Mediterranean coast—and compelled the inhabitants to give up their warships.

War vessels and galleys in those times had sharp prows made for the purpose of running into and breaking through the sides of other vessels. The prow was a beam, with pointed irons fastened to it, and a metal figure resembling the beak or head of a bird or other animal. This beak was called a *rostrum*.

When the Romans captured the warships of Antium

they broke off the beaks and carried them to Rome. There they fastened them as ornaments to the platform in the Forum, from which orators addressed the people. Hence the word rostrum came to mean a platform or pulpit for public speaking, and in this sense it is now used in our own language.

APPIUS CLAUDIUS CAECUS

I

Soon after the defeat of the Gauls there lived in Rome a great man named Appius Claudius. He belonged to one of the highest families of the city. He was consul for two years, and for several years he held the office of censor (312-308 B.C.).

The censor was a very high and important officer. He was not only head of the department for taking the census, but he had charge of the collecting of the taxes, the erecting of public buildings, and the making of roads and streets.

Appius Claudius was a great soldier. Every Roman citizen had to be a soldier, and every man who was consul had to be able to lead armies and to fight and win battles. But Appius Claudius was chiefly famous for the great public works he planned and directed in Rome, which at that time was a city with a population of about three hundred thousand. One of these works was an aqueduct which brought water to the city from a lake eight miles distant. The Roman aqueducts were the best in the world. Some of them that were built over two thousand years ago are still in use.

But the greatest work of Appius Claudius was the making of a road from Rome to Capua, a distance of one hundred and twenty miles. This road was called the Appian Way in honor of Appius. It was also called the "queen of roads" because it was so well built. Parts of it are still in existence. The Romans had good roads as well as good aqueducts. They were the best road-builders in the world.

While he was censor Appius Claudius very much improved Rome. He was called "the greatest of his countrymen in the works of peace." Even after he retired from office he had great influence in public affairs. His advice was asked by both plebeians and nobles.

Once during the first war which the Romans had with the Greeks the advice of Appius was of great benefit to Rome. At that time there were many Greek settlements in the south of Italy. One of the Greek towns was called Tarentum. It was built close to the sea and had a very good harbor.

Many of the people of this town were well educated. In those days the Greeks were mostly an educated people. They were fond of learning and of art. They called the Romans barbarians and were not friendly to them.

Once when a Roman fleet entered the bay of Tarentum, the people of the town attacked it and after taking five of the ships put the crews to death. When the news of this outrage reached Rome the Senate sent ambassadors to demand satisfaction. One of the ambassadors was a man named Lucius Posthumius. When they arrived at Tarentum they were met by a noisy crowd of people of the town, who made fun of their dress.

The Romans wore an outer dress called a toga. It was a large white woollen cloth, in the shape of a half circle, four or five yards long and of nearly the same width. In putting on this garment they doubled it lengthwise,

then passed one end over the left shoulder and under
the opposite arm and again over the left shoulder, the
other end reaching nearly to the ground in front. The
Tarentines laughed at the toga of the Roman ambassadors. They said it was a dress fit only for savages.

In a short time the ambassadors were taken to the
public theatre, where the people had assembled to hear
the message from Rome. Posthumius spoke to them in
Greek, but as this was not his own language he pronounced many of the words in a peculiar way, and the
Tarentines laughed. The Roman went on, however, in a
dignified manner and finished his speech as if he had
not noticed the insult.

Just then a Tarentine moved forward to the place
where Posthumius stood and threw some dirt on his
white toga. The ambassador held up the soiled garment
with his hand and said that Tarentum would be made to
suffer for the outrage. Then the theatre rang with
laughter and offensive cries.

"Laugh on," said Posthumius, "you may laugh now
but you shall weep hereafter. The stain on this toga shall
be washed out in your blood!"

Then the ambassadors left the theatre and at once set
out for Rome. When they appeared before the Senate
Posthumius showed the stain on his toga as proof of the
insult offered to Rome by the Tarentines. The Senate at
once declared war on Tarentum and sent a powerful
army to attack it.

II

At this time the Tarentines had no general they
thought would be able to fight the Romans. So they sent
across the sea to Epirus, in Greece, for the king of that
country to come and help them. The name of this king
was Pyrrhus. He was a great soldier and commander

and was nearly always engaged in war. He consented to help the Tarentines and crossed over to Italy with a great army in which there was a number of fighting elephants.

When Pyrrhus entered Tarentum he made himself master of the city. The Tarentines were very fond of plays and amusements of all kinds. Pyrrhus closed the theatres, stopped all the amusements and made the people drill as soldiers all day long.

As soon as he was ready to fight he marched out with his army of Greeks and Tarentines against the Romans, and there was a great battle near the city of Heraclea. Both sides fought well for hours, but the Greeks at last began to fall back. They could not stand against the steady, fierce attacks made by the Romans.

Then Pyrrhus brought his elephants upon the field. He had seventy of them, and they were thoroughly trained to fight. They would run into the ranks of the enemy, knock the soldiers down and trample them to death, or lay hold of them with their trunks and throw them high into the air.

As the elephants stood in line waiting for the order to charge, the Romans looked at them with wonder and fear. They knew nothing about elephants, for they had never seen any before. And when the huge beasts came charging furiously across the field, making strange noises, many of the Roman soldiers were terribly frightened and began to run away. The elephants killed hundreds of them, and in a few minutes the Roman army was put to flight.

It was saved from entire destruction by only one thing. A Roman soldier was brave enough to rush at an elephant while it was charging and cut off a part of its trunk with his sword. The animal, wild with pain, turned and ran back to the Greek lines, trampling down the soldiers and causing a great deal of confusion. In the excitement the Romans managed to escape across a river to a friendly city where they were safe.

Pyrrhus won the victory, but he lost thousands of men. When he saw the great number of his soldiers that lay dead on the field, he exclaimed:

"A few more such victories and I must return to Epirus alone!"

III

Shortly after the battle Pyrrhus sent his friend and favorite minister, Cineas, to Rome to offer terms of peace to the Senate. Cineas was a very eloquent man. Often when Pyrrhus could not conquer people in battle, Cineas by his clever speeches induced them to submit to the king and be his friends. This was why the Greeks used to say, "The tongue of Cineas wins more cities than the sword of Pyrrhus."

Cineas proposed to the Roman Senate that the Romans should not make war any longer on the Tarentines, nor on any of the Italian tribes that had helped them, and that all the lands Rome had taken from these tribes in past years should be given back. If the Romans would agree to these terms, then Pyrrhus would be their true friend.

The terms were not good for Rome, but Cineas was so smooth-spoken and so pleasant in proposing them that many of the senators were inclined to accept them. One day while they were discussing the matter in the Senate a thrilling scene occurred.

Appius Claudius was still living in Rome. He was very old and had become blind. For this reason he got the name *Caecus,* a word which is Latin for *blind.* But his mind was remarkably clear, and he had not lost interest in public affairs. When he heard that the Senate was going to accept the terms offered by Pyrrhus he rose

74

from his bed declaring that he would go and speak against the proposal.

So he was carried by his slaves to the Senate house, and his sons led the aged man to his seat. He began his speech amidst the deepest silence. His youth seemed to come back to him. Once more he was the bold censor of thirty years before. In fiery words he spoke against the plan for peace, saying it would be base and cowardly to yield to the Greek king.

"Let us fight on," he said, "as long as we have soldiers. Shall we submit to this Greek invader merely because we have lost one battle? Never! Never! I say. Better to lose all that we have than to disgrace ourselves by submitting!"

The patriotic old man went on speaking in this way until his strength failed him and he sank exhausted into his seat. His speech had so much effect on the senators that they immediately voted against the proposal of Pyrrhus and ordered Cineas to depart from Rome.

Then the war was carried on vigorously. A great battle was fought at Asculum, and again the Romans were defeated by the Greeks. But they were not discouraged. The Consul Curius Dentatus fought another battle against Pyrrhus at Beneventum, and won a glorious victory. The Greeks were utterly defeated, and Pyrrhus soon afterwards left Italy and returned to his own country.

Then the Romans speedily took possession of Tarentum and made its people pay well for their insult to the Roman ambassadors.

REGULUS

I

The next great war the Romans engaged in was with Carthage. It was about the possession of the island of Sicily, in the Mediterranean Sea. It began not long after Pyrrhus left Italy and was the first of three wars called the Punic Wars. Punic means Phœnician and the people who founded Carthage came from Phœnicia, so Carthage was called a Punic or Phœnician colony.

When the first Punic War began both Rome and Carthage were very rich and powerful. Rome had great armies and great generals. Its common soldiers, too, were remarkably brave and patriotic. It was very successful in its wars. Before it began to fight Carthage it had conquered nearly all Italy.

Carthage, also, had fine armies, but its greatest strength was in its navy. No other country in the world at that time had so many ships of war and trading ships. The ships of the Carthaginians went everywhere in the Mediterranean. Some of them even went past the

Pillars of Hercules, as the rocky capes at the Strait of Gibraltar were then called, and sailed for some distance on the Atlantic Ocean.

The Carthaginian ships were small, but they were very strong. The warships were built to carry a good many soldiers, as well as sailors and oarsmen. They had great rounded iron prows, which could do much damage to an enemy's ships when run up against them. Each ship had a mast and large sail, but it was also rowed with oars by many oarsmen who sat on long benches, placed one above the other. With the sail and the oars the ship could be made to go very fast through the water.

Carthage was in North Africa, in the country now called Tunis. It stood at the head of a beautiful bay of the Mediterranean. It was a large and handsome city and had a great commerce.

II

Many years before the beginning of the first Punic War Carthage conquered a great part of Sicily and made it a Carthaginian colony. But the Romans wanted the island, and so under the pretence of protecting an Italian tribe that had settled there they sent an army into Sicily. This was how the first Punic War began.

Both Rome and Carthage fought fiercely, and for a long time neither had much advantage over the other. At first the Romans had no warships. Up to that time they did not need any, for all their fighting was on land. But when they began war with the Carthaginians they found that they must have ships to carry their soldiers to Sicily and to fight the Carthaginians at sea. So the Romans set to work to build ships and to train men to row them, and in a short time they had a great navy.

In the ninth year of the war the armies and fleets of Rome were put under the command of a general named

Marcus Atilius Regulus. He was a great hero and patriot. He had been a general before the Punic War and had often led the Romans to victory. After years of good service, fighting and winning battles for his country, he went to live on his little farm and, like Cincinnatus, he cultivated it with his own hands. A story is told of him which well illustrates ancient Roman honor and patriotism.

Until Regulus took command the Punic War was carried on only in Sicily and on the Mediterranean. But he thought that Rome should fight the Carthaginians in their own country, and so he organized an immense army and navy to invade Carthage. He had three hundred and thirty warships of the largest size and about sixty thousand soldiers.

In those times, in fights at sea, they had an engine called a boarding bridge. One end of it was fixed to the deck of the ship. The other end, which was free, could be swung round and on to an enemy's ship, and it had a heavy iron spike underneath, so that when it fell on the deck it would sink into it and thus hold the enemy's vessel for the attacking party to board it.

When everything was ready Regulus set sail for Africa. Soon after starting he met a large Carthaginian fleet, and in a short battle he destroyed it. Then he sailed on and after landing in Africa began a march towards Carthage. On his way he captured several towns, and he met and defeated a Carthaginian army. He then continued his march until he met another army of Carthaginians. This army was commanded by Xanthippus, a famous general of Sparta, in Greece, who happened to be in Carthage at that time. In the battle that followed the Romans were defeated, and Regulus was made prisoner and taken off to Carthage.

III

But the Romans had other generals and other armies, and they carried on the war and defeated the Carthaginians in many battles.

At last the Carthaginians thought it better to try to make peace, and so they sent ambassadors to Rome to propose that the war should be stopped on certain terms, which they were ready to offer. They sent Regulus with the ambassadors, but they made him swear that he would return to Carthage if the Roman Senate should refuse to agree to their terms. They thought that in order to gain his own freedom Regulus would try to get the Senate to accept their proposals. Regulus agreed to go and made the promise required.

"I give you my word of honor," said he, "that I will return if your terms are not accepted."

Then he set out for Rome with the ambassadors. As he approached the gates of the city, thousands of people came forth to welcome him and to escort him through the streets. But he refused to enter.

"I cannot enter Rome," said he. "I am no longer a Roman officer, but a prisoner of Carthage. Do not urge me to enter the gates. I am not even worth exchanging for a Carthaginian prisoner."

The people, however, insisted that he should enter the city, and so amid shouts and cheers he was escorted to the Senate house.

In a little while the Carthaginian ambassadors presented their proposals, and the Senate began to consider them. After some discussion Regulus was asked to give his opinion whether the terms ought to be accepted or not.

Regulus at first was unwilling to speak in the Senate. He said that by becoming a prisoner he had lost the honor of being a senator.

"I am no longer a Roman senator," said he. "I am a

prisoner of Carthage."

The Senate, however, insisted that he should speak. Then Regulus said that the Senate ought not to accept the terms of peace offered by Carthage. He thought that they were not good terms for Rome, and he advised the Senate not to agree to them.

But the Senate was inclined to accept the terms for the sake of Regulus himself. If peace were not made he would have to go back and remain a prisoner in Carthage, or perhaps he would be put to death. Therefore the Senate was for agreeing to the Carthaginian terms. But Regulus again spoke strongly against them, and at last the Senate decided to reject the Carthaginian proposals.

IV

Regulus now prepared to return to Carthage, but his family and friends clung to him, saying:

"You must not go! You must not go!"

To all their appeals he made but one answer:

"I have given my word of honor to return, and I cannot break it."

So Regulus returned to Carthage with the ambassadors. When the people of that city heard that by his advice their terms had been rejected they were very angry. They had wished very much to make peace with Rome, for the long war had cost them a great many lives and a great deal of money, and they wanted to stop it. Therefore they were enraged against Regulus and they put him to death in a very cruel way.

The war between Rome and Carthage continued for some years more, but at last the Carthaginians were defeated in a great sea battle near the coast of Sicily. They were then obliged to give up Sicily and pay a large sum of money to the Romans as a fine. This was the end of the first Punic War (241 B.C.).

SCIPIO AFRICANUS

I

But peace did not last long between Rome and Carthage. Some years after the end of the first Punic War the Carthaginians attacked and took possession of a town in Spain, the people of which were friends and allies of Rome. This caused the second Punic War, which began B.C. 218.

One of the great soldiers of this war was Publius Cornelius Scipio. In the latter part of his life he was called Scipio Africanus, on account of the great victories which he won in Africa.

Scipio was a brave soldier from his youth. When only seventeen years old he fought in a battle and saved his father's life. He was always gallant and heroic in war, so he soon became noted in the Roman army and rose to high rank. And although he was a member of a noble family, he was well liked by the plebeians and they elected him "ædile."

The ædiles were magistrates or judges. They were

also superintendents of public buildings and of the games and shows of which the Roman people were so fond.

When Scipio was about twenty-seven years of age, he was appointed to command the Roman army that was fighting the Carthaginians in Spain. Carthage had conquered some parts of Spain, and Rome had conquered other parts, and the two nations were often at war about places in that country.

When Scipio went to Spain many of the people there were against him, but they soon became his friends. Whenever he took a city he allowed the chiefs who were captured to go free, and he gave presents to many of them. He always showed great respect to women and children who were taken prisoners. In those times it was the cruel custom to make slaves of women who were found in towns that had been taken in war. But Scipio never did this in Spain. He always let the women go free.

One day a beautiful Spanish girl who had been taken prisoner was brought before him. She seemed very much frightened, but Scipio spoke kindly to her and told her that no one should harm her. While speaking with her he learned that a young man who was her lover had also been taken prisoner by the Roman soldiers. He sent for the young man and said to him:

"Take your sweetheart and go. I set you both free. Go and be happy and in future be friends of Rome."

And so by many acts of kindness Scipio gained the friendship of the Spaniards. After a while they began to join the Romans and gave them great help in their war against the Carthaginians.

II

When his services were no longer needed in Spain,

Scipio returned to Rome. He got a great reception in the city. There was a grand parade in his honor. He brought home an immense quantity of silver, which he obtained from the rich Spanish mines and from the cities he had taken. The silver was put into the Roman treasury to pay the expenses of the war.

Soon after he returned from Spain Scipio was elected consul. The Carthaginian general, Hannibal, was then in Italy with a large army. This Hannibal was one of the greatest generals of ancient times. When he was but nine years old his father, who was also a great general, made him take an oath that he would hate Rome and the Romans forever. Then he took the boy with him to Spain and gave him a thorough training as a soldier.

When his father died Hannibal became commander of the Carthaginian army in Spain. He was then little more than twenty-one years old. He fought well in Spain for some time and was well liked by his soldiers. Suddenly he resolved to make war on the Romans in their own country and to go by land to Italy. So he got ready an immense army and set out on his march. In passing through France he had to cross the broad River Rhone. This was not easy to do, for there was no bridge. He got his men over in boats, but he had a number of elephants in his army and they were too big and heavy to be taken across in that way. The boats were small and the elephants were afraid to go into them. Hannibal therefore got rafts or floats, made of trunks of trees tied together, and in these the elephants were carried over.

After crossing the Rhone Hannibal marched over the Alps into Italy. He and his army suffered many hardships in making their way over those snow-covered mountains. He had often to fight fierce tribes that came to oppose him, but he defeated them all, and after being defeated many of them joined his army and brought him provisions for his soldiers.

Very soon Roman armies were sent against Hannibal, but he defeated them in many battles. Once his army got into a place near high hills where he could not march further except through one narrow pass between the hills. The Roman general, Quintus Fabius, sent four thousand of his troops to take possession of this pass, and he posted the rest of his army on the hills close by.

Hannibal saw that he was in a trap, but he found a way of escaping. He caused vine branches to be tied to the horns of a large number of the oxen that were with his army. Then he ordered his men to set the branches on fire in the middle of the night and to drive the oxen up the hills.

As soon as the animals felt the pain they rushed madly about and set fire to the shrubs and bushes they met on the way. The Romans at the pass thought that the Carthaginians were escaping by torchlight. So they hastily quit their posts and hurried towards the hills to help their comrades. Then Hannibal, seeing the pass free, marched his army out and so escaped from the trap.

Quintus Fabius was very slow and cautious in his movements. The Romans had been defeated so often that he thought the best plan was to harass Hannibal in every possible way, but not to venture to fight him in a great battle until he should be sure of winning. For this reason the Romans gave Fabius the name of *Cunctator*, which means *delayer*, and so the plan of extreme delay or caution in any undertaking is often called a *Fabian* policy.

But in spite of the caution of Fabius Hannibal gained many great victories. His greatest victory was at the battle of Cannæ, in the south of Italy. Here he defeated and destroyed a Roman army of seventy thousand men. And for several years after this battle Hannibal remained in Italy doing the Romans all the harm he could.

At last Scipio thought it was time to follow the plan of Regulus. So he said to the Senate:

"We have acted too long as if we were afraid of Hannibal and Carthage. We defend ourselves bravely when we are attacked, and so far we have saved Rome from destruction; but we do not make any attacks on our enemies. We certainly ought to do this, for our armies are strong and fully ready to meet the Carthaginians."

Scipio then proposed that an army led by himself should go to Africa and carry on war there. He believed that if this were done Hannibal would have to go to Africa to defend Carthage.

Perhaps on account of what had happened to Regulus, the Senate did not like Scipio's plan. Nevertheless, it gave him permission to go to Africa, but would not give him an army. Scipio then raised a splendid army of volunteers and sailed across the Mediterranean Sea to Africa.

III

Scipio tried for some time to obtain the aid of Syphax, a powerful king of Numidia, in Africa. But Syphax decided to join the Carthaginians. So Scipio found two great armies ready to fight him. One was the army of Carthage, with thirty-three thousand men, commanded by Hasdrubal Gisco, and the other was the army of Numidia, with sixty thousand men, commanded by King Syphax.

But Scipio found in Africa one strong friend, and that was a Numidian prince named Masinissa. This prince had a host of supporters among his countrymen and was therefore able to bring a large force of good soldiers to the aid of the Romans. He was of great service to Scipio in many ways.

When everything was ready the Roman army, with

Masinissa's force, encamped about six miles from the camps of the enemy. Scipio sent spies among the Carthaginians and the soldiers of King Syphax, and from them he learned that both armies were lodged in huts made of stakes and covered with reeds and dried leaves. He resolved to set those huts on fire.

So one very dark night the Roman army left its camp and marched silently to the plain occupied by the enemy. Then a division of the Romans went to the encampment of the Numidians and a soldier crept cautiously from the Roman lines and set one of the huts on fire. The fire spread rapidly, and in a few minutes the whole camp was in flames.

The Numidian soldiers, suddenly awakened by the fire, fled from the burning huts without their weapons and made frantic efforts to escape from the camp. Hundreds of them were knocked down and trampled to death in the rush and confusion; hundreds more lost their lives in the fire. Those who got to the open country were attacked by the Romans and killed. The ground was covered with the bodies of the slain. King Syphax and a few horsemen managed to escape, but the rest of the vast Numidian army was destroyed.

In the meantime the Carthaginians had been aroused by the noise in the camp of the Numidians. They thought that the fire had been caused by an accident, and some of them ran forward to assist the Numidians. But the greater number stood in a confused throng, without their arms, outside their camp, looking at the fire with terror.

While they were in this helpless state the Carthaginians were suddenly attacked by the Romans with Scipio at their head. Many were killed, and the others were driven back into their camp, which was immediately set on fire in a number of places. Then there was a frightful scene. Thousands of Carthaginians, struggling to escape the fire, were slain by the Romans, while thousands more perished in the flames. Hasdrubal Gisco, the commander, and some of his officers escaped, but only a few of the others. In less than an hour there was little left of the Carthaginian army.

IV

Scipio now began to march towards the great, rich city of Carthage. He captured a number of towns and a great deal of treasure. In a few weeks, however, the Carthaginians were able to form another army of thirty thousand men, and then they came boldly forth to meet Scipio.

A fierce battle followed. The Romans were driven back for a time, but with wonderful courage they charged the Carthaginians again and again and at last totally defeated them.

The Carthaginians now sent a message to Italy requesting Hannibal to come to the relief of his country. The renowned general did not want to leave Italy, for he hoped to be able to take Rome; but he thought it best to obey the call of Carthage, so he sailed for Africa with his army.

After arriving in Africa Hannibal led his army to a wide plain near Zama, a town not far from Carthage. Here he awaited the Romans.

Hannibal had great admiration for Scipio, and he desired to see him before engaging in battle. So he sent a messenger to Scipio requesting an interview. The request was granted, and the two generals met.

They greeted each other cordially, and each complimented the other on his victories and greatness as a soldier. Then Hannibal proposed terms of peace to Scipio.

"We will give Spain and the islands of Sicily and Sardinia to Rome. Then we will divide the sea with you.

87

What more would you have? Rome and Carthage would then be the two great nations of the world."

Scipio thought it was too late to make terms.

"We must fight it out," said he, "until one side or the other is vanquished."

The generals then parted, and the next day the two armies were drawn up in battle array. On each side there were about thirty thousand men, but Hannibal had a herd of fighting elephants.

The battle was long and severe. Both armies fought heroically, and there was terrible slaughter. But Hannibal's elephants were of little use to him, as the Romans frightened them by blowing trumpets and hurling balls of fire at them. At a moment when the lines of the Carthaginians were breaking, a strong force of Roman horsemen came up suddenly in the rear and overpowered all before it. This won the battle for the Romans. When Hannibal saw that the battle was lost he fled from the field with a few friends (202 B.C.).

Scipio was now master of Carthage. He compelled the Carthaginians to pay him a vast amount in gold and silver and to give up some of their towns and lands. He also compelled them to destroy their great fleet of warships and to promise not to make war in future upon any people without the permission of the Romans.

When Scipio returned to Rome he entered the city at the head of a grand procession. The greatest honors were paid to him, and he was called Scipio Africanus.

Some years afterwards Scipio met Hannibal at the court of the king of Syria. The two generals had a friendly conversation and Scipio asked Hannibal who he thought was the greatest general that ever lived. Hannibal answered:

"Alexander the Great."

"Who was the second?" asked Scipio.

"Pyrrhus," replied Hannibal.

"Who the third?"

"Myself," answered Hannibal.

"But what would you have said," asked Scipio, "if you had conquered me?"

"I should then have said," replied Hannibal, "that I was greater than Alexander, greater than Pyrrhus, and greater than all other generals."

CATO THE CENSOR

I

On a farm near Tusculum, a little town about fifteen miles from Rome, there once lived a boy named Marcus Porcius Cato. His father and his grandfather before him had been farmers and he, too, expected to be one.

When he was about seventeen Hannibal's army crossed the Alps into Italy, and young Cato became a Roman soldier. When the war ended the country boy had become a man, stern and forceful. He attracted the attention of a neighbor, a rich man, who persuaded him to go to Rome and practice law.

In time he was elected to office, and he did his duty so well that he rose higher and higher, until he became one of the consuls. That same year a rebellion arose in Spain, and Cato led an army against the Spaniards. It is said that in four hundred days he captured four hundred villages. On his return to Rome he was honored with a triumph.

Shortly after this he was sent to Greece, where Antiochus was attacking Greek cities that were friendly to Rome. He defeated Antiochus in the Pass of Thermopylae and won great fame as a soldier.

Cato was a very hard man; hard on himself, hard on his friends. And although he was rich and held office in a great city, he lived a hard life, taking no pleasures and saving his money. He ate the plainest food and drank the same cheap wine that he bought for his slaves.

He thought that the luxury and extravagance of the rich were taking away the strength of Rome. In order to put a stop to these things Cato asked the people of Rome to elect him censor. The patricians opposed him bitterly, but he was elected by a large majority. One of the first things he did was to expel from the senate several senators who were leading improper lives. He had a heavy tax put on carriages so as to compel people to walk. He also placed a tax on jewels, handsome dresses, carpets, and fine furniture. So well did he do his work that he is always known in history as Cato the Censor, just as if he were the only man who ever held the office. A statue erected in his honor says nothing about his victories in Spain or at Thermopylae, but only that, "When the Roman Republic was degenerating, Cato restored it by strict discipline."

II

In the later years of his life Cato was sent to Carthage to look into a certain matter for Rome. The trouble was this: You will remember that Carthage had agreed to make war upon no nation without the consent of the Roman Senate. A few years later, Masinissa, who was a friend of Rome, attacked the Carthaginians, and they appealed to Rome for protection. This was refused, and the people of Carthage took up arms to defend themselves against Masinissa.

Cato was sent to Carthage to find out who was to

blame. When he arrived in the city he was surprised to find it large and strong and flourishing. Only twenty-six years had passed since Scipio Africanus had conquered Carthage, and yet Cato saw crowds of young men on the street, stacks of arms in the arsenals, and a forest of masts in the harbor. The city itself was rich and prosperous.

Cato returned to Rome and warned his countrymen that Carthage must be destroyed. From that time forward whenever he made a speech in the senate, no matter upon what subject, he always ended it by saying, "And my opinion is that Carthage must be destroyed." In time, the words of Cato had their effect, and war was declared against Carthage.

The troops had already embarked when envoys from Carthage reached Rome and offered to do whatever might be asked. The Roman Senate promised that the laws and liberties of Carthage should not be touched, but demanded hostages. So three hundred children of the leading families of Carthage were sent to Rome. When the Roman army reached Carthage the consuls insisted that the Carthaginians should give up their arms. This was done and the Carthaginians asked if the Romans required anything more.

Then one of the consuls said, "Your city must be destroyed, and you must move ten miles inland from the sea." The Carthaginians now saw that they had been deceived. They closed their gates and determined to defend themselves to the last. They asked an armistice of thirty days, so that an embassy might go to Rome. It was granted, and thus a month of time was gained. During this time men, women, and children went to work to make arms to defend their homes. The women even cut off their hair to furnish strings for the bows of the war machines with which stones were hurled at the enemy.

The embassy failed in its mission to Rome and the siege of Carthage began. It lasted three years.

The son of Paulus Æmilius had been adopted by the son of Scipio Africanus and had taken the name Scipio. He was sent to Carthage and about a year after his arrival forced an entrance into the city and captured it (146 B.C.). The walls were torn down and the buildings set on fire. Cato who was so largely responsible for the war did not live to see its end. He died almost two years before the city was destroyed.

The Senate honored Scipio with the title Africanus, which the older conqueror of Carthage had borne.

The young Scipio won fame not only in Africa but also in Spain, where he was sent against the Numantians. These brave people had defeated two Roman armies, but Scipio soon succeeded in shutting them within the walls of Numantia. Around its walls he built walls of his own behind which his soldiers were safe from attack. Food soon became scarce in Numantia. At the end of fifteen months the citizens were starving. They were willing to lose their lives, but Scipio stayed behind his own walls and refused to fight. Rather than trust to the mercy of Rome the Numantians killed themselves.

In time all Spain was forced to submit and become a Roman province.

THE GRACCHI

I

Between the second and third Punic wars there lived in Rome two brothers named Tiberius and Caius Gracchus, commonly called the Gracchi. They were very good men and great friends of the common people.

The mother of the Gracchi was Cornelia, a daughter of Scipio Africanus. She was an excellent woman, and she was very proud of her two sons. She taught them to be brave and manly and always to stand up for the people.

One day a rich lady, while on a visit to Cornelia, showed her some magnificent jewels. When they had looked them over the lady said:

"These are my jewels; now let me see yours."

Just at that moment Tiberius and Caius, who were then boys, came into the room. As soon as she saw them Cornelia called them to her and, putting her arms around them, said:

"These are my jewels."

When Tiberius and Caius grew up to be men they took the side of the people in a quarrel that had been going on for a long time between the plebeians and nobles. The quarrel was about land. Whenever the Romans conquered a country in war they took possession of a portion of the land of the conquered country. Such land was called public land, and for many years after the founding of the city the custom of dividing parts of the public lands among all the citizens was strictly observed.

But in later times this custom was changed. Instead of part of the public lands being divided among all the citizens, it was divided among only the nobles, and the plebeians got none at all. The lands were tilled by slaves, and all that was raised went to the nobles. So the poor soldiers who won the lands by hard fighting were without farms to till, and some of them even without homes. They continually demanded that the old law, for a fair division of the lands among all the citizens, should be carried out. The nobles laughed at the demand.

But Tiberius Gracchus came forward boldly as the champion of the poor. He declared that the nobles should give up the lands they had unjustly taken, and that the people should have their fair share. His words made the nobles very angry, and they became his bitter enemies.

II

But the people honored Tiberius and made him one of their tribunes. The tribunes were supposed to look after the people's interests, but sometimes they were not faithful to their duty. As we have already said, they had a great deal of power. They could sit at the door of the Roman Senate, and when a law was proposed that they did not like they could say, "We veto it!" and then the law could not be passed.

Whenever the tribunes wanted a law passed they proposed it at the meeting of all the people in what was called the Assembly of Tribes. The common people had a great deal of power in this Assembly, and any law proposed by the tribune was generally passed. Then the tribunes had the power to compel the consuls to carry out the law.

Not long after Tiberius Gracchus became tribune he proposed a law that each noble might have five hundred acres of the public land for his own use and two hundred and fifty more for each son, and that the remainder of the lands should be equally divided among the poor citizens.

This law was passed, and then the nobles had to give up a large part of the lands they had seized. So the poor citizens got good farms.

About this time Attalus, the king of Pergamus, a country of Asia, died, leaving all his money to the Romans. The nobles tried to get this money for themselves, but Tiberius had it divided among the poor citizens.

Of course this made the nobles still more angry with Tiberius, and they resolved to get rid of him if they could. So on election day, when the people were voting to make Tiberius tribune for a second term, some nobles went to the voting-place and raised a disturbance. But the friends of Tiberius drove them away. Then the nobles started a report that Tiberius was trying to induce the people to make him king.

Afterwards they gathered their friends and slaves and began fighting with the people. No arms were used, but stones were thrown, and sticks, broken benches, and other things hastily caught up, served as weapons. There was a dreadful tumult for a while, and many persons were killed.

Tiberius was in the midst of his friends bravely defending himself against an attack by a party of nobles, when suddenly he stumbled and fell to the ground. In a moment the nobles rushed upon him. One of them struck him on the head with a piece of wood and killed him. Then they took his body and threw it into the Tiber.

III

Tiberius was now out of the way, and the nobles began to seize the lands that had been divided among the people. But Caius Gracchus suddenly appeared in Rome and declared that he had come to take his brother's place as the friend of the people. He had been with a Roman army in Spain when Tiberius was killed.

The people now elected him tribune and he began to carry out his brother's plans. For this reason the nobles hated him as much as they had hated his brother. They said that he was a dangerous man and was planning to make himself king. One day as he was passing through the Forum a strange man said to him:

"I hope you will spare the Republic!"

The friends of Caius were angry at these words, and they fell on the man and killed him.

The nobles and their followers then armed themselves. The plebeians also gathered in great numbers ready for a fight. Caius was asked to lead them, but refused. He did not want them to fight with the nobles. He knew that the nobles would be satisfied with his own death, so he ordered a slave to stab him to the heart. The order was obeyed, and thus perished the last of the Gracchi (121 B.C.).

MARIUS

I

At the time of the death of Caius Gracchus there was in Rome a great man named Caius Marius. This man came forward and said to the people that if they would elect him tribune he would get them their rights.

The people elected him tribune and, true to his word, he did everything he could to improve their condition. He was afterwards elected consul seven times, and for a long while he was the greatest man in Rome.

Marius was a tall and very powerful man and had a strong will. When he said he would do anything he would do it in spite of all difficulties. He was a very great soldier. Many people thought him the best of the Roman generals.

He succeeded in a war against Jugurtha, king of Numidia, after other generals had failed. He took many cities from Jugurtha and at last captured the king himself and all his treasure.

Jugurtha was brought to Rome and compelled to

walk behind the chariot of Marius in a grand triumphal procession. He was afterwards put into a foul dungeon and left there to die.

The nobles did not like Marius. He was the son of plebeian parents and he had taken the side of the plebeians against the nobles. Therefore the nobles hated him, and they would have done everything they could against him, only that they needed his help to protect Rome from very dangerous enemies.

A host of barbarian people, called Cimbri, Teutones, and Ambrones, had left their homes on the shores of the Baltic Sea and invaded the southern lands. They were strong, fierce men, and they laid waste every country they passed through. They defeated several Roman armies that were sent against them. Some of the tribes of Helvetia (the country now called Switzerland) joined them and one of those tribes defeated and killed a Roman consul and made his army pass under the yoke.

The Romans were, therefore, very much frightened. They thought that the barbarians would soon be in Italy. So Marius was appointed to go against them with a great army. He crossed the Mediterranean into Gaul and met the Teutones and Ambrones near the city of Arles on the River Rhone. The Cimbri had already gone to Italy.

Marius first made a strong entrenched camp. He wanted to give his men time to get accustomed to the manners of the strange enemy before attempting to fight them. The Roman soldiers had shown fear at sight of the barbarians. They had never before seen such people.

The Teutones were like giants. They had large, wild, staring eyes and long hair, and they made terrible war-cries. The Ambrones and the Cimbri were as savage in appearance. The king of the Teutones was very tall and so active that he could leap over six horses placed abreast.

When the barbarians saw that the Romans would not fight, they began to taunt and insult them. They walked up and down in front of the Roman camp day after day, calling the soldiers cowards.

"Why don't you come out and fight us like men?" they cried. "Are you afraid? Come out, come out; we are in a hurry! We are going to Rome after we kill you!"

Marius had hard work to keep his men from rushing out upon the barbarians. He did not yet want to fight, but he said to his soldiers:

"When the proper time comes we will give these savages all the fighting they want."

One day a gigantic Teuton chief, with a long shield and spear, came up to the very entrance of the Roman camp and called loudly for Marius himself to come out and fight. The great general laughed heartily at the impudence of the barbarian, and he sent out a gladiator to fight with him in order to give sport to the Romans.

Gladiators were men who fought one another in the shows at Rome for the amusement of the people. They were usually slaves and were very strong, active, and well-trained fighters.

It did not take the gladiator long to defeat the Teuton. In a few minutes he laid the savage giant low, and the Romans shouted with joy at the sight.

After the Teuton was killed the Romans still remained in their camp. Marius was not yet prepared to fight. At last the barbarians got tired waiting and they started off to march to Italy.

II

So great was the number of the barbarians that it took them six whole days to march past the Roman camp. When all had passed Marius left his camp and followed them by slow marches. Before long the two armies arrived at the city of Aix on the south coast of Gaul.

Marius thought it was now time to fight, so he led out his fine army against the enemy. The first battle was fought with the Ambrones. They astonished the Romans with their war-cry. They held their shields upright and at a little distance from their mouths and shouted: "Ambrones! Ambrones!" as if to terrify the Romans by letting them know who they were. Then they rushed furiously across the field.

The Romans met the charge with wonderful courage. Their lines were scarcely broken. Three times they drove back the enemy, and then they themselves moved steadily forward with their whole force. They cut down the Ambrones by thousands, took many prisoners, and sent the others fleeing away in terror.

Next day there was another battle. The Teutones and Ambrones together attacked the Romans, but the Romans were again victorious. When the battle was over it was found that more than a hundred thousand barbarians had been killed or taken prisoners.

Marius now turned his attention to the Cimbri, who had gone to Italy. They had encamped on a beautiful, fertile plain near the River Po, and were enjoying the warm Italian sun and the sweet fruits of the country.

But Marius was not very long in reaching the same place with his victorious army. When the Cimbri saw the Romans marching on to the plain where they were encamped, they were astonished. To gain time they sent a messenger to Marius to ask him to give them lands to live on in Italy.

"Give us," said the messenger, "lands in Italy for ourselves and for our friends, the Teutones and Ambrones, and we will all live at peace."

"Never mind the Teutones and the Ambrones," said Marius, "they have lands already. We have given them some which they will keep forever. We will give you the same."

Then a battle began between the two great armies. The foot soldiers of the Cimbri were formed into an immense square, and the men in the front ranks were chained to one another by iron chains so that they could not run away. There were fifteen thousand horsemen, wearing on their helmets the heads of wild beasts.

The battle was a hard one for a while, but it did not continue long. Time after time the Cimbri were driven back, and at last they were put to flight. Thousands of them were killed, and thousands made prisoners.

When Marius and his soldiers returned to Rome they got a splendid reception. There was a parade through the streets, and a great feast was given to the people. A large sum of money was divided among the soldiers to reward them for their brave conduct.

Marius was now in high favor at Rome. The nobles did not dare to speak a word against him. He was elected consul seven times, so that he was master of the Republic for a long time.

In the sixth year that Marius was consul the war called the Social War broke out. It lasted for three years. It was a war with some of the nations of Italy which Rome had formerly conquered. The people of those nations did not want to separate from Rome, but they wanted to have the right of voting as the Romans themselves had. Rome refused to give them this right, and at last they resolved to go to war.

All the greatest Roman generals of the time took part in this war. One of them was a young noble named Sulla. He was a very successful soldier and won a number of great victories. The nations were defeated in the war, but Rome soon granted them most of the rights they had asked for.

The nobles gave great praise to Sulla for his victories in the Social War. They declared that he was a better general than Marius. So many fine things were said about the young noble that Marius became jealous and did a very foolish thing. He suddenly left his army in the field and came back to Rome. He complained that he was nervous and he shut himself up in his house and refused to see any of his friends for weeks.

The nobles then started a story that Marius was getting silly and weak-minded from old age. He was about seventy at this time, and the nobles said he ought to retire from the army. This made the old hero angry and he declared he was as strong in mind and body as any of the young Romans.

One morning he went to the place where the young men of Rome used to practise athletic sports, and for two or three hours he wrestled and ran and leaped with as much skill and strength as any one. Some of the nobles who happened to pass by saw him and were very much amused.

About this time Sulla was elected consul on account of his victories in the Social War. Shortly afterwards Rome declared war against Mithridates, King of Pontus in Asia Minor, who had cruelly put to death a number of the citizens of a Roman province in Asia.

The Senate appointed Sulla to command the Roman army in this war. But as soon as he left Rome with his army one of the tribunes proposed at an Assembly of the people that the command should be taken from him and given to Marius. The Assembly agreed to this and Marius accepted the appointment. He sent word to the army, which was not far from Rome, that he would come in a short time to take command.

When Sulla heard this he became very angry. He called his soldiers around him, told them what had been done, and asked them if they would submit to be the slaves of Marius and his party.

"No, no!" cried the soldiers, "we will not submit. We want you for our general."

"Then follow me to Rome," said Sulla, "we will teach Marius and his friends that they must not insult us."

So the soldiers marched quickly back to Rome with Sulla at their head. They declared that they would take the city out of the hands of rebels, as they called the friends of Marius. When they entered the city they were met by Marius and his followers and there was a battle, in which Marius was defeated. Then a law was passed declaring Marius a traitor and that he should be put to death.

But Marius fled from Rome with some friends and went down the Tiber in a boat to the Mediterranean. He sailed along the coast and then he and his companions went ashore to seek for food. They wandered through the country for some time without seeing any one. At last they met a farmer, who gave them something to eat. He told them that horsemen from Rome were riding through the place searching for Marius.

They were frightened at this and they ran into a thick wood where they stopped all night. But while his companions were downcast Marius was cheerful and hopeful.

"This bad state of things," he said, "will last only a short time. I know it, because the gods have revealed to me that I shall be once more consul of Rome!"

But next day Marius was taken by the horsemen. He saw them coming and waded far into a great marsh and hid himself among some high, thick reeds. The horsemen rode into the marsh and found him, and they put a rope round his neck and dragged him to the shore. Then they shut him up in a hut and began to think what they should do with him.

At last they decided to put him to death at once. They thought this would please Sulla, and that perhaps he would reward them for it. So they gave a sword to a slave and sent him to kill Marius. The slave entered the hut and stood for a few moments looking at the great general. Marius glared at him like a wild beast and said in a stern voice:

"Slave, will you dare to kill Caius Marius?"

The slave started back in terror and ran out of the hut. Then he threw down his sword at the feet of the soldiers and cried out that he could never have the courage to slay Marius.

It was now decided to send Marius out of the country. So he was taken to a ship and carried to Africa. After going ashore he wandered through the country until he came to the place where Carthage once stood. Nothing now remained of the famous city but a mass of gloomy ruins, for the Romans had entirely destroyed it a few years before in the third Punic War. In these ruins Marius lived for a short time. One day a soldier came to tell him that the governor of Africa wanted him to leave the country.

"Go to your governor," answered Marius, "and tell him that you saw Caius Marius sitting on the ruins of Carthage."

Not long afterwards, when Sulla was away fighting King Mithridates, there was great trouble at Rome. One of the consuls named Cinna, aided by many of the plebeians, attempted to get the control of public affairs, but was defeated by the nobles. Then Cinna and his followers were forced to leave the city. They organized an army among the Italians who had been complaining of not getting their rights from Rome, and they sent to Africa for Marius to come and be their commander.

When Marius arrived he made an attack on Rome and soon captured it. Then he marched in through the gates at the head of his army and took possession of the city. At the next election the people elected him consul.

Marius now resolved to have vengeance on the nobles who had driven him from Rome. And for several days the old Roman, surrounded by a guard of freed slaves, went through the city seeking the nobles in their houses, in the temples, in the Forum, and everywhere that they could be found, and killing them without mercy.

These were dreadful days. Some of the noblest men of Rome were put to death. None of Sulla's friends was spared. Even his wife and children were harshly treated and forced to leave the city.

Marius did not stop the bloody work until he had killed all his enemies that he could find. But his triumph was short. He died in a little more than two weeks after he had become consul for the seventh time.

SULLA

I

We have said something of Sulla, but there is much more to be told about him, for he was a very remarkable man, and he did remarkable things in Rome. His full name was Lucius Cornelius Sulla. He belonged to a very noble family. When he was a young man he was very fond of study and became an excellent scholar. He was also a good speaker and often made eloquent speeches in the Forum on public affairs.

He was a large, strong man, with red hair and a ruddy face. He was a very great soldier and one of the greatest of Roman generals. They called him "the Lion," he was so brave in battle, and he was so successful in war that he also got the name of *Felix*, a Latin word which means *happy* or fortunate.

II

One of the greatest wars that Sulla was in was a war against the Greeks. Rome had conquered Greece some

107

time before, and the governors of many of the Greek cities were Romans. These governors were very cruel to the Greeks; therefore the people hated them. Mithridates, King of Pontus, knew this, and he offered to send armies to Greece to help to drive the Romans out of the country. The Greeks were very glad of this, and they prepared for war against the Romans.

Sulla arrived in Greece with a strong army and began a march through the country. He captured several of the cities and compelled them to submit to the Roman governors. Then he marched on to Athens, the capital city of Greece. But he found that it was occupied by Archelaus, one of the generals of King Mithridates, who had brought from Asia Minor an army to help the Greeks.

Athens at this time was one of the most strongly fortified cities in the world. Its walls were seventy feet high, and they were made of huge, thick blocks of hard, smooth stone. It took thousands of men many years to build these massive walls. The city was also well supplied with food, so that it could hold out against a siege for a long time.

For several weeks Sulla attacked Athens furiously day by day, but it was all in vain. He could not take the city. His soldiers tried many times to mount the high walls, but they could not do it.

At last Sulla had battering-rams made. These were engines for breaking down the walls of towns. They were long, heavy beams of wood, with iron at one end, formed like the head of a ram. This was why they were called battering *rams*. At first they were worked by men with their hands and bodily strength, as you see in the picture. In later times they were hung from a cross beam, so as to swing back and forward, and the iron end was made to strike against the wall with great force.

When a number of battering-rams were ready, Sulla

began another attack on Athens. But at dead of night a party of Athenians came out of the city and burned all the battering-rams. Sulla quickly had new ones made, and after months of hard labor the Romans at last succeeded in breaking down the walls and taking Athens. They plundered the beautiful city and destroyed many fine works of art. It is said that they carried off more than six hundred pounds of gold and silver.

Sulla remained in Athens only long enough to establish Roman authority there once more. Then he departed with his army and marched to Chaeronea, another town of Greece, where there was a force of one hundred and twenty thousand men, which King Mithridates had sent to help the Greeks.

The Romans numbered only about forty thousand men, but Sulla was not afraid to fight the immense army of Mithridates. By placing his troops in good positions at the beginning of the battle, and afterwards by moving them skillfully from one point to another, he was able to win a great victory.

This was a remarkable battle in one respect. Although there were furious charges and hand-to-hand combats, in which thousands upon thousands of the soldiers of Mithridates were slain, the Romans lost only a few men. We are told that when the roll-call of the Roman army took place after the battle only twelve men failed to answer to their names! The army of Mithridates had lost one hundred and ten thousand men; the Romans only twelve men!

But perhaps we ought not to believe that so very few Romans were killed, for it seems hardly possible that it could have been so. It is certain, however, that Sulla gained a great victory. He also defeated another army sent by Mithridates soon afterwards.

Then Archelaus, the general of the army of Mithridates, begged for peace. Sulla made terms that were very good for Rome, and Archelaus and Mithridates had to accept them. Mithridates had to give the Romans a large sum of money and seventy ships of war and to promise to be the friend of Rome in future. Thus the war with Greece ended.

III

Sulla now prepared to return to Italy. He had heard how his friends in Rome and his wife and children had been treated by Marius. He was greatly enraged, and in his letter to the Senate, telling them of his victories in Greece, he said:

"In return for my services, which have brought honor and glory to Rome, my wife and children have been driven from their home, my house has been burned, and my friends have been put to death. I am now going back to punish those who did these things."

When the letter was read to the senators, they were very much alarmed, for they knew that if Sulla did as he threatened it would cause a dreadful civil war in Rome. In reply to Sulla they begged him not to make war on his own countrymen, and they promised to do their best to bring about a friendly understanding between him and the followers of Marius. Sulla answered that he did not want any understanding with them.

"I want no friendship with my enemies," he said. "I am able to take care of myself. It will be well for them if they can take care of themselves."

Soon afterwards he set out for Italy with his army. Rome was then under the power of the Marian party. This party was led by Cinna and by Marius the Younger, the son of the great Marius. When they heard that Sulla was coming they raised an army and went forth to drive him back. Young Marius said:

"Now it will be decided who shall be the master of Rome!"

A battle was fought between the two armies. It was

long and severe, and for a time it seemed as if the Marians would win. Even Sulla himself had no hope of victory. But soon very bad blunders made by the Marians turned the tide of battle in his favor, and he was victorious. He took six thousand prisoners.

IV

Sulla now entered Rome as its master, and a cruel master he proved to be. He first got himself appointed dictator for as long a time as he wished to hold the office. Then he commanded that all the followers of Marius should be slain. So they were hunted out of their hiding places and all put to death without mercy.

When every person that was known to have been connected with the Marian party was killed, the people thought Sulla would cease his murderous work, but he did not. He went on killing this one and that one—now a poor man and then a rich man—until at last the Romans became dreadfully frightened. "When will he stop?" they said to one another in trembling tones.

One day a senator had the courage to ask Sulla if he would please to say whom he intended to spare from death. Sulla coolly answered:

"I have not yet made up my mind, but if it is the wish of the Senate I will shortly make out a list of persons who must die!"

And Sulla really did make out a list of persons he intended to kill. It was called a PROSCRIPTION LIST and was hung up in the forum. Oh, how anxiously the poor, terror-stricken Romans went to that list to read the names! And if a man saw that his name was not there he went away with joy in his heart. But if his name was there he covered his face with his toga and ran off to hide himself.

The next day another and a longer list of proscribed persons was hung up, and the day after still another list.

Any one who killed a proscribed person got a large reward in money, but if anybody helped a proscribed
person to escape he was punished by death. This
dreadful work was continued until many thousands of
people in Rome and throughout Italy were slain.

Then Sulla had his Triumph in the streets of Rome. It
was the most magnificent procession that had yet been
seen in the city. There were hundreds of beautiful horses
drawing bright, golden chariots; there were long lines of
soldiers in glittering armor; there were numbers of
slaves, and there were huge wagons containing gold
and silver and other precious things, which Sulla had
got in Greece after his victories over Mithridates. The
dictator himself rode in the most splendid chariot of all.
He seemed like a king, and indeed was a king in power,
though not in name. This was what was called a
Triumph.

Sulla, for his own protection, had a bodyguard
formed of slaves who had belonged to the people he
had proscribed and put to death. This bodyguard is said
to have numbered ten thousand men, and they were
called Cornelii, after Sulla's family name.

Under the rule of Sulla his own will was law. He
could do whatever he pleased. But he did not remain
dictator a long time. In about a year after his Triumph
he seemed to have got tired of ruling and resigned the
office. Then he left Rome and went to reside in his
country house on the beautiful Bay of Naples. Here he
spent the rest of his life, passing his time partly in
feasting and merriment and partly in study. He died
78 B.C.

POMPEY THE GREAT

I

Not long after the death of Sulla, a new enemy to Rome appeared upon the Mediterranean Sea. A large number of people who lived on the coasts of Asia Minor built and armed fleets of ships, sailed along the shores of Italy, and attacked and plundered Roman vessels.

The sea-rovers, or pirates, as the Romans called them, had more than a thousand well-built, fast-sailing ships. Many of them were adorned with richly gilded bows and sterns, purple sails, and silver-mounted oars. They seized trading-vessels, robbed them, and killed every person on board.

Often, too, the pirates committed robberies on land. A boat's crew from a pirate ship would go ashore, put to death all the farmers in the neighborhood, and lay waste their farms. So in a short time the pirates made themselves masters of the Italian coasts, and kept the people in constant excitement and terror.

But at last the Romans resolved to make war upon

the robbers, and selected a very popular young man named Cneius Pompey to be the general. The people had great confidence in Pompey. They said that he was the only one who could put down the Mediterranean pirates, and demanded that he should be sent to do the work.

Pompey was a fine-looking man, with very pleasant manners. He had made himself famous as a soldier by brave deeds in wars in Spain and Africa, and was generally called Pompey the Great. His father had been a great commander, and the boy had lived in camps and taken part in wars almost from childhood. He had had many adventures during his army life and had always shown the qualities of a hero. He fought on the side of Sulla in many battles against the Marians, and he was thought to be one of Sulla's greatest generals.

The Roman Senate, therefore, yielded to the demand of the people and appointed Pompey to go forth against the pirates. He accepted the command and promptly set to work to carry out the important undertaking.

He gathered fourteen powerful fleets. He kept one of them for himself and put the others under the command of good officers. Then he divided the Mediterranean into thirteen districts, and sent a fleet to each district to hunt the pirates.

With his own fleet he sailed as far as the Strait of Gibraltar and then turned back towards Italy. On the way he chased the pirate vessels before him as he met them, until they were stopped and seized by some of the thirteen fleets stationed here and there all over the Mediterranean. The pirates were thus caught in a trap. Thousands of them were killed in battles with the different fleets, and their vessels were burned. The remainder soon surrendered to the Romans, and in three months the sea was cleared of pirates.

Pompey was much praised for this great work, and the

people said he was just the man to take charge of the war against Mithridates. This king had again attacked a Roman province in Asia, and the Romans resolved to punish him. But Mithridates was a very powerful man. He had great armies; he was a skillful general, and he defeated the Romans in many battles. The Roman people, therefore, resolved to send Pompey against him. Pompey was much pleased to be placed in command of a great army, and he proudly started off with his soldiers for the eastern lands.

II

Pompey remained in Asia several years and won many great victories. He conquered a number of countries and put Roman governors over them. Then he came back to Rome, bringing kings and princes as prisoners, and an enormous amount of gold and silver and other valuable things to enrich the Republic and himself. He was welcomed in a magnificent manner and he had a Triumph such as was given to great and victorious generals.

But Pompey now began to think of making himself master of Rome during his life-time. He had greatly pleased the people by his victories in war, and they were praising him on every side. How to keep their favor, and by it to get power was what now occupied his mind. He had been consul before, but he was now elected again, and then he set about providing various sorts of amusements for the people. He believed that if the people were amused they would be less likely to object to his taking the powers of the government entirely into his own hands.

He built a theatre large enough to seat forty thousand persons. This was the first great theatre erected in Rome. It was of stone and very strongly made. It had no roof, and the rows of seats rose one above another in a

115

half circle. At one end there was an immense stage on which all the performances took place.

In this grand theatre Pompey gave some very wonderful exhibitions from time to time. He had lions, elephants, and other wild animals brought from Asia and Africa at a great expense. These animals were let loose upon the stage and gladiators fought them in full view of the people in the theatre.

There were also thrilling combats in the theatres between the gladiators themselves. They fought each other savagely until one was wounded and fell upon the stage. Then the victor would turn towards the audience to find whether they wished him to kill the wounded man. If the people wanted this they would stretch out their hands with the thumbs down; if they did not want him killed they would hold their thumbs upward. If he had shown skill and courage and fought well they would give the sign to let him live, but if he had not made a brave fight they would turn down their thumbs and the unfortunate man would be instantly killed.

Slaves and prisoners taken in war were taught to be gladiators in schools established for the purpose. There were hundreds of these trained fighters always ready for the combats. The Romans were very fond of such amusements, and great crowds of men, and women too, attended the theatre whenever there was a fight of gladiators.

By giving the people a great deal of amusement of this kind on a grand scale, Pompey became the great popular favorite in Rome, and while the people were entertained at his theatre he managed the government to suit himself.

III

At this time the Romans ruled a vast territory, which

included not only all Italy, but Greece, Spain, Syria, Egypt, Turkey, Switzerland, and parts of France and Germany. Country after country had been conquered during a long series of years, and millions of people of different races and languages were subjects of Rome.

Rome itself was a city with a population of about half a million. It covered a very large area, including the famous seven hills. Its streets were narrow and crooked, but well-paved and clean. In the centre of the city were a number of large squares in which there were handsome buildings. There were magnificent temples and baths, and the houses of the nobles and wealthy plebeians were very large and splendid. Many of the fine houses were built of marble, with great pillars in front. Elegant furniture and handsome carpets and rugs filled the rooms.

There were many rich men in Rome at this time. Most of them had obtained the greater part of their wealth by plundering the conquered countries. They lived in a very magnificent manner, gave splendid dinners and entertainments, and had hundreds of slaves to attend upon them.

The slaves were a large class who were brought to Rome from many nations conquered in war. Many of them belonged to high families in their own country, and were well educated. Some of them were physicians, and others were good scholars and could read and write for their masters. The best cooks, builders, tailors, and farmers were slaves. In fact it was by slaves that nearly all the skilled work in Rome was done.

There were markets in Rome where slaves were sold. The slaves to be sold were placed on a platform. Labels hung from their necks, showing their age and what they were able to do.

The Roman children were taught to read and write Latin, which was their own language. They were also taught arithmetic and history. Most of the teachers were well-educated slaves.

Rome, then, was very rich and very powerful in the time of Pompey, and for many years Pompey was very popular. At one time he became dangerously ill while visiting Naples. Then the people showed their great love for him in many ways, and when he recovered there were public thanksgivings throughout Italy. On his journey home great crowds came out to greet him as he passed through the towns, and when he arrived at Rome he was received with unbounded joy.

Pompey had now a very strong hold on the affections of the people, so he cared little for the efforts made by a very ambitious Roman named Julius Cæsar to win public favor. But Cæsar was a man of strong will and great energy. He had resolved to be the ruler of Rome, and he spared no labor to accomplish his purpose. Pompey at last became alarmed at Cæsar's efforts, but it was then too late. He was defeated by Cæsar in a great battle and soon after lost his life. How these things came about we shall learn in the next story.

JULIUS CAESAR

I

Of all the Roman heroes the greatest was Caius Julius Caesar. He was a very remarkable man in many ways. He was remarkable as a soldier, statesman, scholar, and as an orator. He wrote a history of his own wars which is one of the best ancient histories that have come down to us. It is called *Caesar's Commentaries*, and it is used as a text book in all schools where Latin is taught.

This famous Roman was tall, handsome, agreeable in his manners, and of a gay disposition. He liked songs and stories, and even when he was a great general he often was as merry and frolicsome as a boy. Sometimes, however, he was stern and cruel instead of kind and forgiving.

Caesar was a member of the Julian family, which was one of the first families in Rome. Four Caesars of this family had been consuls of Rome in one century.

The aunt of Julius Caesar was the wife of the great leader, Marius. Naturally, Sulla was Caesar's bitter enemy and did all he could against him. "In that young man there is many a Marius," Sulla is reported to have said. However, by keeping out of Rome, Caesar was able to escape the traps laid for him at Sulla's orders. As soon as Sulla died Caesar returned to Rome.

Although he was a rich noble, he became a friend of the plebeians and always supported their cause. He spoke a great deal in the Forum upon political questions, and the people looked upon him as their champion. They elected him to several public offices, one after the other, and thus his influence and power were much increased. At last he was appointed governor of Spain, which was then ruled by the Romans.

On his way to Spain he stopped for a night at a little village among the mountains. One of his companions remarked that perhaps in that small place the people had their contests and their jealousies, as well as people in large cities.

"Poor as this village is, I would rather be first here than second in Rome!" said Caesar.

Caesar was very successful in Spain, and the Romans were so pleased with his conduct that when he came home they made him consul. During his consulship he had many good laws passed. When about forty years old he was given command of an army, and for some years followed the life of a soldier with wonderful success.

The Roman armies were formed of regiments called *legions*. Each legion contained over three thousand men, who were sometimes called legionaries. The weapons of the legionary were a short sword and a long spear called a *pilum*.

Besides spears and swords the Roman soldiers used slings for hurling stones against the enemy. They also had a machine called a *ballista* for throwing stones too heavy for handslings.

The military standard of the Romans was a figure of

an eagle borne on the top of a pole. Each legion had one of these and the soldier who carried it was called the *eagle-bearer*. Other standards also were used by the *cohorts* or companies into which the legions were divided.

Caesar's first great battles were in Gaul. The Romans called all the inhabitants of that country Gauls, although they were of many nations and spoke different languages. The Gauls were brave, but Caesar proved to be a great general, and in a few years he conquered all Gaul.

The Roman soldiers had great confidence in Caesar. When he led them they believed victory was certain. He was strict in his discipline, but very friendly and pleasant with the men, and he often gave them praise. He himself shared in their hardships. Day after day he marched on foot at their head through heat and rain and snow, and fought with them in the front ranks.

On one occasion Caesar built a very remarkable bridge. He wanted to get across the River Rhine with his army, to punish some German tribes who were in the habit of attacking the friends of Rome in Gaul. There was no bridge. The Germans used to get over in small parties by swimming, or in small boats. But a large army could not cross in this way without a great deal of trouble and loss of time, so Caesar resolved to build a bridge. He quickly set his men to work and they finished the bridge in ten days, though all the wood had to be cut down in the forests and carried to the river side.

One of Caesar's greatest victories in Gaul was the taking of the Alesia. This town had very strong walls all round it and it was defended by a great army of Gauls commanded by a brave chief named Vercingetorix. Caesar surrounded the town with his army and prevented food from being sent in to the inhabitants. He also defeated an army that came from other parts of Gaul to help the Alesians. Vercingetorix then had to come out from the town and give himself up to Caesar.

After many conquests in Gaul Caesar sailed over with an army to the island of Britain, now called Great Britain. The natives were a wild, fierce people, and they fought bravely against Caesar and his army. But the Romans were victorious, and they took possession of Britain, and for over four hundred years the island was a part of the Roman Empire.

II

Caesar was engaged eight years in his wars in Gaul and Britain. It is said that during these years he conquered three hundred tribes or nations, took eight hundred cities, fought battles with three millions of men and made a million prisoners. He obtained immense quantities of treasure in the conquered lands, and he himself, as commander of the victorious armies, kept a large part of it as his own share, so that he became very rich.

Caesar's wonderful victories made him a great man in Rome. The plebeians rejoiced at the success of their leader and favorite and were ready to welcome him with the highest honors whenever he should return to the city.

But Caesar had now made up his mind to become the master of Rome. So he began to plan and to work to destroy the power of Pompey, who at that time ruled public affairs in Rome almost completely.

In order to gain still greater favor Caesar sent a number of his friends to Rome to spend immense sums of money in various ways to please the people. They got up splendid games and feasts; they divided large quantities of corn among the poor; and they paid the debts of hundreds of men who had influence among the plebeians. The people knew that all this was done at Caesar's expense, and they praised and loved him for his generosity.

Pompey, with a great show of authority, now ordered Caesar to disband his army and send the soldiers to their homes, for he said that Caesar had no need of an army any longer, as he had finished his work in Gaul. But Pompey, too, had an army at this time in Spain, and Caesar said to him:

"If you will disband your army, I will disband mine."

This made Pompey very angry, and he got the Senate to pass a law declaring that Caesar was a public enemy and must be put down. One senator asked Pompey what he should do if Caesar should come to Rome with his army.

"What should I do?" cried Pompey, in a tone of contempt. "Why, I have only to stamp my foot and thousands of men will spring up to march under my orders."

At that time Caesar was with his army in the northern part of Italy. When he heard what the Senate had done he called his soldiers together and made an eloquent speech. He told them of the injustice that Pompey and the Senate had done to him, and he concluded by saying:

"This is my reward for all that I have done for my country. But I shall go to Rome and establish an honest government of the people, if you, my brave soldiers, will be faithful to me."

The soldiers answered with a loud shout, saying:

"We shall be faithful to you. We will stand by you to the last."

Caesar than started with his army and marched rapidly through northern Italy until he came to the banks of a little river, at that time called the Rubicon, and known as the southern boundary of Gaul. What river this was no one can now exactly tell, but it is supposed that it was some one of several small rivers which flow into the Adriatic Sea south of the River Po.

Caesar halted his army at the Rubicon and forbade any one to cross it until he gave the order. He stood for some time on the banks in deep thought, as if trying to decide whether he should cross the river and proceed, or give up his dangerous undertaking. He was still within his own territory as commander of Gaul; if he should cross the Rubicon he would be on territory directly under the government of the officers at Rome. By law it was made an act of treason, to be punished with death, for any Roman general to enter this territory with an army, without permission of the Senate.

"We can retreat now," said Caesar to some of his officers who stood near him, "but once across the Rubicon it will be too late to draw back."

While Caesar was talking a shepherd came along from a field close by, playing lively music on a reed pipe. The soldiers gathered around him to listen to the music, and some of them began to dance. One of Caesar's trumpeters stood among the soldiers, with his trumpet in his hand. The shepherd saw the trumpet, suddenly seized it and walked to the bridge over the Rubicon, which was but a few steps off. Then he put the trumpet to his lips, sounded the stirring notes for an advance of the troops and began to march across the bridge.

"A sign from the gods!" shouted Caesar. "Let us go where we are thus called. The die is cast!"

So saying, he turned his horse right into the stream and rode across the Rubicon, followed by his army. It was a daring thing even for Caesar to do, and the phrases, "he has crossed the Rubicon," "the die is cast," are now often used to mean that a bold or dangerous step has been taken from which there is no drawing back.

There was no one to oppose Caesar as he marched through Italy. On the contrary, city after city surrendered to him. There was very little fighting. In most places the people seemed glad to have him as their ruler, and gave him a warm welcome and feasted his soldiers. He had only words of kindness for every one, even for those who were against him, and he won hosts of friends and supporters all along his route.

There was great alarm at Rome when it was learned that Caesar was advancing toward the city. The supporters of Pompey became terrified, and the rich nobles gathered up their money and other valuables and fled. Pompey could do nothing to defend the city against Caesar, and at last he too ran away. He went to Greece to raise an army to fight Caesar.

When Caesar arrived at Rome he met with no opposition. He entered the city amid shouts of welcome from the people. He harmed no one, but he set up a new government and organized a new Senate. He was now the master spirit of the republic.

After arranging everything to his satisfaction in Rome, he went to Spain and defeated Pompey's generals there. Then he came back and turned his attention to Pompey himself.

In the meantime Pompey had been very busy gathering an army in the eastern countries controlled by Rome. In one way and another he collected fifty thousand men. They were stationed on the coasts of Macedonia and Greece. There they waited for Caesar and his army to cross the Adriatic Sea to give them battle.

Caesar had a great deal of trouble in getting across the stormy sea with his army of forty thousand soldiers, but at last a landing was made in Greece. Then the two armies had some skirmishing, but no great battle.

This continued for months. Pompey at one time would gain the advantage, and Caesar at another time. But it was evident that neither of the great rivals was in any hurry to risk the chance of defeat in a general battle. They knew well that such a defeat would entirely ruin the one that was defeated.

But at last the two armies met for battle on the plain of Pharsalia, in Thessaly, a district of Greece. The soldiers on both sides were mostly armed with spears and broadswords. Some carried slings to hurl large stones, and others had bows and arrows. The greater part of the fighting, however, was done with swords.

Eighty thousand men were engaged in the battle, about forty thousand on each side. It was a brave, heroic struggle and lasted for hours. Both armies fought splendidly, but in the end Pompey's army was forced back to its camp, after dreadful slaughter. For a few minutes the camp was bravely defended against the attacks of Caesar's soldiers and then had to be abandoned. The battle did not last long after this. Pompey's great army was utterly beaten.

Pompey himself, with a few followers, fled to the seashore and sailed across the Mediterranean to Egypt. There he was treacherously murdered by order of Ptolemy, the Egyptian king.

Caesar gained a splendid victory at Pharsalia, but he was not yet master of the Roman Empire. The rich nobles and senators formed armies to fight him in Asia Minor, Africa, and Spain. Caesar went with an army to Asia Minor, attacked his enemies, and won a great battle at a place called Zela. This victory was so quickly gained that in sending news of it to Rome Caesar wrote the famous despatch, *"Veni, vidi, vici,"* which is, in English, *"I came, I saw, I conquered."*

He had equal success in Africa and Spain. In a very short time he destroyed the armies opposed to him. Then he returned to Rome and had the grandest Triumph ever seen in the city.

The celebration lasted four days, and during that time Rome was in a high state of pleasant excitement. Thousands of persons from the surrounding country came to the city to witness the magnificent show.

On each day there were splendid processions, in which there were great numbers of gorgeous chariots, drawn by beautiful horses and filled with Caesar's principal officers. Behind them marched hundreds of soldiers bearing banners on which were pictured scenes from Caesar's important battles. Herds of elephants and camels from Asia and Africa appeared in the procession, and there were also long lines of prisoners carrying valuable articles obtained by Caesar in the lands he had conquered.

In addition to the processions many kinds of entertainments were provided for the people, such as plays, circus exhibitions, combats between gladiators, wild-beast hunts, and chariot races. There were also feasts served to all the people of the city. It was a time of unbounded enjoyment and delighted the Romans so much that they became very devoted to Caesar.

There was now no opposition to him. Both the nobles and plebeians were willing, and even glad, to have him as their ruler. He was chosen dictator for life and put in command of all the armies of the Empire. He was called *imperator*, which means *emperor*.

The people gave him the title of *Father of his Country*. Statues of him were erected in the public buildings and squares. A grand chair, made somewhat like a throne, was placed in the Senate chamber, and whenever he came to listen to the debates he sat in this chair, as if he were king.

Caesar now had laws passed making many improvements in the government. He also carried out a number of plans to make Rome of more importance as a commercial city. He erected magnificent buildings, made aqueducts to bring plenty of water to the city, established a great library, and did many other things which were of much benefit to the people.

One of the most useful things he did was to make a new calendar. Before his time the Romans had not a very clear knowledge as to the length of a year. At one time they had only ten months in their year. Afterwards they had twelve, but they counted only 365 days in every year. They did not know or they did not give attention to the fact that the real length of a year is 365 days, 5 hours, 48 minutes, 50 seconds. They did not reckon the extra hours, minutes, and seconds, and so their calendar got quite wrong in the course of a number of years. Caesar corrected the error by making one year in every four have 366 days, and the calendar thus corrected was called the *Julian Calendar*.

Caesar now possessed all the glory and power of a king, and it began to be believed that he wanted to be a king in reality. The Romans had not had a king for five hundred years and would not have one. Their feeling against kings was so strong that none of the men who had ruled Rome, at times with almost kingly power, had ever dared to call himself king.

One day an intimate friend of Caesar saluted him in public as king. Caesar replied:

"I am not king, but only Caesar."

Some of the nobles, however, felt certain that he meant to make himself king, and they formed a plot to kill him in the Senate house, on the Ides of March, that is, on the fifteenth of March. The Romans had certain days in their months which they called Kalends, Nones, and Ides.

One of the persons who made the plot against Caesar was Junius Brutus, a highly respected Roman. It is said that he was a descendant of the Junius Brutus who, five centuries before, had helped to overthrow the tyrant King Tarquin. Brutus was an intimate friend of Caesar, but he thought that Caesar intended to destroy the Republic by making himself king, and therefore he joined the plot against him.

As the Ides of March drew near the plan for putting Caesar to death was carefully arranged and settled. An augur, or fortune-teller, one day stopped Caesar in the street and said to him, "Beware the Ides of March!" but the great conqueror laughed at the warning.

On the appointed day the plotters met in the Senate chamber, ready to do the wicked deed they had planned. When Caesar entered the chamber, all present rose to greet him. He bowed and smiled pleasantly to the people and took his usual seat. Now was the fatal moment.

As had been arranged, one of the plotters went up to him with a request for the pardon of a prisoner. Then the rest crowded around his chair, as if to urge him to grant the request. Caesar seemed somewhat alarmed at the crowd and rose from his chair. At this moment he was stabbed in the side with a sword. Then there were loud outcries in the chamber, and all was excitement and confusion.

Caesar used his stylus to defend himself. The stylus was an instrument made of iron, with a sharp point on one end for writing on wax tablets, and with the other end smooth, for rubbing out a word when necessary. For writing on parchment or paper a pen made of reed was used. Educated Romans carried their stylus and tablet in their pockets. From the name of the instrument the word *style* is now used to mean a particular manner of writing.

Caesar had nothing but his stylus to defend himself with. He fought bravely, until he saw his friend Brutus coming to strike him. Then he cried out, "You, too, Brutus!" and made no further resistance.

They stabbed him until he fell dead. Then they went out of the Senate and through the streets of Rome with Brutus at their head. They told the people what they had done and rejoiced at the deed. They said the death of Caesar saved the Roman Republic.

But the people were very angry and threatened to put to death those who had killed Caesar. They would have done this only that Brutus and his friends fled from the city.

There was a grand funeral service in honor of Caesar. The body was laid in the Forum, and a famous Roman named Mark Antony made an eloquent funeral speech over it. He praised Caesar and spoke so bitterly against Brutus and his party that the people were more angry than ever. This Mark Antony was afterwards a very powerful man in Rome.

Caesar died forty-four years before Christ was born. Of course his death did not save the Roman Republic. It had, indeed, already ceased to exist in all but the name. Rome was no longer a republic, but an empire and, as we shall see, the family of Caesar gave it its first emperor. All the emperors adopted the name of Caesar as part of their title.

CICERO

I

Marcus Tullius Cicero was a prominent man at Rome for some time in the latter years of the Republic. He was a great orator—one of the greatest the world has ever known. His principal speeches have been preserved and are read and studied at the present day.

He often spoke in the Forum before large audiences, and by his wonderful eloquence delighted all who heard him. Both the nobles and plebeians admired him for his learning, his oratory, and his manly qualities.

Cicero was a tall, graceful man, with an intellectual and rather handsome face, and very bright, black eyes. He was so great a favorite that he was chosen to fill several public offices and at last was elected consul.

In the early part of his year as consul there was a mysterious plot formed in Rome by some nobles of bad character, old soldiers, and others ready for any mischief. What their real object was no one seemed to know. But it was said that the conspirators wanted to overthrow the government and set up a new one of their own.

There was a senator named Sergius Catiline, and many believed that he was at the head of the plot. He had a bad reputation, and for some time the other senators had looked upon him with suspicion. There was no proof, however, that he was engaged in any unlawful proceedings, so no charge could be made against him.

But one day a young woman, named Fulvia, came to Cicero and gave him some important information about the plot and Catiline's part in it. She said that she had a lover who was one of the plotters, and that he had told her some of their secrets. She was greatly frightened, for she thought that there might be bloodshed in Rome if the plot went on, and she felt it her duty to tell Cicero about it.

Cicero immediately went to the Senate and made a powerful speech. He charged Catiline with being the leading person in a plot to overthrow the government. There was great excitement at his words. Catiline was present, and he boldly denied the charge and defied Cicero to prove it.

"If Consul Cicero is afraid of my doing harm in Rome," said he, "I am willing to place myself as a prisoner in the hands of any senator."

"I do not think it is safe to have you in the city," replied Cicero, "and do you expect any one to take you into his house?"

After a great deal of exciting talk the Senate laid aside the charges against Catiline for a while.

II

A few weeks later, in a city near Rome, there was an uprising of the people against the public officers. This caused a great deal of alarm, and Cicero said it was the beginning of the plot that he had charged Catiline with forming.

Then he hurried to the Senate, where Catiline was, and made a great speech against him. He called him a traitor to his country. Catiline turned pale and began to tremble. He attempted to speak, but the senators shouted, and hooted and hissed him. Those who sat near him got up in disgust and took seats in another part of the chamber, leaving the conspirator sitting by himself. At last Catiline ran out of the Senate, furious with anger, and threatening revenge. Then he mounted a horse and rode quickly out of the city.

Shortly afterwards Cicero learned the names of nine Roman citizens who were leaders in the plot, and he had them arrested. He declared in the Senate that they had planned to murder the senators and the high officers, and to burn Rome. The senators declared at once that the nine must die, and so Cicero had them put to death.

Catiline now fled to the mountains called the Apennines and there raised a force of twenty thousand men. Two armies were sent against him from Rome. A battle took place, in which Catiline's army was defeated and he himself killed.

Thus ended what was known as the Catiline Conspiracy. Cicero's action in helping to destroy it greatly pleased the Romans. In the Senate he received much praise and honor. It was even declared that he was the "Father of his Country."

Antony did not like Cicero, and when the Triumvirate was formed, the great orator was put to death by Antony's order.

AUGUSTUS

I

The first of the long line of Roman emperors was Octavius, called in history Augustus. He was the grandnephew of Julius Cæsar. Although he was scarcely twenty years old when Cæsar died, he was very ambitious. He often said that he should one day be at the head of the Roman Empire.

"I shall rule Rome like Cæsar," he would say to his companions. "You may laugh at me now, but the time will come when I shall be master of the Romans."

Shortly after Cæsar's death Octavius began to take an active part in political affairs. At this time Mark Antony was in control of Rome and was managing everything to suit himself. He had been an intimate friend of Cæsar and commanded one of his armies. He obtained a great deal of power, but he was not liked very much either by the nobles or the plebeians. He was a bad ruler, and nobody trusted him.

Once Antony tried to prevent Octavius from being elected a tribune of the people. "I will be a tribune in spite of you," Octavius said, and he set to work with all his energy to get the office. There was a severe struggle on election day, but the boy was successful.

After this Octavius hated Antony and planned in secret to bring about his downfall. And he succeeded in all he attempted to do. From a tribune he advanced steadily, step by step, to more important offices. At last he obtained command of an army and marched his soldiers to northern Italy, where a war was going on. While in this region he met Antony with his army. The two began to quarrel and at last came to blows. Then the army of Octavius fought the army of Antony, and the northern plains were reddened with the blood of the soldiers.

When the fighting had gone on for some time, Octavius sent to Antony and asked him to stop it. He pretended that he was very sorry he had begun to fight with Antony and asked for his friendship.

"Let us be friends and work together," he said to Antony. "By joining our armies we shall be able to do some good."

The fighting was then stopped, and the two generals had a meeting. They agreed to unite their armies, and to invite another Roman general, named Lepidus, who had a large army, to join them. Lepidus accepted the invitation and came to have a talk with Antony and Octavius. They agreed to a plan by which they themselves were to rule Rome together. This rule, or government, was called a *triumvirate*, and Octavius, Antony, and Lepidus were called *triumvirs*, a word which means *three men*.

II

After making all their arrangements, Antony, Octavius, and Lepidus started for Rome with their armies and took possession of the city. Then they began to kill those that they thought were their enemies. More than two thousand Romans were slain. They would have killed Brutus only that he was then in Greece, where he had gone after Cæsar's death to raise an army to fight Antony and his friends. Antony and Octavius now went with an army to Greece to fight Brutus. Both armies met at Philippi, in Macedonia, and then there was a battle in which the army of Brutus was defeated. After the battle Brutus requested one of his slaves to kill him. The slave refused, but when Brutus still pressed him to do it, he held out his sword and Brutus killed himself by falling upon it.

It is told that some time before the battle of Philippi, as Brutus was sitting one night in his tent, a vision or spectre appeared to him and said, "I am thy evil genius, Brutus; we shall meet again at Philippi." It is also said that the spectre again appeared to Brutus on the night before the battle of Philippi and told him that his death was at hand.

There was no one now to interfere with Antony, Octavius, and Lepidus, and they managed everything in Rome as they liked. They pretended all the time to have great respect for the Senate and the officers of government who had been elected by the people.

After a short time Antony went to some of the Eastern countries that were a part of the Roman Empire, and Lepidus went to Africa. Octavius was left in Rome to attend to its affairs. He then began to plan to get rid of Antony and Lepidus, so that he might rule Rome himself. With this object he raised a great army and determined to make war on his rivals.

Sextus Pompey, a son of Pompey the Great, was at this time in control of the island of Sicily. He was always making trouble for Octavius, and he was aided by Lepidus, who had come from Africa to Sicily with his army. One day Octavius sailed over the Mediterranean Sea to Sicily, with thousands of soldiers, destroyed the army of

Sextus, and induced the army of Lepidus to leave him. Lepidus was then taken prisoner.

"Now to put an end to the power of Antony!" said Octavius to himself, when he returned to Rome from Sicily. So he went to the Senate and accused Antony of treason in Asia and Africa and asked that war be declared against him. The Senate declared war, and Octavius began to make great preparations for it.

Antony was in Egypt when he heard of the declaration of war. He laughed scornfully at the idea of Octavius being able to beat him. Then he gathered an army of more than a hundred thousand men and a fleet of several hundred warships, and set out to meet Octavius. He had with him Cleopatra, the beautiful queen of Egypt, whom he had married, and she had a fleet of her own, numbering sixty ships.

Octavius had about as many soldiers and ships as Antony. The two fleets met near a place called Actium, on the coast of Greece, and fought a battle. For several hours the fight went on bravely, but neither side gained any great advantage. Suddenly Cleopatra sailed away with her fleet, and Antony quickly followed her with a few ships. Thus he deserted his men while they were fighting.

The sailors and soldiers of the deserted fleet kept on fighting for a short time and then surrendered to Octavius. A few days later a part of Antony's army, which was encamped on the shore near Actium, also surrendered.

Antony went back to Egypt with Cleopatra. His friends and supporters then left him, and his power was gone. Soon after, he stabbed himself, and so died. It is said that Cleopatra died from the bite of a poisonous serpent called an asp, which she placed on her arm on purpose to kill herself.

Octavius continued to fight in different parts of the Empire until he defeated every one who dared to oppose him. Then he went back to Rome with a great deal of glory and riches and let it be known at once that he intended to be the master of the government. Although he pretended to protect the rights of the people, he made himself consul and also assumed other high offices which greatly added to his power. Thousands of soldiers were at his call, and finally he became very much like a king.

The Senate asked him if he would wish to be appointed dictator for life, but he thought it wise to refuse this office. The Senate then gave him the name of Augustus, which meant that he was worthy of respect. The word *augustus* in the Latin language means sacred. He called himself emperor, and, as Emperor Cæsar Augustus, he ruled the Romans all the rest of his life, a period of about twenty-seven years. And when Augustus became emperor the Republic of Rome was no longer in existence.

What were known as the Prætorian Guards were organized by Augustus to protect himself and uphold his authority as emperor. These guards were about ten thousand in number, and they were composed of the most trusty soldiers of the Empire. Each soldier had high rank and large pay, and had to serve for many years. Whenever Augustus appeared in public he was attended by some of the Prætorian guards, and they looked very imposing with their handsome uniforms and glittering swords and spears.

Augustus made many good changes in the government. He very much improved the condition of the plebeians. His principal ministers were two able men named Agrippa and Mæcenas, who gave him very valuable assistance.

Whenever these wise men saw that the Romans were getting uneasy and beginning to grumble, they would advise the emperor to distribute corn or money to the poor, or to give the people grand exhibitions to amuse them. Augustus would follow the advice, and by so doing made himself very popular.

During his long reign Augustus had many splendid palaces, temples, and other buildings erected in Rome, and they made the city very beautiful. Augustus also founded cities in various parts of the empire. He encouraged literature and art and was himself an author. In his time the famous Roman poets, Horace, Vergil, Varius, and Ovid lived, and also the great historian Livy, who wrote the history of Rome from the earliest period down to his own time. Vergil was the author of a celebrated poem called the *Æneid*, which tells of the wanderings and adventures of the Trojan hero Æneas.

It was in the reign of Augustus that Jesus Christ was born in Bethlehem, a town of Palestine, or Judea, in Southwest Asia. Judea was then part of the Roman Empire.

NERO

I

On the death of Augustus in the year 14 A.D. his stepson Tiberius became emperor. He was a cruel tyrant. He put to death a great many people only because he thought they were his enemies. A Roman emperor could put to death any one he pleased. If he did not like a person, he would charge him with some crime and order his soldiers to kill him. Tiberius had many people killed in this way, but he was himself killed by the commander or general of the Prætorian Guard.

The next two emperors were Caligula and Claudius. They also were tyrants and put many people to death without just cause. It is said that Caligula once wished that all the Roman people together had but one head so that he might cut it off with one blow.

But the next emperor was a still greater tyrant. His name was Nero. He became emperor in the year 54 A.D. He was the son of a wicked woman named Agrippina. This woman married the Emperor

Claudius and got him to appoint her son, Nero, his successor, instead of his own little son, Britannicus. Then she killed Claudius by poison, and Nero became emperor.

Nero was a tall, strong, good-looking, bright youth. He was fond of games, and could play well on several musical insruments. When he first became emperor he seemed to be affectionate and kind-hearted, and he did a number of good things. Once, when he was asked to sign a warrant for the execution of a man condemned to death, he exclaimed:

"I wish I had never learned to write, for then I shouldn't have to sign away men's lives!"

Then all the people around him cried:

"What a noble young man our emperor is! What a good heart he has!"

But in a very short time it was found that Nero was not at all kind or merciful, but that he was a cruel and wicked man.

His mother Agrippina expected that when her son was emperor she herself would be the real mistress and would rule the Roman Empire as she pleased. Nero was only a boy, she thought, and he would not want to take upon himself the cares and burdens of government.

And for a while Agrippina did rule Rome. She had a woman she hated put to death and she punished several other persons who had offended her. She made some of the richest Romans pay her large sums of money. But Nero soon put an end to his mother's power. One day he said to her:

"I, not you, am the ruler of the Empire. You have no right to take any power upon yourself and you must not do so again. Whenever you want anything done you must ask me to do it for you."

"Ask you?" cried Agrippina, in a rage. "How dare you talk this way to me who made you emperor? You the emperor! You are not the rightful emperor. The true heir to the Empire is your stepbrother, young Britannicus, the son of Claudius!"

Then there was a fierce quarrel between Nero and his mother, and at last he turned her out of his palace and ordered her never to appear there again.

But what she had said alarmed him very much. He feared that Britannicus might be made emperor, and therefore he determined to get him out of the way as soon as possible.

At this time there was in Rome a dreadful woman named Locusta, who made poisons and sold them secretly to any one who wanted them. Nero went one night to this woman and said:

"Make me a strong poison—so strong that it will kill a person like a flash of lightning!"

Locusta made the poison and gave it to him. He tried it on a pig, and it killed the animal in a few moments.

"Ha!" said he, "this will do the work."

Now, Britannicus lived in the palace with his stepbrother and next day, when dinner was served, Nero put some of the poison into a cup of wine which he knew the boy was to drink. The moment Britannicus drank it, he fell to the floor dead. Then Nero said to the guests who were at the table:

"Do not be alarmed. It is nothing. My poor stepbrother always was subject to fits."

The attendants carried the body of Britannicus out of the room, and the dinner went on gayly.

II

A little while after he had poisoned his stepbrother, Nero made up his mind to get rid of his mother, also. He was afraid that as long as she lived he would not be safe as emperor. She might stir up the people against him any day. So he went to see her and pretended that he was sorry he had ill-treated her. He kissed and caressed her so affectionately that she was entirely deceived.

Then the cruel son made a plan to drown his mother. He had a ship so built that by pulling out certain bolts and pins it would suddenly fall to pieces and sink. He then hired a wicked captain and crew to do his bidding, and got his mother to take a sail in the ship down the Tiber.

Agrippina took a maid with her and went aboard. She was in a happy humor, because her son, as she thought, was so kind to her. When the ship came to a certain place in the river where the water was very deep, the sailors pulled out the bolts and pins. Then the ship began to fall apart and to sink.

The sailors sprang into the river to swim to the shore, and Agrippina and her maid jumped overboard. The maid was killed by a sailor, but Agrippina was picked up by the crew of a fishing boat.

Nero was greatly troubled when he learned of his mother's escape. He believed that now she would certainly try to have him removed from the throne. So he sent some men to kill her in her house, and they did so in a most cruel manner.

III

None of the emperors before Nero lived so grandly as he did. He had a splendid marble palace at Rome, containing immense quantities of beautiful furniture, gold and silver ornaments, and works of art of the finest kind. On the pleasant shores of the Mediterranean Sea he had several houses where he lived in the summer and autumn months. Wherever he went he had, as his court or companions, three or four hundred richly dressed men and women, with many slaves to wait upon them. They traveled in chariots covered with ivory and gold and drawn by beautiful horses.

Nero was famous for the splendid dinners he gave in his palace. The rarest and most costly food and wines were spread upon the tables in great plenty, and when the feasting was over troops of actors and dancers would give performances which lasted until late at night.

Sometimes, at these dinners, Nero would play on a harp or flute, and sometimes he would act portions of plays or recite poems which he himself had composed. He was a very clever musician and actor, and he wrote very good poetry.

One evening a fire broke out in Rome and raged furiously for a week. Half the city was burned, and hundreds of people lost their lives. Some of the Romans said that Nero had started the fire and had prevented it from being put out. Most of the six days during which the fire lasted he spent in a high tower, enjoying the sight. He played on his harp, sang merry songs, and recited verses about the burning of the ancient city of Troy.

After the fire was put out Nero said that it had been caused by the believers in the religion of Christ. At this time there was a very large number of Christians in Rome. But most of the Romans still worshiped their old pagan gods, and they hated and ill-treated the Christians.

When Nero declared that the Christians had caused the great fire, the people began to persecute them in a dreadful manner. Many of the Christians were hanged, some were covered with pitch and burned, and others were hunted to death by savage dogs. During the time of this persecution the Apostle Paul was beheaded and the Apostle Peter was crucified, as Christ had been crucified thirty-one years before.

After a short time Rome was rebuilt in a greater

magnificence than before. Nero built for himself an immense and splendid palace on the famous Palatine Hill. This palace contained so many ornaments of gold that it was called the Golden House.

In governing the Empire Nero was very harsh and cruel. He often put innocent men and women, and even his own friends, to death. He killed his wife in a fit of passion. He did so many wicked things that at last the Romans got tired of having such a tyrant to rule them, and they formed a plot to dethrone him and make some one else their emperor.

But the plot came to nothing, because a slave who had heard of it went to Nero and told him all about it. The Prætorian Guards seized the leading plotters and put them to death. Nero then became more wicked than he had been before. He even accused his old tutor Seneca, and the famous poet Lucan, of taking part in the plot against him, and he sent them an order to put themselves to death. Seneca was a very good man and a great writer. When he received the cruel order from Nero, he knew that if he did not obey it the tyrant would send some one to kill him, so he had the veins of his arms cut open and he died after much suffering. Lucan also obeyed the tyrant's order. While dying he repeated lines from one of his own poems.

IV

This wicked emperor reigned fourteen years. But at last there was a rebellion against him, and the soldiers elected Galba, the Roman governor of Spain, to be the new emperor.

Then Nero acted like a miserable coward. He was afraid to stay any longer in Rome, for most of the people hated him and favored Galba. So he mounted a horse and rode out of the city to the home of a trusty slave. But while he was there he received word that the

Senate had condemned him to death and that horsemen had been sent out to capture him.

"Now dig a grave for me," he said to the slave, "and I will kill myself!"

At this moment the galloping of horses was heard.

"Hark! They are coming to kill you," cried the slave. "Use the dagger while it is time and save yourself from disgrace!"

With trembling hand Nero placed his dagger at his throat, but did not have the courage to use it. The slave then seized it and plunged it into the emperor's throat, and the wicked Nero fell dead.

TITUS

I

During the two years that followed the death of Nero, there were three emperors, Galba, Otho, and Vitellius. They were generals of Roman armies, and were made emperors by their soldiers. But they reigned only a few months each, and they did nothing of importance.

Vitellius was a glutton. He took pleasure only in eating and drinking. He would often visit the houses of rich Romans without invitation and take breakfast with one, dinner with another, and supper with another. After breakfast he thought only about dinner; and when dinner was over he began to think of what he would have for supper.

The next emperor was Titus Flavius Vespasian, commonly called Vespasian. He also was an army general. When he was made emperor by his soldiers he was in Palestine. He had been sent there by Nero with an army to punish the Jews who had rebelled against Rome. As soon as he was declared emperor he returned to Italy and left his son Titus Flavius, called in history simply Titus, to carry on the war against the Jews.

Titus captured Jerusalem after a siege of six months, and his soldiers took possession of all the valuable things they could find. Then they burned the city to the ground. The famous temple was also destroyed, and thus was fulfilled the prophecy of Christ that not one stone of the building should be left upon another. When Titus returned to Rome he had a grand Triumph, and a beautiful arch was built in his honor. This arch is still in existence.

II

Vespasian died in 79 A.D., and then Titus became emperor. One of the remarkable things Titus did during his reign was to finish the Colosseum, which had been begun by his father.

The Colosseum was the largest theatre in the world. It had seats for over 80,000 people. It was first called the Flavian Amphitheatre, from the family name of the emperors who built it. Inside it had seats all round the ring, or arena, and as the word *amphi* means *around*, they called the great building an amphitheatre. In later times it got the name of Colosseum. The Greeks used the word *colossus* as a name for any very large statue, and because the Flavian Amphitheatre was so large it was called the Colosseum. In our own language we use the word *colossal* to describe anything of immense size.

In the Colosseum they had many kinds of amusements. When it was first opened the shows and games lasted for a hundred days, and 5,000 wild beasts were killed in the arena by gladiators. The arena was a vast space fenced round about with a strong wall, and around it were circular tiers or rows of seats, one behind the other, like steps of stairs. Sometimes the arena was turned into a lake by letting water flow into it from

148

pipes. Then they put ships upon it and had sham fights in imitation of a battle at sea. This sort of show was called *naumachia*, which means a fight with ships. It was first introduced into Rome by Julius Cæsar, who had a lake dug for the purpose in the Campus Martius.

The Colosseum is still in existence, but it is partly in ruins. From the picture, which shows it as it now is, we can form an idea of how grand a building it once was.

Besides finishing the Colosseum, the Emperor Titus also built splendid baths. They were called the Baths of Titus. The Romans were very fond of baths. Wealthy citizens used to bathe several times every day, and often they spent the greater part of the day at the baths, where there were finely furnished rooms.

It was in the reign of Titus that the cities of Pompeii and Herculaneum, in the south of Italy, were destroyed by an eruption of Mount Vesuvius. A famous Roman author, Pliny the Younger, saw the eruption from a distance and wrote a description of it. He tells that a fiery cloud of cinders, stones, and ashes burst from the top of the mountain and rained down upon the country all round, destroying towns and villages and people. The ruins of Herculaneum were accidentally discovered by workmen in 1709, and the ruins of Pompeii were discovered some years later.

Titus was a very good emperor. He always did everything he could for the welfare and happiness of the people, and he was so much liked by everybody that he was called the "Delight of Mankind." It is said that one night he thought he had done nothing during that day for the good of any person, and that he cried out, "I have lost a day."

TRAJAN

I

On the death of Titus his brother Domitian became emperor. He was a very bad man and took pleasure only in doing cruel and wicked things. It is said that one of his amusements was catching flies and sticking them with pins. Once when a visitor called and inquired whether there was any one with the emperor, the servant answered, "No, not even a fly."

It is not to be supposed that such an emperor could have been liked by the people. Even his soldiers hated him, and at last they formed a plot against his life and killed him in his own palace.

Nerva, who had been a favorite of Nero, was the next emperor, but he was an old man and died after a reign of two years. He was succeeded by his adopted son Trajan, who became emperor in 98 A.D. and reigned for nineteen years.

Trajan was a good man and a brave soldier. At the time he became emperor he was governor of one of the

Roman territories or provinces in Germany along the banks of the Rhine, and he resided at Colonia, now called Cologne.

Not long after his return to Rome Trajan was engaged in a war with the King of Dacia. This was the name of the country lying north of the Danube River. The greater part of it is now [1904] called Hungary [Romania after WWI]. The Dacian king, whose name was Decebalus, had frequently made raids into neighboring countries which belonged to Rome, and robbed and killed many of the people. Trajan resolved to punish Decebalus, and so he set out with a large army and marched into Dacia. The war continued three years, for the Dacians were brave and skillful fighters; but at last Decebalus was defeated in a great battle and he had to come to Trajan and humbly beg for peace. He agreed to be a vassal of Rome; that is, to hold his kingdom subject to the control of the Roman emperors.

But in less than a year Decebalus again attacked his Roman neighbors, and Trajan had again to march against him with an army. The Dacians were once more defeated in a great battle, and Decebalus, after failing in an attempt to escape, put an end to his own life. Dacia was then made a Roman province.

During this year Trajan built a remarkable bridge across the Danube. Before that time bridges were built of wood, but in the bridge over the Danube Trajan used stone for the piers, which were of great size. The bridge had twenty-two arches, and its ruins, which are still to be seen, show what a wonderful work it was.

When Trajan returned to Rome after his victory over Decebalus he had a grand Triumph, and there were games and shows in his honor which lasted a hundred and twenty days. It is told that during these celebrations 10,000 gladiators fought in the amphitheatre and 11,000 wild animals were killed in the arena.

A marble column was erected in honor of Trajan's

victories in Dacia. This monument is still standing in Rome. It is called Trajan's Column. Many scenes showing battles and other events in the Dacian war are engraved upon it from the base to the top.

II

Trajan also had wars in Asia, and he won many victories. He conquered Armenia and Mesopotamia and added them to the empire. But he did not live to return to Rome. He died in a town in Asia Minor, which in honor of him was afterwards called Trajanopolis.

The Romans were much grieved at the death of Trajan, for he had been a good emperor and had done much to benefit the people. He built fine roads and canals and bridges in Italy and the provinces. He greatly improved and beautified the Circus Maximus. This was the place in which the Romans had their horse races and chariot races. It was built in the hollow between the Palatine and Aventine hills, and it had seats for 250,000 people.

Trajan also made a forum in Rome, which was called after his name the Trajan Forum. In the centre of this forum the Trajan Column was built, and around it were temples and libraries established by the good emperor. For a long time after Trajan's death the people of Rome, whenever they got a new emperor, used to wish that he would be "as great as Augustus and as good as Trajan."

Some great writers lived in Rome in the time of Trajan. One of them was Plutarch, who wrote the famous book called "Plutarch's Lives." This book, which you will perhaps some day read, contains an account of the lives of many great men of Greece and Rome. The historian Tacitus, the poet Juvenal, and Pliny the Younger, already mentioned, also lived in the time of Trajan.

Pliny the Younger was so-called to distinguish him

152

from his uncle, Pliny the Elder, who lived in the time of Nero and was the author of a celebrated work on natural history.

MARCUS AURELIUS

I

The next emperor was Trajan's cousin Hadrian. He was a good ruler and did a great deal to improve the city of Rome. He traveled through many parts of the empire to see that the people were justly governed and that the public officials were doing their duty. He visited Britain, which was then a Roman province, and he caused a strong wall to be built from sea to sea across the country near Scotland, to prevent the fierce tribes of the north from making raids upon the Roman settlements in the south. Some of the remains of this wall are still to be seen.

Hadrian also built a great tomb in Rome, which was called Hadrian's Mole. He and many other Roman emperors were buried in this tomb. It is now known as the Castle of St. Angelo.

When Hadrian died a very good man named Antoninus was made emperor. He showed such filial regard for Hadrian, by building a temple in his honor, that he was called Antoninus Pius. Under the emperors who ruled before his time the Christians were very cruelly treated. They were not allowed to have churches or places of worship, and numbers of them were put to death in the most shocking manner. Often Christians were thrown into the arena in the Amphitheatre and devoured by wild beasts.

In those times the Christians of Rome held their religious meetings in underground passages dug for burying places. These Catacombs, as they were called, were near the walls of the city and altogether were hundreds of miles in length. Along both sides of the tunnels were openings, one above another, in which the dead were buried. Many of the Catacombs have been explored in recent times. They are among the "sights" which visitors to Rome are always eager to see.

Antoninus Pius was very friendly to the Christians. He gave orders that they should be allowed to practice their religion and that any one who interfered with them should be punished.

The next emperor of Rome was a very remarkable and a very good man. His name was Marcus Aurelius. He governed the empire justly and well for nearly twenty years. He began to reign in the year 161 A.D. He was the adopted son of the good Emperor Antoninus. For some time before the death of Antoninus, he held a high office and helped to govern the empire.

As soon as he became emperor Aurelius invited a young man named Verus to share the throne with him. Verus had also been adopted by Antoninus. The generous act of Aurelius surprised everybody. Never before was there a Roman emperor who wanted to give half of his power to another person, and it seemed strange to the people that Aurelius should do so. But Aurelius said:

"I think my adopted brother has a right to be emperor with me."

And so Verus was made emperor with Aurelius, and

for the first time Rome was ruled by two emperors. Verus had a great respect for Aurelius. He seldom attempted to do anything in matters of government without asking his advice. But he did not have much to do with public affairs. He cared very little about being emperor and generally spent his time in amusing himself. He was not a good young man, and his conduct gave Aurelius a great deal of sorrow. But after nine years Verus died, and Aurelius was the sole ruler during the rest of his life.

In his youth Aurelius studied under the best teachers in the empire, and so had an excellent education. He always had an eager desire for knowledge and was constantly learning. Even in war times, when he was fighting in the field, he carried a library with him and could often be seen in his tent engaged in study. He was one of the most learned of the Roman emperors, and his intimate friends were scholars and authors.

When a boy of only twelve years he joined the Stoics. These were followers of a famous wise man or philosopher of Greece, called Zeno. This man taught that the people should act according to reason and virtue, and should keep an even temper and a brave heart under all circumstances. He taught also that men should show neither joy nor sorrow, but control their feelings and passions, and submit without complaint to what could not be prevented.

The followers of Zeno were called Stoics, from the Greek word *stoa*, which means a roofed colonnade or porch. It was in a roofed porch at Athens that Zeno taught his doctrine.

The Emperor Aurelius was one of the best and most earnest of the Stoics. He carefully trained himself to control his feelings at all times and to do his duty honestly and faithfully. The Romans never had a purer or nobler emperor, or one more respected and beloved. His style of living was very simple. He had no idle courtiers at his house, and he kept only a few servants. He gave no costly dinners and entertainments. He spent much of his salary to improve the condition of the poor and to provide good schools for their children.

He used to walk through the streets of Rome in plain clothing, attended only by a favorite slave. He returned the greetings of the people with bows and pleasant smiles. Any one could go to him and talk freely, and he encouraged the people to tell him about their troubles so that he might understand how to help them.

He gave the Senate a great deal of power which he thought it ought to have, and gave back to the people many rights and privileges which former emperors had taken away from them. No wonder the Romans loved him and called him a good man.

II

But the reign of Aurelius was full of troubles. In the first part of it the Tiber one day overflowed its banks, and the waters swept away a large portion of Rome, destroying many lives. After this there were dreadful earthquakes, very destructive fires, and other serious misfortunes.

There were also many wars. There was a war with the Parthians, a brave, warlike nation in Asia, who destroyed a Roman army and then invaded Syria. Large armies were sent against them and they were soon conquered and forced to pay homage to Aurelius.

The Parthian horsemen had a strange way of fighting. They were armed with bows and arrows and small spears called javelins, and were mounted on very swift horses. They would make attacks on the rear lines of the Romans, and when the Romans turned to attack them they would lash their horses and ride off as fast as the wind. And while their horses were going at full speed they would turn in their saddles and cast their javelins, or shoot their arrows with wonderfully accurate aim.

After the Parthian war there were wars with a number of wild tribes living in the countries now called Austria and Hungary. The tribes there rebelled against their Roman governors, and Aurelius had years of hard fighting before he could subdue them. He was himself a remarkably brave and able general and gained many splendid victories. So at last he taught the barbarians to respect and obey the Romans who governed them.

Once, while Aurelius was fighting a tribe called the Quadi, his soldiers were hemmed in by the enemy, in a small rocky valley, and suffered greatly from thirst. Suddenly the sky darkened and rain fell in torrents. The thirsty soldiers collected the water in their helmets and drank it eagerly.

While they were drinking, and their lines were in confusion, the Quadi suddenly attacked them in large numbers. The Romans would have been cut to pieces but that there came a violent hailstorm, with lightning and thunder, which stopped the battle. When the storm had ceased, the Romans, much refreshed by the rainfall, boldly fought the Quadi and won a great victory.

Some of the Romans believed that the sudden storm which relieved them so much was caused by the magical power of an African wizard who was with the army at the time. But there was also with the army a legion of soldiers, some 3,000 in number, who were Christians. The Christians had prayed for rain, and they believed that the rain came in answer to their prayers. They said that it was a miracle sent by God to prove the truth of Christianity.

Now Aurelius was a pagan. Some of his Christian soldiers had tried to convert him to their faith, but they had not succeeded. He lived and died a believer in the pagan gods and goddesses. After the strange storm, however, he seemed to have a greater respect for Christianity, and he named his Christian legion of soldiers the "Thundering Legion."

III

Once the commander of the Roman armies in Asia, a man named Avidius Cassius, planned a rebellion against Aurelius. When everything was ready Cassius declared himself emperor and started with his army to Rome to take possession of the city. Aurelius collected his troops and went to meet Cassius; but no meeting took place, for Cassius was killed by his own soldiers, and the rebellion quickly came to an end.

Those who had aided Cassius were brought before Aurelius for punishment. But the emperor would not punish them.

"No, I will not harm them," he said. "I think I have governed the empire too faithfully and liberally to fear plots. I can afford to forgive traitors. Let all the friends of Cassius go free; they are to be pitied rather than punished."

Aurelius was always very industrious and would never waste any of his time. It was a part of his duty as emperor to attend the games and sports in the Colosseum and the Circus. Aurelius cared nothing for such sports and whenever he attended them, he always spent his time at some useful occupation while sitting in the splendid chair of state provided for him. Sometimes he would study his favorite books and make notes from them, and sometimes he would dictate letters and government orders to a secretary. Thousands of excited Romans around him would be shouting their delight at the sports in the ring, but Aurelius would go on calmly with the work he had in hand.

"I do not like to waste my time by sitting here doing nothing," he would say. "To waste time is one of the greatest of crimes."

159

And so, by never allowing himself to be idle, Aurelius was able to do many useful things. He established good schools and hospitals in Rome and other cities of Italy. He introduced new trades so that the poor people could get a much better living than before.

Aurelius always gave great encouragement to art and literature. He welcomed authors and artists to Rome and was always their friend. He established libraries and halls of paintings and statuary. He himself wrote several books.

It is said that with all his virtue the life of Aurelius was not a happy one. He had serious troubles at times in governing the empire, and the cares of a ruler often weighed heavily upon him. His wife, whom he dearly loved, behaved very badly and caused him much anxiety, and his only son was a very bad young man.

So in the latter years of his life Aurelius always appeared melancholy. A smile was seldom seen upon his face. He died at the city now called Vienna, in Austria, A.D. 180.

CONSTANTINE THE GREAT

I

For more than a hundred years after the time of Marcus Aurelius none of the Roman emperors did anything great or remarkable. They were nearly all bad men, and many of them were put to death for their evil deeds.

In the year 307 A.D. the empire had been divided up through many quarrels and wars between generals of the armies. Often an army would declare its commander an emperor, and he would set himself up as ruler of part of the empire. So in this way there came at last to be six persons who claimed to be emperors.

None of them was in any way remarkable except the Emperor Constantine, called Constantine the Great. He was the son of a former emperor named Constantius. When Constantius died the army chose Constantine to be emperor. But he did not go to Rome to be crowned. He remained in Gaul, for he learned that five others had taken the title of emperor in different parts of the empire.

After a while, however, Constantine got messages from people in Rome begging him to come and relieve them from the cruel government of Maxentius, who was acting as emperor there. But Constantine was a wise man. He thought it would not be well for him to leave Gaul and enter into a fight with Maxentius, so he paid no attention to the messages.

At last Maxentius openly insulted Constantine and threatened to kill him. Then Constantine was aroused to anger, so he gathered a great army of good soldiers and set out for Rome. He marched over the Alps and in a short time was fighting the army of Maxentius on the plains of Italy.

The first battle took place near Turin. The soldiers of Maxentius were clad in steel armor; but Constantine's men fought them so fiercely that their armor was of little use to them, and they were speedily defeated. There was another battle at Verona, where Constantine was again the victor.

The third battle took place on the banks of the Tiber, near Rome. Maxentius had more soldiers than Constantine, but he was not a good general, so he was easily beaten. He himself was drowned while fleeing across the Tiber.

After the battle Constantine entered Rome amidst the cheers of the people. A little while afterwards he told an interesting story to a Christian bishop named Eusebius. He said that while he was marching through northern Italy, on the way to Rome, he was constantly thinking about the Christian religion. It had been spreading in every civilized country for more than two centuries, and Constantine thought that he, too, should become a Christian and no longer worship pagan gods. But he could not make up his mind to do so.

One day while he was in front of his tent, with his officers and troops around him, there appeared in the heavens an enormous cross of fire. A little on one side of the cross were these words in the Greek language, "By this, conquer." The words are sometimes given in the Latin form, *In hoc signo vinces*, the translation of which is, "Through this sign thou shalt conquer."

Constantine was astonished at the wonderful vision, and he gazed at it until it faded away. He could not understand what it meant and was greatly troubled. But that night he dreamed that Christ appeared to him in robes of dazzling white, bearing a cross in His hands, and that He promised him victory over his enemies if he would make the cross his standard.

Constantine now declared himself a Christian and had a standard made in the form of a cross, with a banner attached to it bearing the initial letters of the name of Christ. This banner was called the *Labarum*, and it was afterwards the standard of the Roman emperors.

When Constantine became a Christian himself he began to take the Christians into his favor. He made some of them high officers of the government; he built Christian churches and destroyed the pagan temples. He also made the Christian religion the religion of the empire, and he had the sign of a cross painted on the shields and banners of the Roman armies.

Thus, after many, many years of terrible persecution, the Christians were befriended by the Roman emperor, and soon they became very powerful. Thousands of Romans were converted to Christianity, and the churches were crowded with worshipers.

II

Constantine also very much improved the Roman laws and system of government. He put a stop to the dishonest practices of the officers and established just methods of carrying on public affairs. He disbanded the famous Prætorian Guards, which had been an evil power in Rome for centuries. Many other reforms were carried out by Constantine, who seemed anxious to do what was right and what was for the best interests of the people.

Under Constantine's rule, therefore, Rome was happy and prosperous. To show their gratitude to him for his noble deeds the people erected in his honor a grand marble arch in the central square of the city and inscribed on it:

'TO THE FOUNDER OF OUR PEACE.'

Four of the six emperors who had at one time ruled the empire were now dead. But in the east there was one emperor named Licinius. Constantine attacked him, scattered his armies, and took away from him the greater part of his territory.

The two emperors then became friends, but after some time they had a quarrel and went to war again. Each had a large army and a fleet of warships. Two great battles were fought, and Constantine won both. Licinius soon afterwards died.

Now for the first time Constantine was sole emperor, and for more than fourteen years he ruled the immense Roman empire. He built the most magnificent palace Rome had ever seen. He surrounded himself with hundreds of courtiers and lived in great splendor.

After a time he resolved to move the capital of the Empire to a more central place than Rome, and he selected Byzantium, an ancient city of Thrace, at the entrance to the Black Sea. To this city Constantine sent numbers of workmen to make alterations and improvements, and he changed its name to Constantinople, which means *city of Constantine*. He spent vast sums of money in erecting gorgeous buildings, making aqueducts, constructing streets and public squares, and in doing the many other things proper to be done in the capital of a great empire. The finest statues and other works of art that could be obtained in Greece, Italy, and the countries of Asia were brought to make Constantinople beautiful.

When everything was ready Constantine with the officers of his government removed to Constantinople. He lived for about seven years afterwards. There were no further wars, except a slight conflict with a tribe called the Goths, and the people of the empire were contented and prosperous.

Constantine died in Constantinople at the age of sixty-three, after a reign of nearly thirty-one years. He was the first Christian emperor of Rome.

END OF THE WESTERN EMPIRE

Most of the Roman emperors after Constantine were either cruel tyrants or very worthless persons, who spent their time in idle pleasure and neglected their duties to the people. A few, however, did some remarkable things and therefore deserve to be mentioned among the Famous Men.

One emperor, whose name was Julian, is called in history Julian the Apostate, because he gave up the Christian religion and tried to establish the worship of the pagan gods again in Rome. Julian also attempted to rebuild the Temple of Jerusalem which, as we have seen, was destroyed by Titus. There was a Christian prophecy that it would never be restored, and Julian thought of rebuilding it to prove the prophecy false. A story is told that as soon as the men began the work balls of fire burst from the ground close by them and they had to stop. They tried again and again and the same thing happened, and at last they had to give up the work altogether.

Not long after he became emperor Julian set out with a large army to conquer Persia. For a while he was very successful and defeated the Persian king in many battles. But one day he was shot in the breast by an arrow and he died soon after. It is said that while he lay wounded he cast a handful of his own blood toward heaven, crying out, "Thou hast conquered, O Galilean." By Galilean he meant Christ, who is sometimes called the Galilean because He was brought up in Galilee.

Not long after the reign of Julian, there was an emperor named Valentinian. He made his brother Valens emperor of the eastern part of the empire while he himself ruled over the western part. And for many years afterwards the empire was ruled in this way by two emperors, one called the Emperor of the East, and the other the Emperor of the West.

On the death of Valentinian his son Gratian became Emperor of the West, and a talented soldier named Theodosius became Emperor of the East on the death of Valens. Gratian was weak and unfit to rule, and he was killed by a Spaniard named Maximus, who made himself Emperor of the West.

Theodosius fought Maximus and defeated him, and afterwards had him put to death. Then he made a son of Valentinian Emperor of the West, as Valentinian II, and gave him as his adviser a chief named Arbogastes. But Arbogastes was soon the real master of the Western Empire. One day Valentinian was found dead in his bed, and Arbogastes then made Eugenius, a teacher, the emperor. Theodosius, who well knew that Valentinian II had been murdered, made war on Eugenius and Arbogastes and defeated them, and until his death, a few months afterwards (in 395), Theodosius was emperor of both East and West.

Theodosius had been a wise ruler, but he did one very bad thing. The people of Thessalonica, a city of Macedonia, a country north of Greece, had killed their governor because he had put one of their favorite circus riders in prison. When Theodosius heard of this he was very angry, and he gave orders that they should be invited to a show in the circus and there put to death. This cruel order was carried out. The citizens of Thessalonica were invited to come one day to the circus to see a grand show. Thousands came, and as soon as they had taken their seats a troop of soldiers under the command of one of the generals of Theodosius entered the building and massacred them all without mercy. Over six thousand men, women, and children were killed.

At this time Theodosius resided in Milan, a city of north Italy. At the same time there lived in Milan a bishop named Ambrose, who was a good and holy man. When Ambrose was told of the massacre at Thessalonica he was greatly shocked. He severely reprimanded the emperor and would not permit him to enter the door of the church until he had done penance for the sin he had committed in so cruelly putting to death many innocent persons.

The successor of Theodosius as Emperor of the West was his son Honorius, who reigned for twenty-nine years; but the actual ruler during all that time was a soldier named Stilicho, who was the emperor's guardian. Honorius was a simpleton and had no desire or ability to attend to the affairs of the government.

The Goths and Vandals and other barbarous tribes from the north and east of Europe now began to overrun the Western Empire and to threaten Rome itself. Twice the great city was actually captured and plundered; the first time by the Goths under Alaric, and next by the Vandals under a bold warrior named Genseric. About those barbarian chiefs and their exploits you will perhaps read in *FAMOUS MEN OF THE MIDDLE AGES*, a companion volume to this book.

To defend the seat of their empire against the attacks of its enemies the Romans were obliged to withdraw their forces from several of the outlying provinces, including Britain, which was now left to its native inhabitants. For more than fifty years afterwards a number of men without much ability took part in ruling what was left of the once mighty empire. One of these was called by the high-sounding name of Romulus Augustulus. He was the son of Orestes, the general of the army of Italy and had been made emperor by his father. He was the last of the Western emperors.

Among the Italian soldiers there was a huge, half-savage man named Odoacer, who belonged to a wild northern tribe. He was a favorite of the army because of his courage and strength. He resolved to be the ruler of Italy, so with the army at his back he put Orestes to death, took Romulus Augustulus prisoner, and forced him to give up the title of emperor. Then Odoacer became king of Italy in the year 476 A.D.

By this time the world had nearly entered that period which is known as the Middle Ages, and many of the other countries which had been parts of the Roman Empire were either ruling themselves or defending themselves against new invaders. Gaul was invaded and conquered by German tribes called Franks, from whom the country subsequently got the name of France. Britain, abandoned by the Romans, was soon after conquered by other German tribes. And so at last the great Roman Empire had crumbled to pieces, and Rome, so long the Mistress of the World, as she was called, had fallen from her proud position of grandeur and power into that of a second or third rate city.

But the Empire of the East continued to exist for centuries afterwards, with Constantinople as its capital. It included many of the countries of Asia, Africa, and eastern Europe which had formerly belonged to the undivided Empire. In course of time the power of the Greeks, aided by the influence of the Greek division of the Church, became supreme at Constantinople, and so the Empire was also called the Greek Empire, and sometimes the Byzantine Empire, from the ancient name of the capital.

In the fourteenth century the Turks, or Mohammedans, then very powerful in southwestern Asia, began to make inroads on the empire. They conquered and took possession of several of its provinces, and in 1453 they captured Constantinople, which has since been the capital of the Turkish, or Ottoman Empire, the ruler of which is known as the sultan.

FAMOUS MEN OF GREECE

PREFACE

The study of history, like the study of a landscape, should begin with the most conspicuous features. Not until these have been fixed in memory will the lesser features fall into their appropriate places and assume their right proportions.

The famous men of ancient and modern times are the mountain peaks of history. It is logical then that the study of history should begin with the biographies of these men.

Not only is it logical; it is also pedagogical. Experience has proven that in order to attract and hold the child's attention each conspicuous feature of history presented to him should have an individual for its center. The child identifies himself with the personage presented. It is not Romulus or Hercules or Cæsar or Alexander that the child has in mind when he reads, but himself, acting under similar conditions.

Prominent educators, appreciating these truths, have long recognized the value of biography as a preparation for the study of history and have given it an important place in their scheme of studies.

The former practice in many elementary schools of beginning the detailed study of American history without any previous knowledge of general history limited the pupil's range of vision, restricted his sympathies, and left him without material for comparisons. Moreover, it denied to him a knowledge of his inheritance from the Greek philosopher, the Roman lawgiver, the Teutonic lover of freedom. Hence the recommendation so strongly urged in the report of the Committee of Ten—and emphasized, also, in the report of the Committee of Fifteen—that the study of Greek, Roman and modern European history in the form of biography should precede the study of detailed American history in our elementary schools. The Committee of Ten recommends an eight years' course in history, beginning with the fifth year in school and continuing to the end of the high school course. The first two years of this course are given wholly to the study of biography and mythology. The Committee of Fifteen recommends that history be taught in all the grades of the elementary school and emphasizes the value of biography and of general history.

The series of historical stories to which this volume belongs was prepared in conformity with the foregoing recommendations and with the best practice of leading schools. It has been the aim of the authors to make an interesting story of each man's life and to tell those stories in a style so simple that pupils in the lower grades will read them with pleasure, and so dignified that they may be used with profit as text-books for reading.

Teachers who find it impracticable to give to the study of mythology and biography a place of its own in an already overcrowded curriculum usually prefer to correlate history with reading and for this purpose the volumes of this series will be found most desirable.

THE GODS OF GREECE

I

In the southern part of Europe is a little country called Greece. It is the home of a nation called the Greeks, and Greeks have lived in it for more than three thousand years. In olden times they believed that before they came to the land it was the home of the gods, and they used to tell wonderful stories of what happened when the gods lived in the country. One of these stories was about a god called Cronos, and his children.

Cronos was the first king of the gods. He had a wife named Rhea. His mother told him that one of his children would take his kingdom from him. He determined that this should never happen, and so he swallowed his children as soon as they were born. His cruelty distressed Rhea very much, and when a sixth child was born she made a plan to save its life. She gave Cronos a stone wrapped in baby-clothes, and this he swallowed.

Then Rhea took the child and hid him in a cave. And though the cave was dark he filled it with bright light;

so she named him Zeus, which means brightness. We call him Jupiter.

Jupiter had one of the strangest nurses that a baby ever had. It was a goat. However, she took such good care of him that when she died she was changed into a group of stars, which shine in the sky to this day.

When Jupiter grew up he went to war against his cruel father. Cronos persuaded some giants, called Titans, to help him in fighting Jupiter. These Titans were so strong that they pulled up hills and mountains and threw them at Jupiter as easily as boys throw snowballs at one another. Jupiter soon saw that he must find some match for the Titans. So he asked another family of giants to aid him. They were called Cyclops, or Round-Eye, because each had only one eye, which was round and was in the middle of his forehead. The Cyclops were famous blacksmiths, and they made thunder and lightning for Jupiter. So when the Titans hurled mountains, Jupiter hurled back bolts of thunder and flashes of lightning. The battle was a terrible one. Jupiter was the victor.

After this great battle Jupiter made Cronos bring back to life the children whom he had swallowed, and then he gave to each of his brothers and sisters a part of the kingdom of their wicked father. He made himself the king of the gods, and for his own kingdom he took the blue sky. He made his sister Here, whom we call Juno, the goddess of the clouds and queen of all the gods.

To his brother Poseidon, whom we call Neptune, he gave the ocean, and he made his brother Hades, whom we call Pluto, king of the regions under the earth and sea.

He made his sister Demeter, whom we call Ceres, queen of the grains, the fruits and the flowers.

His sister Hestia, whom we call Vesta, he made the

goddess of fire and gave her charge of the homes and hearthstones of men.

II

When the kingdom of Cronos had been divided, the new rulers found a great deal to do. In the depths of the sea Neptune built a palace whose floor was of snow-white shells and blood-red coral, while the walls were of shining mother-of-pearl. When the waves above his palace were wild, Neptune would yoke his brazen-hoofed horses to his chariot and, standing with his trident, or three-pronged spear, in his hand, would drive swiftly over the water. And as the brazen hoofs of the horses trampled upon the waves the sea became calm.

The underground world of Pluto was a dreary region. It was the home of the dead. Round it flowed a black river called the "Styx," or "Hateful." The only way to cross this river was in a ferryboat rowed by a silent boatman named Charon. At the gateway of the under world was the terrible watch-dog Kerberus, or, as we spell the name, Cerberus. When the old Greeks buried a person they put a coin in his mouth and a barley-cake sweetened with honey in his hand. The coin was to pay Charon for taking the spirit across the Styx and the cake was to be thrown to Cerberus, so that, while he was eating it, the spirit might pass unnoticed into the spirit-land.

No goddess was willing to be Pluto's wife and live in his world of gloom. So he was very lonely. One day he visited the upper world in his chariot drawn by four handsome coal-black steeds. He saw a beautiful maiden, named Persephone, whom we call Proserpine, gathering flowers in a meadow. Pluto at once bore her off to his kingdom of darkness and married her. Thus she became the queen of the lower world.

This made life much pleasanter for Pluto, but it was

very hard for Proserpine. She loved sunshine and flowers, and she grieved for them so much that at last Jupiter took pity upon her and persuaded Pluto to let her come back to the land of light for a part of every year. When she made her yearly visits, the flowers that she loved so dearly bloomed for her, the grass grew green, and it was spring. When the time came that she must return to Pluto, all the flowers drooped and died, the grass turned brown, and bleak winter followed.

The sisters of Jupiter had a great deal to do in their fair kingdoms. Every spring and summer Ceres caused the different kinds of fruits and grains and flowers to grow. As she could not do all this work alone she had thousands of beautiful maidens, called nymphs, to help her. There was a wood-nymph in every tree to make its leaves green and glossy and to color its blossoms. There was a water-nymph in every spring that bubbled out of the hills, and one in every stream that flowed through the valleys. The nymphs of the springs and brooks watered the plants and crops of Ceres and made them grow.

Vesta was the sister to whom had been given charge of the home and hearthstone. She caused the fires to glow, which burned on the hearth and made home cheery and gave warmth to the family and to strangers who came to see them. In every city and town of Greece a fire sacred to Vesta was always kept burning.

III

In his kingdom of the sky Jupiter dwelt in splendor, but he was not always happy; for although Juno, his queen, was a lovely in face and form, she was more beautiful than good-tempered; and sometimes she and Jupiter had bitter quarrels.

One of the sons of Jupiter was named Hermes or Mercury. He wore golden sandals and carried a wonderful wand. On the heels of the sandals were wings with which he could fly through the air like a bird. Because he could travel so swiftly he became the messenger of the gods.

Another son of Jupiter was Hephaestus, whom we call Vulcan. He was the god of fire and the friend of workers in metals. He had a great forge under Mount Ætna, and there he made wonderful things of iron and brass. The round-eyed Cyclops were his blacksmiths. One day Vulcan was rude to his father, who to punish him hurled him from heaven. Vulcan fell upon rocks and broke his leg and ever after that was lame.

Ares, the terrible god of war, whom we call Mars, was another son of Jupiter. He delighted in battle and bloodshed.

Apollo and his twin sister Artemis, or Diana, were also children of Jupiter. They were both beautiful. Apollo's beauty was so great that when we wish to say that a man is handsome in face and form, we say, "He is an Apollo." Apollo and Diana were great favorites with Jupiter, who made Apollo the god of the sun, and Diana the goddess of the moon. To each he gave a silver bow, from which they shot arrows of light.

The most wonderful daughter of Jupiter was Athene, whom we usually call Minerva. One day the king of the gods had a headache from which he could get no relief; so he sent for Vulcan. When the great blacksmith arrived at his father's palace Jupiter said to him, "Split open my head with your axe." As soon as Vulcan had done this, a maiden goddess, clothed in armor, sprang from the head of Jupiter. The maiden was Minerva, the goddess of wisdom.

IV

Most beautiful of all the goddesses was Aphrodite, or Venus, who sprang from the foam of the sea. She was the goddess of love. Several of the gods wished to marry her. Jupiter decided the matter strangely by giving her to Vulcan, the ugliest of all the gods.

Venus had a son named Eros, or Cupid, the god of love. He carried a bow and arrows, and if one of his arrows pierced the heart of a mortal, that mortal fell in love.

There was a fair goddess named Iris, who caused the rainbow to brighten dark storm-clouds, and often bore messages from heaven to men.

There were also many other gods and goddesses. Three sisters were known as the Graces. They made mortals gracious and lovable, friendly and pleasant in their ways.

There were three other sisters called the Furies. Their forms were draped in black, and their hair was twined with serpents. They punished wicked people and gave them no peace as long as they lived.

Higher than all gods and goddesses were three weird sisters, called the Fates. Not even Jupiter could change the plans of the Fates. Whatever they said must come to pass always happened. Whatever they said should not happen never took place. When a child was born, one of the sisters began to spin the thread of its life. The second decided how long the thread should be. The third cut the thread when the moment came for the life to end.

After men came to Greece and dwelt there the gods and goddesses withdrew to the far-away peaks of Olympus, the highest mountain in Greece, and made their home there.

DEUCALION AND THE FLOOD

Upon Olympus there was for every god a shining palace of brass, built by Vulcan and the Cyclops; and every day the gods gathered in the great banqueting hall of Jupiter to feast upon ambrosia and drink nectar from goblets of gold.

At the banquets they were served by a lovely maiden named Hebe, who was the goddess of youth. While they feasted Apollo played on his lyre and the Muses sang. The muses were the nine goddesses of poetry, arts, and sciences. Even in our own language playing and singing are called "music" in memory of them.

Sometimes the gods came down from Olympus to visit the men in Greece and taught them what we call the "useful arts." Minerva, the goddess of wisdom, showed them how to harness horses and plow the ground. She showed the women how to spin and weave.

Ceres, the great earth-mother who made the fields fruitful, showed the farmers how to sow wheat and barley. Then, when the grain was ripe, she taught the farmers' wives how to make bread.

Vulcan taught the Greeks how to make plows, spades and hoes and many other things of iron and brass.

When the gods came down now and then from Olympus they found that the early Greeks were very wicked. The kindness of the gods made them no better; so at last Jupiter decided to destroy them by a flood.

A certain half-god, half man, named Prometheus, or Forethought, warned the Greeks of their danger. The only person that heeded his warning was his own son, Deucalion. With Pyrrha, his wife, Deucalion got into an ark as soon as the rain began.

It rained all over Greece for days and days. The rivers and brooks overflowed. The valleys were filled. The trees disappeared. All but the highest mountains were covered. But Deucalion's ark rode safely. At last the rain ceased. For nine days the ark drifted about on the face of the water. Then it grounded.

When the waters had gone down somewhat, Deucalion and Pyrrha found that they were on one of the mountains of Greece, called Parnassus. They left their ark and walked down the mountain. Of all the Greeks only these two were left; and among the quiet hills and valleys near or far not a living creature was to be seen. The loneliness made them fearful. Scarcely knowing whither they went, they came suddenly upon a deep cleft in the rocks. Out of the cleft dense volumes of steam and gas were pouring. Deucalion, who was braver than his wife, peered into the cleft; and while he did so, a wonderful voice came from the depths.

It said, "Cast behind you the bones of your mother!"

"An oracle!" cried Pyrrha.

"An oracle it is!" Deucalion cried.

Long ages before the flood, the gods used some

times to speak with men and give them advice about things that were going to happen. What they said was called an "oracle," a word that means something told by the gods to men.

So now Deucalion and Pyrrha felt sure that one of the gods was telling them something.

But they wondered what the words "Cast behind you the bones of your mother" could mean. After a while Deucalion said:

"Pyrrha, the earth is our mother."

"Very true," said she.

"Then," cried Deucalion, "the bones of our mother must be the stones of the earth."

Both now saw plainly that the oracle meant that they should cast behind them the stones that lay scattered upon the ground. So they went on down the mountain, and as they went they picked up stones which they cast behind them.

Soon they heard the clatter of many feet behind them, and looking back they saw that the stones which Deucalion had thrown had turned into a troop of young men, who were following Deucalion, while the stones that Pyrrha had thrown had become a band of girls, who were following Pyrrha.

Deucalion and Pyrrha were no longer lonely; and they had plenty to do for they taught the youths and maidens the arts of plowing and spinning and weaving that they themselves had learned from the gods before the flood.

Stones lay thick on the face of the land, and the hills were covered with forests. With the stones walls were made, and with timber from the forest roofs and floors were laid, and thus houses were built. Farms were then laid out, fields were sown, and vines and olive trees planted. Soon the valley below Mount Parnassus was crowded with many people. In time the race of Deucalion and Pyrrha spread from valley to valley, up and down the land of Greece.

The people called themselves Hellenes, because one of the sons of Deucalion was named Hellen. Their country, which, as you have learned, we call Greece, they called Hellas.

CADMUS AND THE DRAGON'S TEETH

In a land of Asia, named Phoenicia, lived King Agenor with his queen. They had four children—three sons and a beautiful daughter named Europa.

One morning, as the young people were playing in a meadow near the seashore, a snow-white bull came toward them. Europa and her brothers thought it would be a fine frolic to take a ride on the back of the bull; and the brothers agreed that Europa should have the first ride. In a moment she was on the bull's back, and the bull was capering over the meadow. Then, suddenly, he ran down to the shore and plunged into the sea. For a little while he could be seen swimming through the water, with Europa clinging to his horns. Then both disappeared, and Europa never saw her brothers or her father or her mother again. Still, her fate was not a sad one. At the end of a long ride on the back of the bull she reached that part of the world which to this day is called Europe in her honor. There she married a king, and was queen for all the rest of her life.

But in her old home there was great distress. Agenor sent his sons to look for her and told them not to return until they had found their sister. Their mother went with them. After a long time the two elder sons gave up the search and settled in a strange land. The mother and the youngest son, Cadmus, wandered on until her death. With her last breath she made him promise to go to Mount Parnassus and ask the oracle where he might find Europa. As soon as she was dead Cadmus made haste to Parnassus. When he arrived at the mountain, he found the cleft in the rocks from which long before the oracle had come to Deucalion. Cadmus stood before the stream of gas which poured from it and asked for advice.

From the cleft came a deep roaring sound. Then he heard the puzzling words, "Follow the cow; and build a city where she lies down."

Cadmus saw a cow nibbling tufts of grass by the roadside, not far from where he was standing. He decided to follow her and, with some companions, set out on his unknown journey.

For a long time it seemed as though the cow would not lie down at all, but, finally, she began to double her knees under her, as cows do, and in a second more she was at rest on the ground. Cadmus and his men decided to camp on the spot for the night. They looked about for some water and found a spring bubbling out from under a rock.

Now this was really an enchanted spring. It was guarded by a dragon that had the claws of a lion, the wings of an eagle and the jaws of a serpent. When Cadmus and his men came near, the dragon sprang from behind the rock and killed all but Cadmus.

Luckily, Cadmus had his sword with him, and so, when the dragon, with wide-open jaws, flew at him, he thrust his sword down the fiery throat and into the creature's heart. The monster fell dead, and through the air rang the words, "Sow the teeth of the dragon, O Cadmus!"

Though he saw that it would be hard work to break the great teeth out of the dragon's jaws, Cadmus at once set about the task, When it was finished, he dug the soil with the point of his sword as best he could and planted half of the monster's teeth.

Never had grown such a wonderful crop. For every tooth that was planted a warrior, armed and eager to fight, sprang up. Cadmus gazed in amazement, until a voice in the air commanded, "Throw a stone among the warriors."

Cadmus obeyed, and immediately every warrior drew his sword and attacked one of his companions. The woods rang with the din of the battle. One by one the warriors fell, until only five were left. Cadmus now shouted loudly to them, "Be at peace!" When they stopped fighting, he added, "Building is better than killing." And every man of the five immediately repeated the words, "Building is better than killing."

"Then let us build a city here!" cried Cadmus; for they were standing where the cow had lain down.

The warriors agreed, and all set to work to build a city. They called the city Thebes; and in later days it became very famous.

The land around Thebes was rich and covered with grass. So Cadmus and his friends raised cattle. But there were many robbers in Greece, who often made raids upon the cattle and stole some of the finest animals.

For protection against the robbers a wall was built. It was not a wall laid by masons, but a magic wall built by a strange musician called Amphion. He struck such sweet music from his lyre that the stones danced about and took their proper places in the wall.

When Cadmus was a boy at his father's palace in Phoenicia, he and his brothers and the lost Europa had been taught to read and write; and now that peace and plenty filled his land, he determined to teach his people the arts of reading and writing. So the men of Thebes learned their a-b-c's, and Cadmus' school was the first in Europe where people were taught to read.

But Cadmus was not happy. He was condemned to eight years of punishment for killing the dragon. After the punishment was over, Jupiter gave him Harmony, the daughter of Venus, for a wife, and all the gods came to the wedding feast. One of the wedding presents was a necklace that brought bad luck to any one who wore it, and Harmony had great misfortunes. Bowed with grief, she and Cadmus left Thebes and settled in the western part of Greece. Finally, Jupiter pitied them in their trouble, turned them into serpents, and carried them to the realm of the blessed.

PERSEUS

I

In a Grecian city named Argos lived beautiful Danaë, the king's daughter. An oracle warned the king that he would be killed by Danaë's son. To save his life he ordered Danaë and her child, Perseus, to be shut up in a chest and cast adrift on the Mediterranean Sea.

For two days and nights the chest floated on the water. At the end of that time it struck against some rocks on the shore of an island called Seriphos. There was a little opening in the side of the chest, and peeping through it, Danaë saw a man coming over the rocks toward her. As soon as he was near enough, he threw a fishing net over the chest and drew it ashore.

He broke the chest open and let Danaë out. Then he told her that she had landed upon an island ruled by his brother, Polydectes. His own name was Dictys. He took Danaë and her child to his home.

Years went by, and Perseus grew to be a strong and handsome man. Danaë was still a beautiful woman and

Polydectes fell in love with her. She refused his love, and Perseus also was unwilling that he should marry her. Then Polydectes told Perseus that he was about to marry, and that he wished to give the head of the Gorgon, Medusa, to his bride for a present. Perseus promised to get him the Gorgon's head. This pleased Polydectes. He did not want the Gorgon's head, but he asked for it because he believed that the young man would never return alive if he went in search of it.

The Gorgons were three horrible sisters who lived on a distant island near the land of the setting sun. Their hair was snakes that hissed at all who came near them. They had wings of gold and claws of brass. Two of them were immortal, but the youngest, Medusa, was mortal. Her face was that of a beautiful woman, but never free from a frown; and whoever looked upon it was turned to stone.

When Perseus had made his promise, he went out from the palace and sat on the cliffs of Seriphos. While he was gazing at the white-capped sea, Mercury, the messenger of the gods, appeared before him and promised help from himself and from Minerva, the goddess of wisdom. Minerva would lend her shield, Mercury offered his sword of light, and both agreed to guide him to the land of the setting sun, where the three Gray Sisters lived. These sisters would tell him the way to the home of the Hesperides. The Hesperides were beautiful nymphs who had three magic treasures, which Perseus must get before he could reach the land of the Gorgons.

Leaving Seriphos, Perseus began his long journey to the land of the setting sun. When he arrived there he found the three Gray Sisters. They were the strangest beings that he had ever seen. They had among them only one eye and one tooth, which they passed in turn from one to another.

When Perseus reached their dwelling the door was

wide-open, and so he walked in. He was overjoyed to find the three sisters all taking a nap, with their one eye and one tooth lying beside them; and he quickly seized both these treasures. That done, he awakened the sisters and inquired of them the way to the home of the Hesperides. At first they refused to tell him, but when they found that he had their eye and tooth, they quickly told him how to go. He then gave them back the eye and the tooth.

It did not take him long to reach the home of the Hesperides. It was an island in the Western Ocean. The nymphs had been told by Minerva that he was coming. So when he arrived they gave him welcome and agreed to lend him their magic treasures.

"The distance across the sea to the home of the Gorgons is great," said one of the nymphs to Perseus. "Take therefore these winged sandals of gold. With them you can fly through the air like an eagle."

"The Gorgon's head," said another of the nymphs, "must be kept in this magic wallet, lest you look upon the terrible face and be turned to stone."

"To get near the Gorgons," added the third, "you must wear this cap of darkness, so that you may see without being seen."

The hero then slung the wallet over his shoulder, put the sandals upon his feet, and the cap upon his head, and vanished. As swift as lightning, he crossed the dark waters and reached the home of the Gorgons. They were all asleep. Without looking at them Perseus held up the shield of Minerva and saw reflected upon it the frowning face of Medusa. With one blow from the sword of Mercury he struck off her head, and without looking at it placed it within his wallet. Then he hurried away from the weird place.

The other Gorgons awoke at once and followed him in furious haste; but as he wore his cap of darkness they could not see him, and with his sandal wings he flew so fast that he was soon too far for them to follow.

II

As he was flying along the coast of Africa he heard the sound of weeping. He looked down and saw a beautiful girl chained to a rock at the water's edge. Hastening to her, he took off his cap of darkness that she might see him and exclaimed, "Fair maiden, why are you chained to this rock?"

"Alas!" she said, "I have been offered as a sacrifice to Neptune. You cannot save me, however much you want to."

Her words made Perseus the more determined to help her. "Why is Neptune angry?" he asked. "And who has dared to treat you so cruelly?"

"I am Andromeda, daughter of Cepheus and Cassiopeia, king and queen of this land," replied the maiden. "My mother boasted that I was more beautiful than any nymph in Neptune's palace. Her pride enraged Neptune so that he raised great storms and sent a terrible monster to devour our people. The priests said that if I were offered to him the rest of the people would be spared."

Then with the sword of light Perseus cut the chain which bound Andromeda to the rock. At this moment the monster, huge and ugly, came plowing through the water. Perseus could not be seen because he had put on his cap of darkness, and before the creature could harm the maiden its head was cut off by the sword of light.

On his swift-winged sandals Perseus, with Andromeda in his arms, now flew to the palace of Cepheus and Cassiopeia.

There had been many glad weddings before that of Perseus and Andromeda, but none was ever more joyful. For he was admired as a wonderful hero, and everyone loved the girl who had been willing to give her life to save her people.

After the wedding Perseus went back to Seriphos, taking Andromeda with him. When he reached the island Polydectes was in his palace feasting, and Perseus hastened at once to the banquet hall and said to the king:

"See! I have brought that which you desired."

With these words he held up the head of the Gorgon. The king and his courtiers gave one look and were instantly turned to stone.

The Gorgon's head had now done its work; so Perseus carried it to a temple of Minerva and there offered it to the goddess. Ever after she wore it upon her shield, and its snaky ringlets and frowning face are to be seen upon her statues. The sword of light was given back to Mercury, who also returned the winged sandals, the magic wallet and the cap of darkness to the Hesperides.

III

You will remember that Argos was the birthplace of Perseus, and to that city he now returned, taking Andromeda with him. His grandfather, who was still king of Argos, remembered the oracle that he should die by the hand of Danaë's son and was much alarmed, but Perseus quieted the fears of the king and the two became very good friends. While playing quoits one day, however, Perseus accidentally hit his grandfather with a quoit. The wound caused the old king's death. And thus, as the Greeks used to say, "What had been fated came to pass."

Perseus was overwhelmed with sorrow. He could not bear to live any longer at Argos and therefore gave his kingdom to a kinsman of his, in exchange for the kingdom of Tiryns.

At Tiryns he ruled long and wisely. The gods gave him and Andromeda a glorious place among the stars after their death. With Cepheus and Cassiopeia they can still be seen in the skies not far from where the Great Bear shines.

HERCULES AND HIS LABORS

Greatest of all the heroes of Greece was Herakles, or Hercules, who was born in Thebes, the city of Cadmus. His mother was one of the descendants of Perseus and his father was Jupiter.

Juno, the queen of the gods, hated Hercules. When he was only a baby in the cradle she sent two large serpents to devour him. He grasped the throat of each serpent with his tiny fingers and choked both to death.

When he had grown to manhood he was forced by the will of the gods to become the slave of a hard-hearted cousin of his named Eurystheus, who was king of Mycenae.

Eurystheus set twelve tasks for Hercules. The first was to kill the Nemean lion. This was a ferocious animal that lived in the forest of Nemea and ate a child or a grown person every two or three days. Its skin was so tough that nothing could pierce it, but Hercules drove the lion before him into a cave and, following boldly, grasped the beast about the neck and choked it to death. That done, he stripped off its skin, which he ever after wore as a cloak.

When the Nemean lion had been killed Eurystheus said to Hercules, "You must now kill the hydra that lives in the marsh of Lerna. "

This hydra was a nine-headed water serpent whose very breath was poisonous. It was hard to kill the creature because as soon as one head was cut off two others at once sprang up in its place. This task might have proved too much for Hercules if a friend had not prevented new heads from growing by burning each neck with a firebrand the instant that Hercules cut off the head.

The third of Hercules' tasks was to bring to Eurystheus the stag with golden horns that was sacred to Diana. It lived in southern Greece in the woods of Arcadia. It had brazen feet and could run so fast that Hercules had to chase it for a whole year before he caught it.

"Now," said Eurystheus, "you must kill the boar that roams on the slopes of Mount Erymanthus." This creature laid waste the farmers' fields of barley and wheat at the foot of the mountain. Hercules captured the brute in a net and killed it.

The next command of Eurystheus to Hercules was, "Clean the Augean stables."

The Augean stables belonged to Augeas, one of the kings of Greece. As three thousand oxen were kept in them, and as they had not been cleaned for thirty years, they were filthy. Hercules cleaned them in one day. He dug a great ditch as far as the stables and turned into it the waters of two swift rivers.

II

As soon as this was done Eurystheus said, "you must now kill the birds of Lake Stymphalus." Instead of wings of feathers these birds had wings of arrows which darted out and shot any one who passed by.

Their claws and beaks were of brass, and they fed on human flesh. Hercules killed them with poisoned arrows.

Still Eurystheus hoped to find some task that might prove too much for the hero, so he said, "Bring me the bull of Crete."

This bull was a terrible monster that had been sent by Neptune to ravage Crete, an island not far from Greece. Hercules set out for Crete at once, conquered the bull, rode on his back across the sea from Crete to Greece, then swung the great animal to his own shoulders and carried him to Eurystheus.

Eurystheus now said to his wonderful slave, "Tame the man-eating horses of Diomedes, king of Thrace." He fully expected that this task would be fatal to Hercules. But the hero went to the palace of Diomedes and soon discovered a way to tame the savage steeds. He killed Diomedes and threw his flesh to them, when lo! the man-eating beasts became like other horses and gladly ate oats and grass.

Eurystheus immediately set a ninth task.

"My daughter," said he, "wants the girdle of the queen of the Amazons. Get it for her."

The Amazons were a nation living upon the shores of the Black Sea. It was the custom for the women to go to battle. Bravest of them all was Queen Hippolyte, whom Mars had rewarded for her courage by giving her a beautiful girdle. All Greece had heard of this girdle, and it was no wonder that the daughter of Eurystheus wished to have it.

When Hercules reached the country of the Amazons and made known his errand he found that the queen was as generous as she was brave. She said that she would send her girdle as a present to the daughter of Eurystheus. So it looked as though Hercules was to have no trouble at all with this task. Juno, however, tried to prevent his success. She made herself look like one of the Amazons and went among them and persuaded them that Hercules wished to carry away their queen. A great quarrel then arose between the hero and the Amazons, which ended in a battle. Brave Hippolyte was killed, and Hercules then took the girdle and carried it to Eurystheus.

III

Bring me the oxen of Geryon, Eurystheus now commanded.

Geryon was a monster with three bodies. He lived on an island in the Western Ocean, as the Greeks called the Atlantic Ocean. In the fields of this island grazed Geryon's herd of red oxen guarded by a two-headed dog. At first Hercules did not see how he could reach the island. But the sun-god, Apollo, came to his aid and said to him, "I will lend you the golden bowl in which I sail every night from the land of the Western Sea to the land of the rising sun."

So in the sun's golden bowl Hercules reached the island safely. He slew the two-headed dog, then got the whole herd of oxen into the golden bowl and sailed back.

For the tenth time Eurystheus was amazed. He now commanded Hercules, "Get me some of the apples of the Hesperides."

At the wedding of Jupiter and Juno, the grandest that ever took place on Olympus, Ceres, the great earth-mother, had given to Juno some branches loaded with golden apples. These branches were afterwards planted and grew into trees upon islands in the Western Ocean, far away from Greece. The trees and their fruit were in charge of the nymphs called Hesperides, who had a terrible dragon to aid them. When Hercules was told to get some of the apples of the Hesperides he was puzzled.

At last he went to Atlas, who was the father of the Hesperides, and begged his help. Atlas lived in Africa, opposite Spain. His duty was to hold up the sky, with all it contains, the sun, moon and stars.

"I will get you some of the apples," said Atlas in answer to Hercules, "if you will hold up the sky for me while I am getting them."

The bargain was made. Hercules held up the sky while Atlas went and secured three of the golden apples. Then the giant took the sky again on his shoulders, and Hercules carried the apples to Eurystheus.

The Fates allowed Eurystheus to send Hercules upon only one more of his dangerous errands.

"Go to the gates of the underworld," said Eurystheus, "and bring Cerberus here."

Hercules now, if ever, had need of aid from the gods. They did not fail him. Mercury, the god who guided the souls of the dead to the unseen world, and Minerva, the goddess of wisdom, both went with him to the kingdom of Pluto.

Pluto said that if Hercules could overpower Cerberus without using any weapon he might take the great watchdog to the world of light. Hercules wrestled with the monster, overcame him, and dragged him to the palace of Eurystheus.

This ended the power of Eurystheus over the hero.

IV

Hercules had a friend named Admetus, a king in Thessaly, who was about to die. The Fates had promised that his life should be spared if his father, mother or wife would die for him. When both father and mother refused, Alcestis, his wife, gave her life for him. Admetus was crazed with grief at losing her, and so Hercules went to Pluto's kingdom, seized Alcestis, and brought her to her husband.

Once Hercules became insane and killed a friend whom he greatly loved. The gods punished him for this with a serious sickness. He asked Apollo to cure him, but the god refused, and Hercules tried to carry away the tripod on which the priestess of Delphi sat when the god spoke to her. For this he was deprived of his great strength and given as a slave to Omphale, Queen of Lydia. She took the Nemean lion's skin from him and dressed him as a woman. Then she made him kneel at her feet and spin thread and do a woman's work for three years. After he was again free he did many brave deeds.

Once when journeying with his wife Deianira he reached a river. There was neither bridge nor ferry. Nessus, the centaur, half-man, half-horse, who owned that part of the river, undertook to carry Deianira across while Hercules waded. When Nessus reached the middle of the river he tried to run away with Deianira, but Hercules shot him with one of his poisoned arrows. Nessus, while dying, told Deianira to save some of his blood and use it as a charm to make Hercules love her more.

V

Some years after this, Deianira became very jealous, and the foolish woman sprinkled some drops of the centaur's poisoned blood upon a robe that Hercules had to wear at a sacrifice. When Hercules put on the robe the poison burned like fire. He tried to pull off the garment, but it clung to him, and as he pulled it his flesh was torn.

Seeing now that his end was near, he went to the top of a mountain. There he pulled up some trees by the roots and heaped them together to make his funeral pyre. With his club for a pillow and his lion's skin for a cover, he lay upon the pyre and soon he ceased to breathe. A friend kindled the pyre, and the hero's body was burned to ashes. Then a cloud, gleaming as though on fire, descended through the air, and amid the pealing of thunder the mighty spirit was born to the skies.

There Jupiter made him one of the gods and gave him the beautiful goddess Hebe for a wife.

JASON AND THE GOLDEN FLEECE

In a city of Greece named Iolcus a good man called Aeson was king. His younger brother, Pelias, seized the throne. But Pelias did not enjoy much happiness in his stolen kingdom. He had no fear of Aeson, who was a weak man. But he was very much afraid that Aeson's son Jason, then only a boy, might some day take the kingdom from him.

So he tried to kill Jason, but the child was taken away by night and Pelias never found him. It was said that he was dead. Twenty years passed, and though Jason was never seen in Iolcus Pelias was still afraid that he was alive. Finally, to settle the matter, he consulted the oracle of Apollo.

He received the answer, "Beware of the man who wears but one sandal."

After that Pelias ordered the watchman at the city gate to take notice of the feet of every stranger who entered the city.

Jason had been all these years in charge of Chiron, the centaur, who was the most famous teacher in

Greece. Jason had heard of the wickedness of his uncle, and now that he was a man he determined to regain his father's kingdom.

So one day he set out for Iolcus. On the way he came to a wide stream over which there was no bridge. At the same time a feeble old woman came up and wished to cross. The stream was swollen, and it looked as if she would be swept away by the current and drowned if she tried to wade across. So Jason took her in his arms and carried her over.

That old woman was really Juno, the queen of the gods. She had come down from Olympus to take a journey on earth without telling any one who she was, because she wished to find out if there was any real kindness among men. She never forgot Jason's courtesy; and to her help he owed his success in his career.

In crossing the stream he lost one of his sandals, and so he reached Iolcus with one foot bare. He cared very little about this; but when word was brought to Pelias that a man wearing one sandal had entered the city, the king was greatly alarmed.

"Either I must kill that man," Pelias said to himself, "or he will kill me." He therefore sent a messenger to invite the stranger to the palace, and Jason soon stood before him.

"What would you do," asked Pelias, "if you had in your power the man who was fated to kill you?"

"I should tell him," answered Jason, "to go to Colchis and bring me 'the golden fleece.' "

"Then you shall go," cried Pelias, "You have come to take my kingdom from me; but not till you bring me that fleece will I yield you my crown."

The story of the golden fleece is very interesting.

Many years before one of the Grecian kings, who had a son named Phrixus, was told by an oracle that Jupiter wished him to offer up his son as a sacrifice. The poor father prepared to make the offering. As the young man was standing before the altar and his father was just about to slay him, a ram with shining fleece of gold came down from the sky and stood beside them. Phrixus jumped to the back of the ram. His sister, Helle, who was standing with him at the altar, jumped on behind her brother, and the ram immediately ran off with the two. He went so fast that people who saw him thought he had wings. When he came to the strait which separates Europe from Asia he plunged into the waves. Poor Helle soon fell off and was drowned; and ever after that the strait was called by the Greeks the Hellespont, a word that means the Sea of Helle. It is the strait that is named the Dardanelles' on our maps.

The ram carried Phrixus safely across the strait, and went on until he reached the palace of Aeetes the king of a country called Colchis, which lay on the shores of the Euxine, or Black Sea.

Phrixus felt very thankful for having made such a wonderful journey in safety, so he offered the ram as a sacrifice to Jupiter and nailed the fleece to a tree that was sacred to Mars.

This fleece became one of the wonders of the world; and lest it should be stolen a dragon was set to watch it. Many persons tried to get possession of it, but most, if not all of them, lost their lives in the attempt.

Jason knew all this, but he said at once that he would get the fleece. Before setting out on the journey, however, he went to a place called Dodona to ask the advice of Jupiter; for at Dodona there was a wonderful talking oak which told men the advice and commands of Jupiter. As soon as Jason came near the oak the leaves began to rustle, and a voice from within the tree said:

"Build a fifty-oared ship. Take as companions the greatest heroes of Greece. Cut a branch from the talking oak and make it a part of the prow of the vessel."

All these commands Jason obeyed. The ship was built and a piece of the talking oak was used in making her prow. Jason invited forty-nine of the bravest men of Greece to go on the expedition. He named his ship the Argo, and he and his companions are known as the Argonauts, or sailors on the Argo. One of them was Orpheus, the greatest musician that ever played or sang in Greece. It was said of him that the trees of a forest once danced in wild delight at his music.

This wonderful musician was of very great use on the Argo. The ship was the largest that had ever been built in Greece and it was found too heavy to launch. The strength of all the fifty heroes did not move it an inch. Jason did not know what to do. So he consulted the talking prow, which told him that everybody must get on board and that Orpheus must then play his lyre and sing. No sooner was the music heard than the great ship glided easily into the water, and the famous voyage began.

Another companion of Jason was Hercules, about whose wonderful labors you have already been told. Then there were Castor and Pollux, twin brothers, who did such wonders that after their death the gods took them to heaven, where they still shine as stars in the constellation called the "Twins."

Still another of the Argonauts was a hero named Lynceus, which means the lynx-eyed. He was kept on watch all through the Argo's voyage, because he could see a whole day's trip ahead.

II

After many adventures the Argonauts at last crossed the Black Sea and reached the shores of Colchis. Aeetes received them in a kind manner; but he was not at all pleased when he learned their errand, because there was nothing in his kingdom which he prized so much as the golden fleece.

However, when Jason explained the matter, Aeetes said, "Very will, you may try to get the fleece if you choose to run the risk. But first you must yoke my pair of brazen-footed, fire-breathing bulls and with them plow a field near the grove where the golden fleece hangs. Then you must sow the field with some of the teeth of the dragon that Cadmus killed. And finally, you must fight with the dragon that guards the fleece."

Aeetes felt sure that Jason would lose his life in trying to do all this; for many brave men had been burned to death in the streams of fire that the bulls breathed out from their nostrils.

King Aeetes had a daughter named Medea. She was famed for her beauty and her skill as an enchantress. Fortunately, she fell in love with Jason and now came to his aid.

"Take this ointment," said Medea, "and rub it all over your body. Then the flaming breath of the bulls cannot harm you. At midnight I will go with you to the pasture where the creatures feed."

That night Jason went with Medea and found the bulls in the pasture. The magic ointment saved him from being burned by their fiery breath. He seized and yoked them without any trouble, and very soon the field was plowed and harrowed. Jason sowed the teeth of the dragon and then stood waiting to see what would happen.

Soon points of light glistened here and there in the soil. They were the tops of helmets coming up out of the ground and touched by the rays of the rising sun. In no great while where each point of light had appeared stood a full-armed warrior.

"Throw a stone into the midst of the host!" commanded Medea; and Jason obeyed.

The stone struck one warrior, glanced off to another,

and then to a third. The new-born heroes, not knowing whence the stone had come, became wild with rage, and hacked and battered one another with swords and clubs. At last only one was left and he was fatally wounded.

Then Jason went back to the palace and told Aeetes what he had done, and said that he was ready to fight the dragon that guarded the golden fleece.

At midnight he went with Medea to the grove in which the fleece hung. The dragon rushed with wide-open jaws to devour him, but Medea threw an enchanted potion into the monster's mouth, and he sank to the ground in a death-like sleep.

"Make haste!" cried Medea. "Take down the fleece." In a twinkling Jason had done so. "And now," she added, "we must start at once for Greece; for my father will never let you carry the fleece from Colchis."

Taking Medea with him, Jason made all haste to the Argo. When he reached the shore where the ship lay, his companions welcomed him heartily, and they were filled with delight when they saw the golden fleece. All hurried on board the Argo, the sails were hoisted, and the ship began her homeward voyage.

To get back to Greece the Argonauts had to sail past the Isle of the Sirens. The sirens were maidens with beautiful faces but cruel hearts. They sat upon dangerous rocks on the shore of their island and sang songs of enchanting sweetness. Sailors who heard them would steer nearer and nearer, till their vessels were wrecked on the jagged rocks. The Argonauts escaped this peril through the help of Orpheus. He played his lyre and sang more sweetly than even the Sirens, and listening to him, Jason and his companions steered their vessel beyond the dangerous rocks.

As soon as Jason reached Iolcus again he showed the golden fleece to Pelias, and then hung it up as a thank-offering in the temple of one of the gods. What became of it afterward nobody knows.

While Jason was getting the golden fleece Pelias murdered Aeson. In revenge for this Medea made a plot by which Pelias was killed by his own daughters. Then the son of Pelias drove both Jason and Medea from Iolcus.

THESEUS

I

One of the most violent quarrels that ever disturbed the life of the gods was between Neptune and Minerva.

Cecrops, one of the wisest of the Greeks, was founding a city near the finest harbor in Greece. Neptune wished to be the chief god of the city, and Minerva also desired the honor.

Neptune said that as the city was going to be a great seaport, busy with vessels sailing in and sailing out, it was only right that he, the god of the ocean should be its guardian.

Minerva foresaw that in days to come the men of the city would care much less about commerce than about art and learning. She therefore thought that she, the goddess of wisdom, should be its guardian.

The other gods became very weary of the quarrel, and to bring it to an end Jupiter ordered that the one who should offer the more useful gift to the city should become its chief god.

Neptune then struck with his trident a rock within the city's bounds, and up sprang a war horse ready for battle. Minerva touched the earth, and an olive tree rose on the spot.

Now groves of olive trees, Jupiter knew well, would be far more useful to the people than the finest of war horses. He therefore decided in favor of Minerva. The city became the most famous place in all the world for learning and art, and from Athene, the Greek name of the goddess, it was called Athens.

II

The most noted of the early kings of Athens was Theseus, the son of Aegeus, who was himself a king of Athens. Theseus was born far away from Athens and was brought up by his mother, Aethra, at the home of her father.

Before parting with Aethra at her father's home, Aegeus placed a sword and a pair of sandals under a heavy stone and said to her:

"When the child is able to lift that stone, let him take the sandals and sword and come to me."

Years went by, and when Theseus had grown up, his mother led him one day to the stone and said to him:

"If you are a man, lift that stone."

Theseus lifted it with ease and saw a pair of sandals and a sword.

His mother told him that the sandals and the sword had been placed under the stone by his father, Aegeus, who was king of Athens. "Put them on and seek him in Athens," she said.

He fastened the sword to his girdle and buckled the sandals on his feet. Then he kissed his mother and set out for Athens.

He did not go far without an adventure. A robber called the Club-bearer attacked him. A struggle fol-

210

lowed, in which the Club-bearer was killed. Then Theseus took the robber's club and ever after that carried it himself.

A little farther on he met a robber called Sinis, who was known as the Pine-bender. It was the Pine-bender's sport to pull down pine trees, tie travelers to their tops, and let the trees spring back. His victims dangled from the tree-tops until they perished from pain and hunger. When Theseus came along he bent a pine, fastened the Pine-bender to it, let the tree spring back, and left the robber to suffer the torture that he had inflicted on so many others.

Journeying still farther, the hero reached the dwelling of Procrustes, the Stretcher. Procrustes had a bed which he made all travelers fit. If a man's legs were too long, Procrustes cut them to the right length. If they were too short, he stretched them until they were long enough. Theseus forced Procrustes to lie upon the bed himself and chopped the Stretcher's legs to the right length.

In this manner, fighting often and bravely, Theseus made his way to Athens. When he reached the city and showed his sword to Aegeus, the king knew that the young man must be his son. He was filled with joy and declared Theseus his heir.

III

Every year the city of Athens had to send seven young men and seven maidens to Minos, the king of Crete, to be devoured by a terrible creature, called the Minotaur. It was kept in a place known as the Labyrinth. The Labyrinth was full of winding paths, so puzzling that a person, once in, could not find his way out.

The day that the youths and maidens were to sail to Crete was at hand, and Athens was filled with sorrow.

Theseus made up his mind that never again should the city have cause for such grief. He determined to kill the Minotaur.

"Father," he said to Aegeus, "let me go to Crete as one of the victims."

"No, no, my son!" cried Aegeus, "I could not bear to lose you."

"Ah, but you will not lose me," answered Theseus. "Not only shall I return, but I will bring back in safety all who go with me."

Aegeus at last gave consent and Theseus went as one of the fourteen victims.

The ship's sail was black, an emblem of mourning. As Theseus bade farewell to his father, he said, "I am taking a white sail with me to hoist when we come back. If the black sail should still be set when the ship comes home you will know that I have failed. But I shall not fail."

When the black-sailed vessel reached the shores of Crete there was a great crowd gathered to see the victims. Among the watchers was Ariadne, the lovely daughter of the king of Crete. She was full of pity for those who were to be devoured. When she was told that Theseus had determined to fight the Minotaur, she made up her mind to help him. She could see that he was very strong and she felt sure that he could kill the monster. But she feared that he would starve to death in the Labyrinth because he would not be able to find his way out. So when Theseus went into the Labyrinth she gave him the end of a ball of thread and said:

"I will stand here at the entrance and let the ball unwind as you go in. When you have killed the Minotaur follow the thread back to me."

So Theseus took hold of the thread and went boldly into the Labyrinth. When he reached the center of it the monster came to attack him. Its weapons were stones. Stone after stone was flung by the monster but each was warded off by Theseus, just as a skilful batter wards off a swift ball. At length Theseus was close enough to strike the Minotaur with his sword and the creature fell dead.

Guided by the thread, Theseus quickly made his way back to the entrance of the Labyrinth. There he was joyfully received by Ariadne and the youths and maidens whom he had saved from death.

Theseus and Ariadne had fallen in love with each other, and when the tribute ship set sail for Greece Ariadne was one of the passengers.

On the homeward voyage the ship touched at the island of Naxos. There Theseus had a strange dream. In it he was told by Minerva to leave Ariadne on the island because the Fates intended her to be the wife of one of the gods.

Accordingly, on the island of Naxos he left her, and sailed away to Greece. She afterward did become the bride of one of the gods, who gave her a golden crown, which after her death was changed to a crown of stars that is yet to be seen in the sky on any bright night.

On the voyage from the island of Naxos to Athens, Theseus was thinking so much of Ariadne that he quite forgot to change the black sail for the white one, as he had promised his father to do. This was a most unfortunate oversight, for it brought death to Aegeus and sorrow to Theseus.

Day after day, while Theseus was away, Aegeus had sat on a cliff which overlooked the sea, hoping to catch sight of the white sail. When at last the ship appeared with its black sail still spread, the poor king supposed of course that his son had been devoured by the Minotaur. He threw up his hands in grief, and falling from the cliff into the sea, was drowned. From that day to this the sea has been called the Aegean, or the sea of Aegeus.

When the ship reached the harbor of Athens, Theseus learned of his father's death, and bitterly did he mourn that he had forgotten to hoist the white sail.

He at once became king; and no king ever did more for Athens than he. Yet in spite of his love and labor for the city, the Athenians were not grateful. After a while he went on a journey. He remained away for so long that they chose a new king. When at last he came back and found that the people whom he had loved so well had forgotten him, he left the city and soon died.

The Athenians in later days repented that they had been so ungrateful. They brought his bones to Athens and buried them with great solemnity. Festivals were held in his honor, and he was ranked almost with Minerva herself as a guardian of the beautiful city.

The story is told that centuries after his death he left the spirit-world and helped the Athenians to gain the victory in the greatest battle they ever fought, the battle of Marathon, of which you will read farther on in this book.

AGAMEMNON KING OF MEN

The early kings of Mycenae were descendants of Jupiter. One of these, named Agamemnon, was the most powerful king in Greece in his day, and hence he was called the "King of Men." During his reign occurred the famous Trojan War, which is supposed to have taken place about 1200 years before Christ. All the most famous heroes in Greece took part in it. The story of the events that brought it on is full of interest.

A wonderful wedding took place in Greece. Peleus, the brave king of Thessaly, married the beautiful sea-nymph, Thetis. The wedding feast was held on Mount Pelion near the home of the gods, and to show their love for Thetis all the gods came down from Olympus. Apollo shot sunbeams through the quivering oak leaves and the floor of the forest was dappled with golden light. Nymphs had hung garlands of snow-white roses from tree to tree. Wild vines were covered with blossoms and the air was filled with their fragrance.

But while the Muses were singing their sweetest songs, a golden apple suddenly fell among the gods and goddesses. It had been thrown by the goddess of discord, who was angry because she had not been asked to the wedding.

Mercury, who of course was among the guests, picked up the apple and read to the wedding party the words written upon it, "Let the most beautiful have me."

Juno, Minerva, and Venus each claimed that the apple was hers, and the quarrel of the goddesses ended only when Jupiter said to them:

"Go with Mercury over the sea to Mount Ida, and let Paris, the shepherd, decide the matter."

At once the goddesses, led by Mercury, sped through the air to Mount Ida to find Paris.

Paris was a son of Priam, the king of a rich and powerful city called Troy, which was opposite Greece on the shore of the Aegean Sea. His mother dreamed that he would one day set Troy on fire, and so, as soon as he was born, King Priam ordered one of his shepherds to carry the infant to snow-capped Mount Ida, near Troy, and there leave it to die of cold and hunger.

Five days after leaving the child, the shepherd found it still alive. This made him think that the gods did not wish it to die; so he carried it home to his wife, who brought it up as her own child.

Paris thought himself only a shepherd's boy and tended King Priam's herds while they grazed on the slopes of Mount Ida.

On the date of the wedding upon Mount Pelion, as he sat watching the flock, Mercury and his three companions suddenly appeared before him. The goddesses were all so lovely that when they asked Paris to say which was the most beautiful he was greatly perplexed. Each tried to persuade him to decide in her favor. Juno promised to make him the greatest of kings; Minerva said that she would make him the wisest of men; and Venus declared that she would give him the most beautiful woman in the world as his wife. He awarded the apple to Venus, but by doing so he greatly offended Minerva and Juno.

Not long after this Paris went to Troy and took part in some games that were held at the court of Priam. These games were wrestling, boxing and running races; and the unknown shepherd carried off many prizes. It was soon found out who he really was and Priam heartily welcomed him home.

Meantime, Venus had not forgotten her promise. She advised Paris to sail to Greece, where he would find the most beautiful woman in the world. This was Helen, the wife of Menelaus, king of Sparta.

Paris went to Sparta and with the help of Venus won the heart of Helen and took her away with him to Troy.

When Menelaus found that his wife had been stolen he sent a message to the kings of all the states of Greece and asked them to help him to regain Helen and punish Paris. Now thirty or more of the kings had wished to marry Helen before she had chosen a husband, and all had sworn to aid the one chosen if any one should ever try to take her away from her husband. So as soon as they received the message of Menelaus, in accord with their oath these kings began to make ready for war against the Trojans.

Meanwhile Agamemnon, who was a brother of Menelaus, was already busily preparing for war. His woodsmen were cutting yew trees from which to make bows and gathering reeds for arrows. His smiths were making swords and spear-heads and javelins. In his shipyards hundreds of men were building ships. The roads were alive with countrymen bringing in loads of wheat, barley, bacon, and olives to store in the vessels.

At last one hundred black ships were ready and Agamemnon set sail. A place named Aulis had been selected where the Greeks were to meet. Twelve hundred ships assembled there, and Agamemnon was chosen commander-in-chief.

Just as the ships were about to start for Troy a terrible storm came up. Agamemnon felt sure that one of the gods must be angry with the Greeks and so he consulted a wonderful soothsayer named Calchas.

"Diana is angry, great King," said Calchas, "but not with the Greeks. Thou only hast offended her. Thou hast slain a deer in the forest and boasted that thou hast greater skill in the chase than Diana herself. Never, O King," he added, "can the storm be lulled until thou hast offered thy daughter Iphigenia as a sacrifice on the altar of Diana."

Agamemnon was heart-broken, but he felt that the will of Diana must be done. So he sent a messenger to the mother of Iphigenia to say that Achilles, a Greek prince, wished to marry the girl and that she must come to Aulis at once. This was only a device to get Iphigenia to Aulis.

However, when she reached Aulis and heard the truth from her father, the girl behaved nobly. "My father," she said, "if my death will help the Greeks, I am ready to die."

Her words sent a thrill through all the host and ninety thousand brave men sorrowed. Achilles and Ajax, sternest of warriors, wept, and Agamemnon was wild with grief.

While the girl was lying upon the altar and the priestess of Diana was standing near, the goddess, watching from Olympus, was moved to pity; and, just as the father had lifted his swords to slay the girl, a cloud as bright as shining snow appeared above him. Diana stepped from the cloud, lifted the girl from the altar, and carried her through the air to one of her temples, where she made her a priestess. On the altar lay a white fawn which was sacrificed instead of Iphigenia.

And now the fairest winds blew, the sails of the Grecian ships were set, the fleet sailed swiftly to Troy, and the siege of that city began.

ACHILLES BRAVEST OF GREEKS

Bravest of all the Greeks who went to fight the Trojans was Achilles. He was the son of Peleus and the beautiful sea-nymph Thetis, at whose marriage feast the goddess of discord had thrown the golden apple among the guests.

Thetis herself could never die, and when Achilles was born she determined to make him also immortal. With the child in her arms she went down to the gloomy kingdom of Hades. You will remember that a dark river called the Styx flowed round the underworld. If a mortal were dipped into the Styx no sword or arrow or other weapon could injure him. Thetis held Achilles by the heel and dipped him into the water. In her haste to get out of the underworld she forgot to dip in the heel by which she had held the child. So in that heel, and only there, Achilles could be wounded.

When Thetis heard that the Greeks were going to fight the Trojans she was greatly distressed, for she knew that if her son went to the war he would certainly lose his life. She dressed him as a girl and took him to

Scyros, a far away island of Greece, and left him there in the palace of the king Lycomedes.

Now Calchas had foretold that Troy could never be taken without the help of Achilles. So the Greek princes were determined that he should go with them.

A Grecian chief, called Ulysses the crafty, learned where he was hidden and set out to find him.

One day a peddler appeared at the gate of the palace in Scyros, bringing all sorts of beautiful things for sale. The princesses were wild with delight as the peddler showed one thing after another. Suddenly the blast of a war trumpet rang through the air. Away ran all the girls save one. That one seized a shield and a spear which were among the peddler's wares and stood instantly ready for battle.

Then the peddler, who was Ulysses, knew that he had found Achilles. So he told the young man that all the princes of the Greeks were preparing for war against Troy. Achilles was eager to go with them, and so in spite of all that Thetis had done, her son sailed to Troy with the other Greek princes. For nine years he was the champion of the Greeks.

In the tenth year of the war a great misfortune befell the Greeks. They had taken captive two beautiful maidens, one of whom had been given as a slave to Achilles, the other to Agamemnon. Now it happened that Agamemnon's slave was the daughter of Chryses, a priest of the sun-god Apollo.

The loss of his daughter was a great grief to Chryses, and he prayed to Apollo for vengeance. In answer Apollo drew his silver bow and shot arrows which brought a terrible pestilence into the camp of the Greeks. The tents were soon filled with the dead and the dying.

The soothsayer, Calchas, told the Greeks why Apollo had punished them, and the girl was sent back to her father. The god was satisfied, and his arrows stopped bringing the plague to the Greeks.

But Agamemnon now took the other maiden from Achilles, and this made the son of Thetis so angry that he declared he would help the Greeks no more. For days and days he stayed in his tent, or sat by the seashore and told his wrongs to his mother.

Then the Trojans, learning that Achilles was not fighting, grew bold and at last came out through the gates of their city and drove the Greeks from the field. Hector, a son of Priam, followed them to their ships. Some of the Trojans took lighted torches and tried to burn the Greek fleet. One ship caught fire.

Just then, however, there rushed to the shore a warrior who looked so like Achilles that the Trojans fled from the ships to the gates of their city. The unknown warrior was not Achilles but Patroclus, his devoted friend, who had put on Achilles' armor. The Trojans had mistaken him for the great hero. Even Hector fled before him. But Apollo, who fought on the side of the Trojans, at last shot forth from his silver bow an arrow which struck Patroclus, and he fell to the earth. Hector then slew him and carried off the armor of Achilles as his prize.

When Achilles learned that his friend had been slain he forgot his wrongs and rushed from his tent, shouting the war-cry of the Greeks. He had neither shield nor spear. Yet the Trojans fled at the sound of his voice; and the ships and tents of the Greeks were saved.

The body of Patroclus was then carried into the tent of Achilles, and the hero wept for his friend.

As he sat mourning his mother Thetis rose from her home in the sea and came to comfort him. She then went to Vulcan the great blacksmith, who, you remember, made all things of iron and bronze for the gods, and said:

"Good Vulcan, make for my son such a suit of armor as never mortal has worn."

Soon the forges of Aetna were glowing; the Cyclops' anvils were ringing, and a suit of armor fit for a god was made.

In this armor Achilles made terrible havoc among the Trojans. He scattered them as a wolf might scatter a flock of sheep. He killed Hector at last, tied the body to his chariot, and dragged it three times round the tomb of Patroclus.

Paris avenged the death of Hector by wounding Achilles in the heel. From the wound the great hero died.

Hundreds of Trojans had been killed by the Greeks; but the walls of Troy still stood and not one Grecian warrior had entered the gates.

Troy was kept safe in a wonderful way. In the city was an image of Athene, which the Trojans believed had come down from heaven. It was called the Palladium, from Pallas, another name of Athene. So long as the Palladium stood in its place, Troy could never be captured.

At length, crafty Ulysses, with the help of another Greek warrior named Diomedes, got possession of the Palladium. One night the two climbed the walls of Troy, went to the temple where the Palladium was kept, and carried the image away.

When they returned to the Grecian camp Ulysses advised the Greeks to build a huge wooden horse. When it was finished it was filled with armed men and left standing before the walls of the city. Then the Grecian army burned their tents and sailed away as if they were going home. But really they only went a short distance and hid behind an island not far from the Trojan coast.

One crafty Greek named Sinon had been left behind. He told the Trojans that the wooden horse would protect their city, just as the Palladium had done. So, very foolishly, they drew the horse within the walls.

When night came Sinon released the armed men from the horse and signalled to the Greek fleet with a flaming torch. In a very short time the ships were all back, and the Greek soldiers again were swarming before the walls of Troy. The city gates were opened by Sinon and his companions, and in poured the Greeks by thousands. They slaughtered the sleeping Trojans, sacked the palace of Priam, and burned the city.

And now, after ten long years of fighting, Menelaus recovered his beautiful Helen. Then he and the rest of the Greeks set sail for their native land.

Many of the Trojans were carried away into slavery by their Greek conquerors. Andromache, the beautiful wife of Hector, was given to the son of Achilles, who took her home to his palace, a captive.

THE ADVENTURES OF ULYSSES

I

Ulysses, king of the island of Ithaca, had been very unwilling to go to the Trojan War because there was a prophecy that if he went he would not return for twenty years. So he pretended that he was mad. Yoking an ox and a horse together, he would plow the seashore, and sow the sand with salt.

One of the chiefs suspected that all this was a trick, and to test Ulysses placed the king's infant son Telemachus in front of the plow. Ulysses at once turned the plow to one side and thus showed that he was not mad. He now had no excuse for staying at home and had to go to the war with the other chiefs.

All through the siege of Troy he was of great value to the Greeks, and after the death of Achilles the splendid armor of that hero was given to Ulysses.

As soon as Troy had fallen he set sail on his homeward voyage. If the winds had been fair he might have reached Ithaca in a month. But the story is that it took him ten years.

He had hardly begun his voyage when his fleet was caught in a storm and his ships were blown to the land of the lotus-eaters. The lotus was a plant that made those who ate it forget their homes and friends forever. Two of Ulysses' sailors went on shore for only a few minutes, and having tasted this curious food became so anxious to stay with the lotus-eaters that they had to be dragged back on board their ship.

After leaving the land of the lotus-eaters the fleet sailed to another shore. The sailors saw the mouth of a cavern and near it large flocks of sheep and goats. Ulysses, with twelve of his men, went to examine the cavern and see if any one lived there. They carried with them a skin full of old wine to give to the king of the island if they should happen to meet him.

They entered the cave and saw pens for sheep and goats. They also found several baskets of cheese. It was plain that somebody lived in the place, so Ulysses decided to wait for the owner and buy some of the cheese from him. Meanwhile he and the sailors helped themselves to what they wanted.

Just as the sun was setting the bleating of sheep and goats was heard, and looking through the mouth of the cave the Greeks saw the owner of the place coming toward them.

He was one of the race of giants called Cyclops, who, you remember, forged lighting and thunder for Jupiter to use in the battles with Cronus. On his back the Cyclops carried a bundle of firewood. Before him went a great flock of sheep and goats. The cave was a shelter for him and his flock.

When the giant had driven the sheep and goats inside he followed them in and closed the entrance with a huge stone. Soon he set about milking the goats. As he milked he muttered that thieves had stolen some of his cheeses. When the milking was over he lighted a fire on the floor of the cave and sat down to a supper of cheese and milk.

The fire lit up the corners of the cave where the Greeks had hidden themselves, and the Cyclops soon saw them.

"Who are you?" he growled. "And what business have you here?"

"Noble Sir, " replied Ulysses, "we are Greeks from the island of Ithaca. With the rest of our nation we have fought against Troy for ten years. At last the city has fallen and now we are sailing homeward. A storm blew us to your island and we landed to look for food. In the name of the blessed gods we ask you to give us something to eat and let us go on our way."

"I care nothing for gods!" roared the Cyclops. "But as for men—let me show you how much I like them!"

With that he seized two of the Greeks and ate them up, devouring even their bones. The other Greeks looked on in terror.

Soon after his supper the Cyclops went to sleep; and Ulysses and his companions would have lost no time in killing him if it had not been for the great stone that blocked the door of the cave. All the Greeks together could not move it, and so they let the Cyclops live because in the morning he would roll the stone away.

Next morning, after devouring two more of the Greeks, he did move the stone; but he put it back as soon as he had driven out his flock, and the Greeks were again shut up. In the evening, after the Cyclops had returned and had supped upon two more Greeks, Ulysses thought of his old wine and asked the giant to taste it. Taste it he did, and then quickly drained three cups.

"What is your name?" asked the Cyclops.

"Noman," answered Ulysses.

"Very well, Noman, you shall be the last that I will eat." And with that the giant lay down in a stupor.

Ulysses had sharpened the trunk of an olive tree that the Cyclops used for a walking cane, and he now held the sharp end in the fire until it glowed. Then with the help of four of his men he rammed the red-hot point into the giant's eye.

The monster roared so loudly that he wakened the other giants who lived in caves nearby, and they came running to ask who had hurt their companion.

"Noman!" screamed the Cyclops. "Noman has put out my eye!"

His friends of course understood him to mean that no one had hurt him. They thought that he had had a terrible nightmare from eating roast cheese and so they went back to their caves.

Ulysses now hit on a plan to get his friends and himself safely out of the cave. He bound the big, long-fleeced rams together, three abreast, and fastened a Greek under each middle ram so that every man was completely covered with fleece. He himself managed to cling to a ram that was the largest of the herd.

When the flock was passing out of the cave the Cyclops thought that perhaps the Greeks would try to ride out on the backs of the sheep and goats; so he carefully felt the back of each animal as it went through the door. But he did not feel the Greeks and they all got out safely.

Ulysses then untied his comrades and they ran quickly to their ships, driving before them some of the sheep of the Cyclops. When men and sheep were on board the vessels Ulysses cried out:

"Good-by, Cyclops! What think you now of the gods? They sent me to punish you for your cruelty. Noman is not my name. I am Ulysses, Ithaca's king."

At this the Cyclops picked up great rocks and threw them at the ship of Ulysses. The vessel, however, was not struck, and Ulysses and his men sailed on their way.

The next land reached was an island on which Æolus, the god of the winds, had his home. Æolus treated Ulysses very kindly. The west wind, which could carry the ships to Ithaca in nine days, the god left free. All the others he tied up in a stout leather bag, which he gave to the hero. Ulysses then bade farewell to Æolus.

For some time everything went well. One day, however, while Ulysses slept his crew untied the wind bag, hoping to find money in it. As soon as the winds were set free they blew the ships back to the island of Æolus, who drove them off because he thought the gods were angry with them.

The fleet next reached an island where there were cannibals of great size and strength. They broke up all the ships except the one that Ulysses himself commanded, and then feasted on the sailors.

Ulysses made his escape on a single ship with those of his men that were left. He soon arrived at another island, on which at some distance from the shore he saw a marble palace in the middle of a grove. He sent twenty-two men under the charge of his trusty captain Eurylochus to ask for food.

When Eurylochus reached the palace he was met by a troop of lions, tigers and wolves, which capered about and fawned upon him and his men as so many playful puppies might do. This put Eurylochus on his guard. He made up his mind at once that the palace was the home of a wizard or a witch. At the palace gate he inquired, "Who dwells here? We are strangers seeking food."

"Welcome!" replied a voice from within. "Welcome to the palace of the sun-god's daughter. The best that is here shall be yours."

The voice was that of an enchantress called Circe. It was her delight to change men into brutes. The lions, tigers and wolves that had met Eurylochus were really men who had once sat at her table and drunk her enchanted wine.

Eurylochus refused to eat, but the men who went with him were a gluttonous set. They ate greedily and drank deeply. When the feast was at its height Circe touched them with her wand and changed them into hogs.

Eurylochus returned to the ship and told what had happened. Ulysses then hastened to Circe's palace. On the way Mercury met him and walked with him some distance. As they passed through a wood the god plucked some flowers of a plant called moly and gave them to Ulysses.

"Smell them," said Mercury, "while Circe is talking to you and especially when you drink her enchanted wine."

When he reached the palace the hero was welcomed as his comrades had been. Circe herself put a golden cup full of wine into his hand. Ulysses took the cup and drained it, taking care all the while to smell the moly that Mercury had given him in the wood.

When the cup was empty the enchantress tapped the hero with her wand and said, "Now, turn to a pig and join your grunting companions."

Unchanged, however, Ulysses drew his sword and cried, "Wicked enchantress, you have no power over me. The gods have sent me here to punish you and you shall die."

"I will undo what I have done if you will spare me," she cried.

So Ulysses followed her to the sty, where she touched the swine, one by one, with her magic wand. As each was touched he was changed back to a man. Next the troop of lions, tigers and wolves were touched, and they too were quickly changed back to men.

The other Greeks were then called from the ships

and Circe gave them a feast. After this Ulysses remained on her island for a whole year.

When at last he was going to sail the enchantress gave him some good advice. On the homeward way he and his men would have to pass close to the Isle of the Sirens, as the Argonauts had done long before them.

"To sail by the Sirens' Isle safely," said Circe, "let the men fill their ears with wax and lash you to the mast when the ship draws near to the Isle."

Ulysses and his men then left Circe's island. As they drew near to the Sirens' Isle Ulysses made the sailors fill their ears with wax and lash him to the mast. As they rowed past the Sirens sweet music came over the waters.

"Loose me!" Ulysses cried to his sailors. "Loose me. I must go nearer that music!" But the sailors rowed on. They could hear neither him nor the song of the Sirens.

"Slaves!" cried Ulysses, "Loose me!" But the sailors rowed on.

The music grew fainter and fainter. At last it died away, and the vessel was out of danger. Then the men took the wax from their ears and loosed the cords that bound their chief.

III

After passing the Sirens' Isle Ulysses had to sail through a dangerous strait, now know as the Strait of Messina. In a rocky cave on one side of it dwelt a monster called Scylla that had six heads and six mouths. Each mouth could take in a whole man at once. Near the other side of the strait was Charybdis, a whirlpool that sucked down all ships that came near it.

Ulysses saw that he could not escape both these dangers, and so to avoid Charybdis he steered close to Scylla. He ordered his men to row as fast as they could past the monster's cave; and the ship fairly spun through the water. But Scylla was also quick. Darting out all her heads at once, she seized six of the crew. While she was devouring them the ship sped past her, and Ulysses with the rest of his men escaped.

The hero now wished to continue his voyage without stopping, but his comrades were so tired that he agreed to land for the night on the coast of Sicily. So they pulled their ship up the sandy shore and soon all were fast asleep.

In the morning a storm was howling about them. It would have been certain shipwreck to put to sea. The storm raged for a whole month, and even crafty Ulysses did not know what to do.

Worst of all, their provisions began to fail. So the sailors made up their minds to kill some of the famous fat cattle belonging to Apollo that were kept upon the island. Ulysses had been warned not to kill the animals and had ordered his men to leave them alone.

One day, however, when he was away his crew killed some of the cattle. They lit a fire and were roasting several nice pieces of beef when suddenly all started back in terror. The pieces of beef lowed as though they were living and the skins of the slaughtered oxen got up and began to switch their tails and toss their horns and gallop up and down the shore.

The moment the tempest lulled the men dragged their ship down the shore and pushed off as fast as they could.

They were not far out at sea when, suddenly, blackness covered the sky and a dreadful squall blew up. The ship went to pieces and all the men were drowned except Ulysses, who was washed up on the shore of a lonely island.

The island was the home of the sea-nymph Calypso. She treated the shipwrecked hero most kindly and became so fond of him that she kept him with her seven years, and promised to make him immortal if he would stay with her always.

But Ulysses longed for home. So at last Calypso led him to the other side of her island, and there he saw a forest of stately pine trees. With a keen bronze axe he soon felled twenty trunks; with these he built a raft, and bidding farewell to Calypso he set out on his homeward voyage.

Soon a storm arose. Heavy waves dashed over the raft and broke it to pieces. The hero clung to one log and drifted on it two days and two nights. The wind then lulled, and Ulysses, seeing land near, swam to the shore. Cold and tired, he gathered dry leaves, lay down upon them, and soon fell asleep. He slept all night and all the next morning.

At noon Nausicaa, the daughter of the king of the island, went to the shore with her maidens. Their talking and laughing awakened Ulysses, and the princess, on hearing the tale of his shipwreck, took him home to her father's palace.

Here he was royally welcomed, and the very next day a ship was made ready and he was sent home to Ithaca.

When at dawn the ship reached Ithaca Ulysses was so fast asleep that the crew carried him out of the vessel, wrapped in the rug on which he was sleeping, and laid him upon the sandy shore without wakening him.

When he awoke he did not know where he was. But the goddess Minerva appeared and told him that he was on his own island of Ithaca, and that Penelope, his wife, loved him as much as ever. Then he climbed the rocky heights of the island and went to the cottage of his swineherd, who invited him in. Without telling the swineherd who he was he stayed at the cottage that night.

Next morning there appeared at the swineherd's home Ulysses's son, Telemachus, who had just come back from a long search for his father. Ulysses made himself known to his son and they talked over all that had happened while Ulysses had been so far away.

More than a hundred men from Ithaca and the neighboring isles had come to Ulysses' palace, hoping to marry Penelope. For months and years they had stayed at her palace, feasting and drinking at her expense and demanding that she marry one of them. She told them that she could not wed until she had finished a shroud for her father-in-law, who was old and likely to die. She had spent years in making that shroud and even yet it was not finished,—for every night she had undone what she had woven during the day.

The suitors at last discovered the trick that Penelope was playing and refused to be put off any longer. They insisted that she must choose one of them for her husband. It was while they were doing this that Ulysses reached home.

He planned a way to punish the suitors. He first sent Telemachus to the palace alone to see his mother. Then, dressed as a beggar, Ulysses followed with the swineherd.

When he came to the palace gate in rags and tatters no one imagined who he was, but his old dog Argo knew him and licked his hand. The swineherd led the way into the banquet hall, and a few paces behind him walked the ragged beggar, leaning upon a staff.

The swineherd kindly gave him a seat and invited him to eat and drink of the good cheer on the table. Hardly had Ulysses seated himself when jests and insults were heaped upon him by the suitors. It wrung the heart of Telemachus to see his father so badly used in his own palace, but he kept his temper and waited.

Not long after Ulysses' arrival Penelope entered the banquet hall. She did not know that her husband had returned, but Minerva had told her what to do. So she stood beside one of the columns that upheld the roof of the hall, and said:

"Hear, all who are in this hall of Ulysses! You wish to take the place of my husband. I bring to you his bow. Whoever among you can bend and string it and with it shoot an arrow through twelve rings, him will I wed and him will I follow from this fair home."

Then the suitors, one by one, haughtily tried to string the bow. And, one by one, they utterly failed to bend it.

Ulysses then demanded that he, too, might try to bend the bow. Amid sneers and laughter he was at length allowed to do so.

As easily as a skillful player stretches a cord from side to side of the harp, so without any effort he strung the bow; and forthwith through each and all of the twelve rings an arrow winged its way. It was followed by another which struck the chief man among the suitors dead. Telemachus and two faithful men, who had already locked the doors of the hall, now lent their aid to Ulysses. Arrows flew, swords flashed, and clubs were swung, until all the suitors who had tried to steal his wife and kingdom from Ulysses lay dead on the floor of the banquet hall.

Penelope's joy was great when she learned that the beggar was her husband; and Ulysses' delight at finding that she still loved him made all his weary wanderings seem like a dream.

LYCURGUS

I

About eighty years after the Trojan War the descendants of Hercules with a large band of followers invaded the Peloponnesus, or southern part of Greece, where Agamemnon and Menelaus had once lived. They captured Sparta and made it their capital and after that called themselves Spartans.

The Spartans made slaves of people who were already living in the country and called them Helots or captives. The conquerors divided the land among themselves and made the Helots work their farms.

After about three hundred years had passed it seems that some of the Spartans had grown rich, while others had lost their land and slaves and become poor.

The Spartans who had lost their property were not willing to work like the slaves, and sometimes, when they had no bread for their children, bands of them marched through the streets of Sparta, broke into the houses of the rich and took whatever they could lay their hands on.

During one of these riots, one of the two kings,—for the Spartans always had two kings with equal power,—went out of his palace to stop it. He tried to persuade the people to go quietly home, but they paid no attention to him and a butcher in the crowd rushed up and stabbed him.

The murdered king left two sons. The elder became king, but soon died. The younger was one of the wisest and best men that ever lived in Greece. His name was Lycurgus and after his brother's death every one wished him to become king. But an infant child of the late king was the rightful heir, and Lycurgus refused to be anything more than regent.

For a while he ruled in the young king's name, but some people accused him of wishing to make himself king. So he gave up the regency and went traveling. He visited many lands and studied their plans of government. After being absent several years he came back to Sparta. There he found that the rich were richer and the poor were poorer and more unhappy than when he went away. Everyone turned to him as the only man from whom help could come.

He persuaded the people to let him make new laws for Sparta. The first change that he made was to give every Spartan a vote. There was a Senate of Thirty which might propose laws, but all the citizens were called together to pass or reject them.

Next he persuaded the rich people to divide their land fairly among all the citizens. So now no one had more than he needed, but every one had a farm large enough to raise wheat or barley, olive oil and wine for his family for a year. No Spartan was permitted to work or to engage in any trade, but the slaves were divided, so that every Spartan had slaves to work for him.

Besides the Spartans and the slaves there was another class of men living on the lands of Sparta who were not slaves like the Helots, and yet not citizens like the Spartans. These men were farmers, traders and mechanics. They had to pay taxes and fight when called upon, but neither they nor the Helots had anything to say about the government. There were about 10,000 pure Spartans and about 140,000 in the two lower classes, so you will see that the political power in Sparta was in the hands of a very few men. Their government was what we call an "oligarchy," which means a government by the few.

II

Lycurgus did not wish the Spartans to become traders and grow rich, and it is said that he ordered their money to be made of iron. This iron money was worthless outside of Sparta, so the traders of other countries would not take it in payment for their goods and sold nothing to Spartans.

In those days soldiers fought chiefly with swords and spears; therefore no matter how brave men were, they had to have physical strength to win a victory. Lycurgus made laws that the men and boys of Sparta should be trained in running, boxing, wrestling, throwing quoits, hurling javelins, and shooting with bows and arrows. The girls had nearly the same training.

The feeble and deformed were thought by Lycurgus to be useless. Infants were therefore examined and those that were weak or deformed were not allowed to live. A strong, well-formed infant was handed back to its parents with the order, "Bring up this child for Sparta."

Boys remained at home until they were seven years old. Then they were taken in charge by the State to be trained. The clothing given them was scanty. They went about with their heads and feet bare, and slept on hard beds, or even on floors, with rushes instead of a mattress.

To teach the boys temperance Helots were sometimes purposely made drunk. Thus the boys saw how foolish men become when they drink too much.

One lesson that every Spartan boy had to learn was to endure pain without flinching. Another was that in battle a man might die, but must not surrender. When the young Spartan was leaving home for the field of battle his mother would hand him his shield and say, "Come back with this, or upon this."

Lycurgus was opposed to all expensive ways of living. He thought that luxury was a waste of money and made men weak and effeminate. He made a law that the men should not take their meals at home but in a public dining hall; and there only the simplest kind of food was set before them—bread, cheese, olive oil, and a kind of black broth that was probably made of black beans. Figs and grapes served for dessert. It is said that some rich people were very angry because they had to eat at the public tables and that one young man stoned Lycurgus.

A great change came over the Spartans after they had adopted the new laws and ways of living. Instead of being a nation of idlers they became so strong and brave that when there was talk of building a wall round the city, Lycurgus said, "Sparta's citizens are her walls."

When Lycurgus saw what improvement had been made he told the people that he was going on a long journey. He made them promise that they would not change his laws until he returned.

He never returned. When the Spartans felt sure that he was dead they built a temple in his honor and worshiped him as a god. He left Sparta about 825 B.C. and his laws were not changed for several hundred years. They made Sparta the greatest military state in Greece.

DRACO AND SOLON

I

One of the first Athenians whose doings belong to history is Draco who lived about 600 years before Christ.

At that time the working people of Athens were very unhappy. One reason of this was that the laws were not written and the judges were very unfair. They almost always decided in favor of their rich friends. At last everybody in Athens agreed that the laws ought to be written out and Draco was asked to write them.

Some old laws were so severe that often people had been put to death for very slight offences. Draco changed these severe laws and made new ones a great deal more merciful, and this made the people very fond of him. A story is told about his death which shows that other people besides the Athenians thought a great deal of him. He went to a theater on an island not far from Athens, and when the audience in the theater saw him they threw to him their cloaks and caps to do him honor. Unfortunately, such a pile of cloaks fell on him that he was smothered to death.

Even after the laws had been written the people were not happy, because Draco had not changed some laws that bore very hard upon the poor. These were the laws about debts. If a man borrowed money and could not pay it back at the right time, the man who lent the money might take the borrower's house and farm and might even sell him and his wife and children as slaves. On most of the farms near Athens stone pillars were set up, each of which told that the land on which it stood was mortgaged, or pledged, for a debt. Many of the farmers and their families had been sold as slaves. In time it came to be said that Draco's laws were written in blood.

II

Happily, a very wise and good man called Solon was then living in Athens, and the Athenians asked him to make a new set of laws.

Rich and poor were surprised when they read Solon's new laws. The poor who had lost their farms and houses were to have everything given back to them. Solon thought they had paid so much interest for so many years that their debts should be forgiven. All who had been sold as slaves were to have their freedom and no one was ever again to be sold for debt. Those debtors who had not lost everything were to be forgiven about a quarter of what they owed.

All this Solon called a "shaking-off of burdens," and thousands of people felt that heavy burdens had indeed been taken from their shoulders.

Solon did another good thing for the people. He gave every citizen a vote and all could attend the Assembly of the people, which was like a New England town-meeting.

240

There was a Senate of Four Hundred, which proposed laws, but the people themselves met and passed them. So the people of Athens really made their own laws.

Besides this, the Assembly chose every year nine archons as the rulers of Athens were called. The chief archon was like the mayor of one of our cities and the others like the aldermen. Under Solon's new laws Athens soon came to stand in Greece for government by all the people, just as Sparta stood for government by the few.

III

When Solon saw that his laws were making the Athenians contented and prosperous, he made them promise not to change them for ten years. He then went on a long journey.

One of the countries which he visited was Lydia in Asia Minor. Croesus richest man in the world. He was so famed for his wealth that even now you often hear people say that a man is "as rich as Croesus."

Croesus was very proud of being so rich and wished Solon to flatter him. So he asked Solon, "Who is the happiest man you have ever known?" He expected the Athenian of course to say, "Yourself, your Majesty."

Solon however replied, "An Athenian peasant who never suffered want, who had a good wife and children, and who died on the battlefield for his country."

"Who is the next happiest?" asked Croesus.

"The two next happiest persons whom I have known," said Solon, "were the sons of a certain priestess of Juno. It was her duty to offer a sacrifice in the temple. When the time came for her to go the oxen to draw the cart could not be found. So her sons yoked themselves to the ox-cart and drew her all the way to the temple. She was so much pleased at them that she prayed to

241

Juno to grant her sons the greatest blessing that they could have. The mother's prayer was answered, for the sons lay down to sleep in the temple and never waked. They had done their parts well in the world and they left it without pain or sorrow, beloved and admired by all who knew them."

"But," cried Croesus, "do you not think a rich and powerful king like me is happy?"

"Ah, Croesus," said Solon, "I call no man happy until he is dead. You are rich; you are king of thousands of people; you live a life of luxury; but none of these things proves you happy. When I hear whether or not your life has ended nobly, then I shall know whether or not you were really happy."

Years afterward when Croesus had lost his kingdom and his wealth, he saw how wise this speech of Solon was.

After ten years of travel Solon returned to Athens where he lived in honor until his death.

PISISTRATUS THE TYRANT

When Solon came back from his travels he found that a young kinsman of his, named Pisistratus, was trying to make himself master of Athens. Pisistratus was rich and gave away a great deal of money, and in every possible way showed himself friendly to the people. His large and beautiful garden was thrown open to them, as if it were a park. Men and women of the working-classes were allowed to sit under his shade trees and their children played among his flowers. When the poor were ill he had nice things cooked for them in his own kitchen, and often in the heat of summer he sent to the sick a present of snow, which was a rare luxury. If a poor man died Pisistratus often paid the expense of burying him. Poor people in Athens were very much pleased by this, because they believed that if a person were not properly buried his soul would have to wander a hundred years up and down the bank of the river Styx.

One day, after the kindness of Pisistratus had made him the idol of the Athenians, he drove his chariot rapidly into the market-place. A crowd immediately gathered about him, for they saw that something was the matter. In a state of great excitement he showed some wounds,—which he had really made upon himself, but which he pretended he had received while he was driving along the high road.

"Men of Athens!" he cried, "See what my enemies have done to me because I am a friend of the people." All saw the blood on his face and of course believed what he said. They were very angry, and one of them proposed in the public Assembly that in future fifty men, armed with clubs, should be paid by the State to guard Pisistratus.

Solon begged the people to vote against this. But they had made up their minds and Solon could not dissuade them. The guard was ordered, and Pisistratus took good care that there should be in it a great many more than fifty men. Very soon he had a company of soldiers who were ready to do whatever he ordered. So, just as Solon had feared, he seized the Acropolis, a high, rocky hill which was the citadel of Athens, and made himself master of the city.

After a while the people grew tired of him and he had to leave Athens. However, he came back and regained his power by playing a trick on the people. A very tall and beautiful girl, in full armor, rode into the city standing at his side in a chariot. Minerva herself was said to be bringing Pisistratus back. When the chariot came into view the people shouted with joy and welcomed their old friend.

Soon he was banished a second time, but again recovered his power, and from that day to the time of his death he had full sway over the city.

II

All the states of Greece had in time become republics, except Sparta, and when anyone took the

244

power of a king in any of these states he was called a tyrant. Thus Pisistratus was called the Tyrant of Athens, and yet he was by no means so harsh a ruler as the world might lead us to think. But he was strict. When he got control of Athens it was full of lazy people who lounged all day about the market-place. Pisistratus put all such people to work upon the roads or public buildings.

There were no public schools or libraries in Athens, but Pisistratus did his best to give the people a chance to read and to educate themselves. Books in his days were not printed, but written, and they were so expensive that few people could buy them. Pisistratus had a large collection and he invited all persons, rich or poor, to go to his library and read.

He did another thing for which the Greeks were grateful. For more than two hundred years before his time the poems of Homer had been recited all over Greece. Traveling minstrels sang them before guests in banquet halls, or before public gatherings. Every one loved these poems, and many people knew parts of them by heart. Pisistratus employed learned men to help him write them and put them in proper order. The verses about the Trojan War were arranged to make up the poem called the Iliad, and those about the wanderings of Ulysses to make up the poem called the Odyssey.

Athens never had a wiser or better ruler than Pisistratus. He died 527 B.C.

MILTIADES THE HERO OF MARATHON

I

After Pisistratus died his two sons, Hippias and Hipparchus, ruled over Athens. They governed well until Hipparchus was killed by his enemies. Then Hippias became so cruel that the Athenians banded together and drove him out of the city.

Some time after being driven from Athens Hippias sailed to Asia and begged Darius, king of Persia, to help him regain his power. At that time Persia was the greatest country in the world. Darius, her sovereign, was called "the Great King," or simply "the King," as if there were no other king on the face of the earth. He intended that there should be no other if he could have his way. He made up his mind not only to help Hippias, but also to make himself master of Greece. Persian heralds were therefore sent to every state of Greece to demand from each a tribute of earth and water. If the Greeks had yielded to this demand it would have been the same as saying that all the land and water of Greece belonged to Persia. Some of the states submitted, others proudly refused. The Athenians threw the heralds into a ditch into which the bodies of criminals were thrown; the Spartans threw them into a well and told them, "There you will find both earth and water for your master."

As soon as Darius heard of this he declared war and a little later his fleet, carrying one hundred and fifty thousand men, set sail for Greece. The Persians landed on the Grecian coast and went into camp on the plain of Marathon, twenty-two miles from Athens.

Meantime the Athenians had not been idle. They had collected a force of ten thousand men, and the entire army was under ten generals, each of whom in turn was commander-in-chief for one day. The little city of Plataea, unasked, had sent a thousand volunteers.

The ablest of the Greek generals was Miltiades. He determined to attack the enemy at once, and when his day of command came, on the 12th of August, 490 B.C., he drew up the Greek army in line of battle and moved across the plain. Then he charged upon the Persian army, broke their line, and drove them back to their ships in confusion.

News of the victory was carried to Athens by a soldier, who though wounded ran the twenty-two miles from the field of battle to the city. Reaching the market-place, he rushed into the crowd of citizens assembled there, and crying—"Rejoice! Rejoice! We are victors!"— fell dead.

This news delighted all loyal Athenians, but was very unwelcome to some traitors who had been hoping to hear of a Persian victory. These traitors had gone to a mountain near Athens, and with a polished shield they flashed to the Persian fleet a signal to sail to Athens and capture the city before Miltiades could return from Marathon.

Fortunately, the signal was seen in the camp of the Greeks. Miltiades guessed what it meant and marched back to Athens immediately. So when the Persians approached in their ships they found that if they landed they must again meet the army of Miltiades. They had no wish to do this and sailed away across the Aegean Sea to the Great King's own dominions.

The battle of Marathon showed that the Greeks were equal to any soldiers in the world. They had routed an army of Persians fifteen times as large as their own, and had lost only one hundred and ninety-two men.

The Greeks believed that this splendid victory was won through the aid of their gods and of their god-like hero Theseus, who was said to have fought in the thick of the battle and made terrible havoc among the Persians.

II

Miltiades won great fame in Athens. Honors were showered upon him and whatever he asked was granted. Thinking that he could add still more to his own glory and that of Athens, he asked that a fleet of seventy ships be placed at his command and that he be allowed to do with it as he pleased.

The fleet was granted and with it he set sail for the island of Paros. The people of Paros had helped the Persians in the recent war and Miltiades wished to punish them, but he also hoped to avenge himself upon a personal enemy. The expedition was a complete failure. The town of Paros was not captured, and Miltiades was obliged to give up the siege and return to Athens.

Moreover at Paros his thigh had been badly hurt while he was leaping over a fence so that he came home injured as well as unsuccessful. Upon his return he was accused of having deceived the people and wasted the public money.

When his trial took place he was brought before his judges upon a couch, being too weak to stand or sit. The

248

decision of the court was against him and he was sentenced to pay a heavy fine, which he was too poor to pay. Not long afterward he died of the injury that he had received at Paros.

After the death of Miltiades the Athenians were sorry for their harshness toward him. Remembering only his heroism at Marathon, they buried him with the highest honors on the plain where his great victory was won.

LEONIDAS AT THERMOPYLAE

Leonidas was a son of one of the kings of Sparta. As a boy he was trained in the gymnasium and excelled in all manly sports. As a man he fought in the Spartan army. After the death of his father and his half-brother he became king. Eleven years later he led the Greek army against the Persians, who a second time were threatening Greece. The second invasion of the Persians came about in this way:

The defeat at Marathon had made Darius only the more determined to conquer the Greeks. But four years later, in the midst of his preparations, he died and Xerxes, his son, came to the throne.

Xerxes after a while decided to carry out his father's plans and spent four years in collecting men and horses and ships. His army and fleet were the largest that the world had ever heard of.

The land forces met at Sardis, a city in Asia Minor, and marched to the shore of the Hellespont, which you have already learned is the narrow strait between Europe and Asia. Xerxes ordered his engineers to make two bridges of boats across the strait for the passage of the army. This was done, but the bridges were not strong enough and a storm destroyed them. The loss of his bridges made the king very angry, and it is said that he had the strait scourged with three hundred lashes and a set of chains thrown into it, to teach the water that he was its master.

Two new bridges, stronger than the first, were built and Xerxes then marched his army over them to the European shore of the Hellespont. Here his fleet of twelve hundred war ships and three thousand smaller vessels had already arrived. On a hill overlooking the strait a throne of marble was built, and upon it Xerxes sat and reviewed his land forces drawn up along the shore, and his ships sailing in the strait. It took the army seven days and seven nights to cross the bridges.

After crossing, the land force made its way southward until it reached a high and almost impassable mountain range. Between this range and the sea the roadway at two points was so narrow that there was room for only a single wagon. There were hot sulphur springs near-by, and therefore the Greeks called this narrow part of the road Thermopylae, which means the "Gates of the Hot Springs." We usually speak of it as the "Pass of Thermopylae."

The Persians intended to march through the Pass, but they were stopped by a Greek force under Leonidas, king of Sparta. His band numbered only about four thousand men, of whom three hundred were Spartans, the rest being from several different states.

The Greeks took their stand at the narrowest part of the Pass. Against them Xerxes sent one division of his army after another, but all were defeated and driven back. For two days the fighting went on with great loss to the Persians, while the Greeks lost hardly a man.

At last, when it seemed impossible to overpower the Greeks, a traitor showed a band of Persians a path that led over the mountain. This path was poorly defended by Greeks from one of the northern states. It was easily taken by the Persians, who then marched round behind Leonidas.

Leonidas learned of their approach in time to escape. Some of his army did retreat; but he, with three hundred Spartans and seven hundred men of Thespiae, a little town some distance from Athens, refused to do so. Greece had trusted the Pass to them to hold and they preferred to die rather than leave their post. When some one said that the arrows of the Persians would come in such showers as to conceal the sun, one of the Spartans replied, "So much the better; we shall fight in the shade."

Leonidas was now penned in between two divisions of the Persian army, one at each end of the Pass. Instead of waiting to be attacked he led his men forward against the Persians. The Greeks fought desperately, but they had no chance against such vast numbers. All were slain save one man.

A monument was afterward raised to their memory. It bore the simple inscription, "Stranger, tell the Spartans that we lie here in obedience to their commands."

After the battle Xerxes marched to Athens. He found it almost deserted. All the Athenians had fled save a little band who held the Acropolis. They hurled rocks upon the attacking Persians and for a long time resisted them. At length however the Persians found a place where no guard had been stationed, because the rocky wall was so steep that it seemed impossible to scale it. Here they climbed up and rushed in upon the brave defenders.

The struggle was soon over. Some of the Athenians hurled themselves headlong down the rocky slopes. The rest were put to death and the city fell into the hands of the Persians, who plundered and burned it. Even the sacred olive tree, which had sprung up at Athene's touch, was burned to the ground.

THEMISTOCLES

I

At this time the leading man of Athens was a great statesman and soldier named Themistocles. Some years before when the news had come that Xerxes was collecting an army and intended to invade Greece, the Athenians sent messengers to Delphi to ask the oracle what they should do. Delphi was upon the side of Mount Parnassus, and there stood a temple of Apollo. It was built over the cleft in the rock which, you remember, Deucalion found long ago as he and Pyrrha were coming down the mountain after the flood.

In the inner chamber of the temple just over the cleft, was a three-legged stool called a tripod. When a person wished to consult the oracle the priestess, who was called the Pythia, took her seat on the tripod. In a few minutes her eyes would close and she would begin to talk. The words which she spoke were noted, and the Greeks believed that they were really the words of the god Apollo.

Her answer to the messengers from Athens was:

"When everything else in the land of Cecrops shall be taken Jupiter grants to Minerva that the wooden wall alone shall remain undestroyed, and it shall defend you and your children. Stand not to await the attack of horses and foot from Asia, but retire. You shall live to fight another day. And thou, O divine Salamis, shalt destroy the children of women!"

What do you think this strange answer meant? The Athenians were greatly puzzled by it.

Themistocles said that the "wooden wall" meant ships of war, and that the gods would save the people if they would leave their city and trust to their fleet when the enemy approached. He advised the Athenians to build more ships of war. The people at last came to believe him. Rich Athenians gave him money, and the people voted that the silver which was dug every year from the silver mines owned by the city should be used to pay for building ships of war. And thus by the time Xerxes began his march Athens had a fleet of two hundred ships of war. These vessels were gigantic rowboats, each having as many as a hundred and fifty oars. Each had also a mast with a single big sail, which was hoisted to help the rowers.

The capture of Thermopylae had given the Persians an open road to Athens, and so the women and children of the city and the men who were too old to fight had been sent away in merchant ships to places of safety. A few men stayed in Athens and defended the citadel, as you learned in the last chapter. The rest went out in the war ships with Themistocles to fight behind the "wooden wall."

II

Themistocles and the commanders of the fleets of the other Greek states took their vessels into the narrow strait of Salamis, which lay between the island of Salamis and the shore of Attica. Here the Persians followed them. Themistocles now wished the Greeks to give battle to the Persians, but the Spartan commander and the other Greek leaders were unwilling to risk a battle in the narrow strait. They proposed to retreat. Themistocles was determined, however, that a battle should be fought in the strait; so he sent word secretly to Xerxes that the Greek ships were going to try to get away and advised him to head them off. Xerxes was delighted to get this message, and during the night he sent a part of his fleet up the shore of Attica to the other end of the strait, so as to hem the Greek fleet in between two lines of Persian ships. Next morning the Greek leaders all saw that there was nothing to do but fight, and at once their ships were drawn up in line of battle.

Xerxes' throne had been placed on a high cliff on the shore of Attica, so that he might look down upon the battle. When the sun rose he took his seat upon the throne. He was clothed in his royal robes and surrounded by the princes of his court. Below him were a thousand Persian war vessels, while close to the shore of the island lay three hundred and seventy-eight Greek vessels. It seemed an easy victory for the Persians. The Greeks rowed forward from the shore of Salamis, shouting the cry, "We fight for all." The Persians replied with their war cry, and the battle began. For a time the Persians had the advantage. But their ships were in the way of one another; those in the front could not go back, those in the rear could not come forward. The confusion became terrible. Ship after ship of the Persians sank, some of them rammed by the Greeks, others run down by their own allies. In all two hundred Persian vessels were destroyed and a great number captured, while the Greeks lost only forty.

When Xerxes saw his thousand vessels sunk or captured or rowing away in flight, he determined to go back to Persia.

He at once returned to northern Greece, where he left 300,000 men in command of his brother-in-law, Mardonius. With the rest of his army he marched on to the Hellespont.

Here he found that storms had destroyed his bridges, so that what was left of his army was carried across to the shore of Asia Minor in ships.

III

Everybody in Greece now admitted that Themistocles had been right in his explanation of the oracle that the "wooden wall" would save the people. And "Salamis," as the oracle had said, "destroyed the sons of women"; but they were chiefly the sons of Persian, not Grecian women.

The battle of Salamis brought fresh glory to Themistocles. After some years, however, he became unpopular and was banished from Athens. He stayed at Argos. Then the Spartans, who were his enemies, accused him of treason against Greece. Fearing that he could not get a fair trial at Athens he fled to Persia.

The Persian king gave him three cities to support him, and in one of these he lived until his death in 453 B.C.

ARISTIDES THE JUST

I

Aristides was the rival of Themistocles. Themistocles was wise and brave, but selfish and fond of money. Aristides, too, was wise and brave, but he was also so honorable that the Athenians called him "the Just."

On one occasion he was acting as judge between two men. One of them had spoken unfairly of Aristides and the other came secretly to Aristides to tell him of it. "My friend," said Aristides, "tell me the wrong the man has done to you, not what he has done to me. It is not my cause that I am to decide, but yours."

Aristides opposed many plans that Themistocles wished to carry out, and so at length Themistocles determined to have him banished.

There was at Athens a curious way of getting rid of a citizen. Every year this question was put before the people: "Does the safety of the State require that any citizen shall be banished?" If it was decided that this was necessary the people were called upon to vote. No person's name was mentioned, but every citizen wrote on a small earthenware tablet the name of any man whom he thought dangerous to the state. The tablets were collected and counted, and if the name of any one man was written on as many as 6,000 tablets he had to leave the city for ten years. Banishing people in this way was called "ostracism." We often use the word to-day. It comes from a Greek word meaning an earthenware tablet.

Themistocles and his friends persuaded many of the Athenians that Aristides was a dangerous citizen. So when a public meeting was being held the people were asked if they thought any citizen ought to be banished. No one mentioned Aristides' name, but Themistocles' friends said, "Let a vote be taken." While the vote was being cast a countryman who could not write his own name came up to Aristides and said:

"Friend, will you write the name of Aristides for me on this tablet?"

"Has Aristides ever wronged you?" asked Aristides gently.

"No," said the other, "I have never even seen him, but I am tired of hearing him called 'the Just.' "

Aristides said no more, but wrote his own name on the tablet.

There were enough votes against Aristides to banish him. As he was leaving Athens he prayed the gods that the time might never come when his fellow-citizens should have cause to be sorry for what they had done.

That time came, however. Three years later when Athens was threatened by the Persians the citizens, at the request of Themistocles himself, recalled Aristides. He sailed from his place of exile to the bay of Salamis and went on board the ship of Themistocles only a few hours before the famous battle. Themistocles at once gave him command of one of the Athenian ships, and he did good service in the battle.

II

In the spring following the battle of Salamis Mardonius, the Persian commander who was in Thessaly, tried to bribe the Athenians to become allies of the great king but they refused his offers with scorn. He then marched to Athens and the people abandoned the city, so that it fell into his hands.

The Greeks, however collected an army of one hundred and ten thousand men. Pausanias, a nephew of Leonidas, the hero of Thermopylae, was made commander-in-chief; but Aristides commanded the Athenian troops. Mardonius now retreated from Athens, destroying and burning as he went. The Greeks followed and overtook him near the city of Plataea, and there they defeated him in one of the "decisive battles of the world." Mardonius himself was killed.

It took ten days to divide the spoil and bury the dead. A tenth of the spoil was sent to Delphi and dedicated to Apollo, because the promise of his oracle that "the wooden wall would save the city" had led to the great victory of Salamis. A temple was erected to Minerva, and thank-offerings were made to other gods. "Liberty games" were established, to be held on the battlefield once in four years, and every year the tombs of those who had fallen in battle were to be decorated with flowers. The land upon which Plataea stood was declared to be sacred and the inhabitants of the city were to be always free from attack by other Greeks.

On the afternoon of the very day on which the battle of Plataea was won the Greek fleet gained a great victory over the Persians at Mycale, on the coast of Asia Minor. After their defeats at Marathon, at Plataea, and at Mycale, the Persians never again attempted to conquer Greece.

III

As soon as the victory at Plataea had freed Greece from the ravaging Persian army, the Athenians flocked back to their ruined city and began to rebuild it. Aristides and Themistocles carried on this work hand-in-hand.

It was found that the sacred olive tree on the Acropolis, though burned to the ground, was not killed. From its root had sprung a stout young shoot. This was taken by the citizens as a good omen and rebuilding of the city went on rapidly. The great seaport called the Piraeus was fortified, and a wall was built round the city.

These and other public works required a great outlay of money, and it was needful to put some one whom all the citizens trusted in charge of the fund raised. Aristides was chosen and enormous sums of money were placed in his hands. He used his office solely for the good of the people and never became rich.

When he died, about 468 B.C., the whole nation mourned and he was buried at public expense.

CIMON

I

Y ou remember that when Xerxes was preparing to invade Greece, Themistocles tried to get the Athenians to build ships and quit their city, and trust to the "wooden wall" of a fleet.

One day, while the people were still in doubt about what they should do, a tall and handsome young man, with a bridle in his hand, was seen hurrying through the streets of Athens toward the Acropolis. He entered the temple of Minerva, hung up his bridle as an offering to the goddess, and took down from the walls a shield. He prayed to the goddess and then carried the shield through the streets of Athens to the Piraeus.

The young man was named Cimon. He was the son of the famous Miltiades and belonged to a class of Athenians called knights, who fought on horseback. For him to hang up his bridle in the temple was as much as to say that Athens now had no need of horsemen, but of seamen, as Themistocles was urging.

People were fond of young Cimon because of his

pleasant ways, and when they saw that he thought well of Themistocles' advice a great many who had not liked it changed their minds.

Cimon himself sailed in the Athenian fleet and fought bravely in the battle of Salamis. He distinguished himself so much that not long after the Persians had been driven from Greece he was elected admiral of the fleet.

At that time there were a number of pirates living on the island of Scyros, in the Aegean Sea. They captured the merchant vessels that carried on the trade of the Mediterranean. Cimon took possession of their island and made the Aegean Sea safe for traders.

The island was the one on which Thetis had tried to hide Achilles when the Trojan War began, and somewhere upon it Theseus, the great hero of Athens, had been buried. Cimon made a search for the burial place and found it. He took the bones out of the tomb and carried them to Athens.

When he arrived at Athens and told that he had brought the bones of Theseus the whole city was filled with rejoicing. Games were held and theatrical exhibitions given. The great poets Aeschylus and Sophocles wrote plays for the occasion.

Cimon took so much booty from pirates that after a while he became very wealthy. He was also very generous. His fine gardens were open to the public and people were allowed to gather fruit in his orchard. The Athenians said, "He got riches so that he could use them and then used them so that he got honor." His fellow-citizens almost worshiped him.

II

After some years of fighting the allies of Athens grew tired of warfare. So Cimon agreed to let them furnish ships and money, and he hired seamen and marines from among the Athenians, so that though the fleet was in name the fleet of Greece, it was really Athenian. He drilled his men well in naval warfare and took them on one expedition after another. Thus they became the finest sea-soldiers in Greece.

At one time Cimon learned that there was a Persian fleet off the coast of Asia Minor. Immediately two hundred ships were made ready and he sailed to attack the Persians. They had about twice as many ships as he had, but the Greeks destroyed a great number of the Persian vessels and captured two hundred.

Cimon then disembarked his men and fought a Persian army on land. He completely defeated it and so gained two victories in one day. Immediately after this he was told that another Persian fleet was not far off, and at once he sailed to the spot and destroyed or captured all the ships and the men upon them.

The Persian king was now glad to make peace. He agreed that no army of his should ever go nearer to the Aegean Sea than a day's journey on horseback—about fifty miles—and that none of his war-ships should ever sail near Greece.

The spoil taken on Cimon's great expedition was immense. It sold for so much that the Athenians took part of the money to pay for building the foundations of the great walls called the "Long Walls." These were to connect Athens with her ports and serve also as fortifications. Cimon paid for part of this work out of his own share of the spoils.

It seems strange that the Athenians should ever have turned against Cimon after all his victories. Yet they did. The reason was this:

A terrible earthquake happened in Sparta. The whole city was ruined and only five houses stood unharmed after the shock. One large building fell upon some of the young men and boys who were drilling and killed them.

While everything was in confusion and everybody was filled with alarm, the Helots flocked together from the fields, intending to massacre their masters. Fortunately, one of the kings heard in time that the Helots were arming themselves. He at once ordered an alarm to be given by sounding trumpets, and the Spartans seized their shields and spears and gathered together. When the Helots reached the city and saw the citizens ready to resist them they went back into the country.

But they had a large and powerful army and they persuaded some neighbors of the Spartans to join them. Then they seized a strong fortress near Sparta.

The Spartans were now in a dreadful plight. Their homes were in ruins, their slaves in revolt, and their neighbors aiding the slaves.

In their distress they sent to the Athenians for aid. The great comic poet Aristophanes says, "There was a wonderful difference between the scarlet robe and the white cheeks of the Spartan who came to ask us for troops."

Some of the Athenians advised that none should be sent. They thought it would be a good thing for Athens if Sparta lost her power, for the two cities were rivals. But Cimon persuaded his countrymen to send a large force. He said, "Athens and Sparta are the two legs of Greece. Do not suffer Greece to be maimed and Athens to lose her companion."

So Athenian soldiers went in command of Cimon and fought for the Spartans. But the Helots and their allies were too strong. The fortress was not taken. Then the Spartans suspected that the Athenians had not done their best and they said that they wished no more Athenian help.

This made the people of Athens very angry. They were enraged not only with the Spartans but with Cimon. They declared that any friend of Sparta was an enemy of Athens, and so they banished Cimon.

III

After the Spartans had conquered their slaves they sent an army to attack Athens. A battle was fought not far from the city and the Spartans gained the victory.

Then some one was needed in Athens who could either beat the Spartans or make friends of them. Cimon was therefore recalled from banishment. Not long after his return he made a truce with the Spartans which lasted for several years.

Cimon thought that the best way to keep peace in Greece was to fight the Persians. So he fitted out a fleet and set sail from Athens to attack parts of the "Great King's" dominions.

He really hoped to overthrow the whole Persian empire. Before making any attack he sent friends to the oracle of Jupiter. The god refused to answer the question that they put and gave as a reason, "Because Cimon is already with me." The messengers wondered what this could mean, but when they reached the Greek fleet they found that Cimon was dead.

Some say he died of sickness, others of a wound which he had received while besieging a city.

Before he died he ordered his officers to conceal his death from the soldiers and to carry his body to Athens. This they did.

PERICLES

I

Cimon had a rival named Pericles who was the most able leader Athens ever had. He had the power of a tyrant but he used it for the welfare of the people.

He had many excellent laws passed. One was that a man accused of any crime should be tried by a certain number of his fellow-citizens. This was like our trial by jury, and it gave an Athenian the same rights in a trial that an American citizen has to-day. Another good law proposed by Pericles was that any citizen who fought in the army or navy of Athens should be paid for doing so. Still another of his laws was that if a poor man wished to go to the theater he might get the money from the city treasurer to pay for his seat.

You will remember that Themistocles and Aristides began to rebuild and beautify Athens after it had been burned by the Persians. This work was afterward carried on by Pericles. It was said that he found the city of brick and left it of marble.

Under his orders the white marble Parthenon, or temple of Minerva, was erected on the Acropolis. It was one of the most beautiful buildings in the world.

In front of it stood a bronze statue of Minerva, so large that it could be seen far out at sea. Within was a splendid statue of the goddess, nearly thirty feet high, which was of ivory and gold.

Pericles made Athens strong as well as beautiful. He finished the "Long Walls" which Cimon had begun. These walls were built from the city to her ports, which were about four miles away. Between two of the walls was a roadway, by which in time of war provisions could be safely carried from the harbor to the city.

Sparta was not pleased to hear of the fortifications of her rival. Athens might make herself beautiful if she chose, but she must not make herself strong. The Spartans watched for an opportunity to quarrel with the Athenians, and the opportunity soon came. The people of Corcyra, an island now called Corfu, lying off the west coast of Greece, went to war with the people of Corinth. Athens helped the Corcyreans; Sparta, the Corinthians.

This was the beginning of a contest between Sparta and Athens which desolated Greece for twenty-seven years (431 B.C. to 404 B.C.) It is called the Peloponnesian War, because most of the states in the Peloponnesus took part in it and were allies of Sparta. Athens also had her allies.

Athens was well prepared for war. She had a large sum of money in her treasury, a good fleet, and about thirty thousand soldiers whom she could put into the field.

The Spartans brought a force of sixty thousand men into Attica to attack Athens. Pericles then urged the country people to leave their farms and homes and come into the city. They took his advice, and every vacant spot in Athens was filled with huts and tents. Pericles thought that Athens, protected by the "Long Walls," could stand any siege.

In this he was right, for the Spartans made no headway; but very soon the Athenians were attacked by a foe far more terrible than the Spartans. This was "the plague." So many people were huddled together in the city that it was impossible to keep it clean and healthy. People began to sicken and die by dozens, then by hundreds. The Spartans, fearing that the plague might attack them, retreated across the Isthmus of Corinth into Peloponnesus.

While Athens was in this desperate condition Pericles acted most nobly. The plague carried off his eldest son, his sister, and many of his closest friends. Yet he went among the people, calming and cheering them, and attending faithfully to the affairs of the government. It was only when he laid the funeral wreath upon the lifeless body of his favorite son that he broke down and sobbed and shed a flood of tears.

While the Spartan army was threatening Athens, and when the plague came, many of the Athenians blamed Pericles. But when he was in sorrow all Athens showed him the greatest respect and affection.

Not long after the death of his son, he himself was stricken with a fatal illness. As he lay dying one of those at his bedside spoke of the good that he had done for Athens.

"What you praise in my life," he said, "has been due to fortune. I deserve no credit for it. That of which I am proudest is that no Athenian ever wore mourning because of anything done by me."

His death occurred in the third year of the Peloponnesian War. It was a sad blow to the Athenians, for he was the greatest of all their statesmen.

II

One of the friends of Pericles was Phidias, the sculptor who moulded the bronze figure of Minerva that stood in front of the Parthenon. He carved also the ivory and gold statue of the goddess that was inside the building.

His fame spread over all Greece, and he was invited to adorn the temple of Jupiter at Olympia. For this temple he made his masterpiece. It represented Jupiter seated upon his throne. The statue was so perfect that it was considered one of the wonders of the world.

When Phidias, after several years absence, returned to Athens he was persecuted by the enemies of Pericles, because he was known to be a friend of the great statesman. He was first accused of having stolen part of the gold which had been supplied by the city to decorate the statue of Minerva. Fortunately, when Phidias was working upon the statue Pericles had advised him to fasten the gold on in such a way that at any time it could be taken off and weighed. It was now removed and weighed and the weight was found to be exactly what it should be.

Phidias was then charged with having insulted the goddess Minerva, because he had carved upon her shield a likeness of himself and one of Pericles. On this charge he was cast into prison to await trial.

Before the day of trial came, however, the great sculptor was taken sick and died.

III

Under Pericles Athens was at the height of her glory, and the twenty-eight years during which he was at the head of Athenian affairs are known in history as "The Golden Age of Pericles." At no other time were there in

Athens so many great painters, sculptors, writers, and philosophers.

A celebrated historian who lived during the age of Pericles was Herodotus. He is called "the Father of History."

Another famous historian of those days was Thucydides, who wrote a history of the Peloponnesian War.

ALCIBIADES

I

During the "Age of Pericles" a young man named Alcibiades attracted a great deal of attention in Athens. He was a kinsman of Pericles and was rich and handsome. But besides his money and his good looks there was another thing that made the people of Athens think a great deal of him. He had won the crown three times in the chariot races at the Olympic games.

These games are said to have been established by Hercules. They consisted of boxing, wrestling, running, throwing the javelin, and racing with horses, and were held once in every four years in the valley of Olympia, in the little Greek state called Elis, which lay northwest of Sparta. They were so important that the Greeks reckoned time from the first Olympic games of which they had a written account as we reckon time from the birth of Christ. These games first took place in 776 B.C. The four years from one celebration to another were called an "Olympiad."

None but Greeks might take part in the Olympic

games, and while the contests were going on tens of thousands of Greeks from every part of Hellas watched and applauded. To win the prize in any of the contests was the greatest honor for which a Greek could hope. The victor's name and the name of his birthplace were called aloud by a herald, and before the vast assemblage he was crowned with a wreath of wild olive cut with a golden knife from a sacred grove said to have been planted by Hercules.

His victories in the Olympic games made Alcibiades the idol of the Athenians. The young men of Athens admired him so much that some of them dressed as he did and even imitated the lisp with which he talked. He was, in fact, the leader of Athenian fops.

Unfortunately, he had very bad faults. He was frivolous and thoughtless and, worst of all, he was not sincere.

While talking with Socrates, the great philosopher, who was very fond of him, he could talk as if he were good or at least wished to be; but the next day he might be leading his companions into all kinds of mischief. Yet with all his faults he was a brilliant genius; even serious people admired him and often took his advice.

During the Peloponnesian War he persuaded the Athenians to undertake an expedition against the island of Sicily. He reminded them that Syracuse, the most important city of the island, was an ally of Sparta and an enemy to Athens. This was one reason he gave why the expedition should be undertaken. Another reason was the advantage that would come to Athens if she should add this fertile island to her possessions.

An old Athenian general named Nicias opposed the expedition, but Alcibiades had his way. Ships and men were made ready and were put under three commanders—Nicias, Alcibiades, and a man named Lamachus.

One morning, shortly before the fleet was to set sail, it was discovered that a shocking insult had been offered to one of the gods. Along the streets of Athens, along the country roads, and in front of the houses were busts of Mercury, who was the protector of travelers. Ears and noses had been chipped from these busts in the night. The Athenians were a very religious people, and this insult to the god filled them with terror. All feared that Mercury would punish them by not protecting people walking on the streets and highways.

Many thought that Alcibiades had chipped the busts for a frolic. Soon after the fleet reached Sicily orders were received that he should return to Athens at once to answer the charge. Of course he had to give up his command.

After he did so one disaster after another befell the expedition. The fleet entered the harbor of Syracuse. The Syracusans then blocked the entrance so that the Athenian ships could not get out. In the battle that followed half of Nicias' ships were destroyed. Nicias ran the rest ashore and tried to escape by land, but all were forced to surrender. The old commander was killed, and those of his men who did not die in battle or of starvation were sold into slavery. Not one of the ships of the fleet ever got back to Athens.

II

Alcibiades was either afraid that he could not clear himself, or that he could not get justice in the courts of Athens. He therefore pretended that he was going to obey the order for his return, but instead of doing so he went for refuge to Sparta. When the Athenians heard of this they passed a sentence of death upon him.

In Sparta he was warmly welcomed and by his pleasing ways became a general favorite. The Spartans, however, soon grew suspicious of him and ordered him to be put to death as a traitor to them. He managed to escape and went to Persia. Here again, as at Athens and

273

at Sparta, he made the people fond of him. But after a while the Persian governor, who had been his best friend, saw that he was treacherous and put him in prison. He escaped and went to a place on the Hellespont where he joined the Athenian fleet. There he gave the commanders such advice that they gained a victory over the fleet of the Spartans and the land forces of the Persians. The Spartan admiral was killed. His successor wrote to Sparta, "Our glory is gone. The men are without food. We know not what to do."

Alcibiades now thought that he might venture to go back to Athens. As he had given to the commanders of the Athenian navy the advice which won for them the victory over the Spartan fleet the Athenians repented of having condemned him to death. So when he arrived in the Piraeus, with a small fleet of twenty vessels, he was allowed to land and go to Athens. In a very short time he persuaded the Athenians to give him command of their fleet. Then he sailed across the Aegean to fight against the Persians and Spartans.

Unfortunately, he had to leave the fleet for a short time. During his absence his lieutenant foolishly brought on a battle. The Athenians were defeated, and many of their ships were captured by the Spartans.

With what was left of his fleet Alcibiades then did the strangest thing possible; he attacked a city that was friendly to the Athenians and tried to make slaves of some of the inhabitants. Complaint was made of this to Athens, and the Athenians at once dismissed Alcibiades from the command of their fleet.

After this he lived for some years in Asia Minor, where he owned a castle. One night his castle was surrounded by armed men who set it on fire. He ran through the flames and tried to escape, but his enemies killed him (B.C. 404.)

LYSANDER

The admiral of the Spartan fleet in the last years of the Peloponnesian War was a man named Lysander. He was brave, but he was also cunning and frequently gained the victory by laying a trap for his enemy. It is said that he used to tell his officers, "When the lion's skin is too short you must patch it with that of a fox." This was another way of telling them that if they could not succeed by force they must try cunning.

After Alcibiades had been dismissed from the command of the Athenian fleet a commander named Konon was appointed to succeed him. Lysander decided to set a trap for him. The two fleets came in sight of each other off the shore of the Hellespont, near a place called Aegos Potamos, which means Goat's River. One morning, at break of day, Lysander drew up his ships in line as though he intended to give battle. Later in the day the Athenians rowed toward the Spartans and challenged them to fight, but not a Spartan vessel moved. The Athenians concluded from this that the Spartans were either not prepared to fight, or were afraid. The next day the challenge was again given by the Athenians, and again the Spartans paid no attention to it. The same thing happened the third day and the fourth. By this time the Athenians felt sure that Lysander was afraid of them. Many therefore went on the shore, some in search of provisions, some to take a stroll, some to sleep. Only a small guard was left with the fleet.

As soon as Lysander saw that the Athenians ships were unprotected he rowed swiftly to the place where they were lying and captured nearly the whole fleet. Of one hundred and eighty ships only about ten escaped. Three or four thousand men were taken prisoners, and all were put to death.

One of the vessels that escaped rowed direct to the Piraeus to carry the terrible tidings. It arrived at night, and a sadder night was never known in Athens. The news spread through the city. Every house became a house of mourning. Nobody slept. All feared that Lysander would sail into the harbor with his victorious fleet. This was exactly what he did. All the seaports of Athens were blockaded by the Spartan vessels. The wheat supply was cut off, so that the people of the city were soon half starving.

The Athenians had now neither army nor fleet. After a three months' siege, during part of which time there was a severe famine, the city surrendered.

The only hope of the citizens was that their conquerors might be generous. But in this they were disappointed. The Spartans' terms were hard and cruel. One mile of each of the Long Walls was to be pulled down. Athens was to have no larger fleet than twelve ships of war. The Spartans were to name her rulers.

To wound the pride of Athens as much as possible Lysander had the long walls pulled down to the sound of music, and a part of the work was done on the anniversary of the battle of Salamis, a day always celebrated in Athens in memory of her great victory over the Persians.

Thus ended the Peloponnesian War (404 B.C.). It had been a fierce struggle, and all Greece had suffered. Thucydides, who wrote the history of this war, says that never had so many cities been made desolate, never had there been such scenes of slaughter.

Athens was ruined. She had lost her ships and her army, and she was helpless in the hands of Sparta. Thirty men were appointed by the Spartans to govern the city. They are known in history as the "Thirty Tyrants." Their rule was very harsh. They allowed only 3,000 Athenians to live in Athens. The rest of the people had to leave the city, and Sparta forbade all other Grecian cities to give them refuge. Thebes and Argos, however, boldly defied this cruel order, and many of the banished Athenians went to live in these cities.

After eight months the Athenians, under a leader named Thrasybulus, overthrew the "Tyrants." But in that short time no less than fourteen hundred Athenians citizens had been put to death.

Lysander's capture of Athens made him so popular in Sparta that for some years he was the real head of the government, and he made up his mind to seize the throne.

Before he could carry out his plans, however, he was put at the head of a Spartan force and sent to the city of Thebes, against which the Spartans had declared war. His army was routed by the Thebans and Lysander himself was among the slain.

SOCRATES

I

During the Peloponnesian War a very curious man lived in Athens. His name was Socrates. He must have been the ugliest person in all Greece. His nose was flat, his lips were thick, his eyes were bulging, and his face was like a comic mask; yet he was one of the best and wisest men that ever lived. His father was a sculptor who carved beautiful figures out of marble, and Socrates when a boy helped him and learned the art.

When the Spartans sent their armies to burn the farm-houses of Attica and capture cities that were friendly to Athens, many of the young men of the city went forth to fight for their country. Socrates laid down his hammer and chisel and took up a shield and spear instead. He fought in several battles, and Athens had no braver soldier. Once in winter he was ordered to a country called Thrace. It was very cold and "camping out" was not pleasant. However, Socrates bore the cold cheerfully, although he went barefoot and wore the same clothes that he wore in the warm weather in Athens.

After serving as a soldier for several years he left the army and went home to Athens. Here he became a teacher. He had no school-house. His school was wherever he met persons who were willing to listen to him. It might be in the market-place, or at the corner of streets. On a hot summer day he would go to the harbor of Athens and chat with people who were sitting there in the shade, enjoying the cool sea-breeze. He talked to the young as well as the old, and often he might be seen with a crowd of children about him. The lessons that he gave were simple talks about the best way of living, or what the Greeks called "philosophy."

Socrates was very unlike other teachers in Athens—and almost everywhere else—for he never made any charge for his teaching. This kept him poor. His clothes were often threadbare and shabby, and so were those of his wife Xanthippe. He cared nothing for this; but she did and it is said that she often scolded Socrates because he did nothing to make money, but idled away his time in talking. Once, when he was going out of the house to escape from a severe scolding, she threw a pitcher of water upon him. "I have often noticed, Xanthippe, that rain comes after thunder," said the philosopher.

No man ever had better friends than had Socrates. But no man ever had worse enemies. Some people disliked him because he used to ask them questions which they could not answer without admitting that they were very foolish in their way of living. Others said that he was teaching people not to worship Jupiter and Minerva and the other gods of Athens, and that he was misleading the young men of the city.

One of his enemies was a poet called Aristophanes, who wrote the most humorous plays that were ever acted in Athens. In one of them a wild young man is one of the characters and Socrates is another. Aristophanes made it seem that the teachings of Socrates had caused the young man to become wild. The play did Socrates a great deal of harm, for many people came to believe that he really was advising young men to lead bad lives.

Yet one of the worst young men of Athens once said, "You think that I have no shame in me, but when I am with Socrates I am ashamed. He has only to speak and my tears flow."

Finally, the enemies of Socrates brought against him in the courts the charge of ruining young men and insulting the gods. He was tried and condemned to drink the deadly juice of a plant called hemlock. In Athens condemned persons were usually put to death by making them drink this poison.

No man ever behaved more grandly when unjustly condemned to die than did Socrates.

Before he left the court he said, "My judges, you go now to your homes—I to prison and to death. But which of the two is the better lot God only knows. It is very likely that death is our greatest blessing."

Generally a person condemned to death had to drink the poison the very next day after his trial. But a sacred ship had just sailed from Athens to Delos. This ship carried every year the offerings of the Athenians to Apollo, the chief god of the island, and it was a law in Athens that no person condemned to die should be put to death while she was on her voyage to and fro. So for thirty days Socrates was kept in prison.

During that time his friends were allowed to go to see him. In the prison he talked to them just as he had done in the market-place or on the streets.

Some of his friends told him how sorry they were that he should die innocent.

"What!" said Socrates, "would you have me die guilty?"

On the return of the ship from Delos he was told to

prepare himself for death. He invited his friends to come and be with him at the end. He took with them his last meal and was as cheerful during it as if it had been a feast.

One of his friends asked where he would like them to "bury him."

"Bury *me?*" he said. "You cannot bury Socrates. You can bury my body; you cannot put *me* into a grave."

He spoke about death and the future life and said that death was only the end of sorrow and the beginning of a nobler life.

When the jailer came with the cup of poison Socrates drank it as cheerfully as if it had been a glass of wine. He walked about the cell as he was bidden and then, beginning to feel sleepy, lay down. Soon after this he ceased to breathe.

Plato, who was one of his pupils, says, "Thus died the man who was in death the noblest we have ever known—in life, the wisest and the best."

II

After the death of Socrates (B.C. 399) his work was carried on by his pupil, Plato, who became one of the most famous philosophers of Greece. His lectures were given in the shade of the trees planted by Cimon in the Academy years before.

Besides great philosophers Athens had some famous painters. Two of the most celebrated were Zeuxis and Parrhasius, who lived about 400 B.C. They were rivals. Once they gave an exhibition of their paintings. Zeuxis exhibited a bunch of grapes which had such a natural look that birds came and pecked at them. The people exclaimed, "Astonishing! What can be finer than Zeuxis' grapes?"

Zeuxis proudly turned to his rival's picture. A purple curtain hung before it. "Draw aside your curtain, Parrhasius," he said, "and let us look at your picture."

The artist smiled, but did not move. Some one else stepped toward the curtain to draw it aside, and it was then discovered that the curtain was part of the painting.

"I yield," said Zeuxis. "It is easy to see who is the better artist. I have deceived birds. Parrhasius has deceived an artist."

It is said the Zeuxis died laughing at a funny picture that he had painted of an old woman.

XENOPHON

I

One day as Socrates was walking through a narrow street in Athens he met a young man who was remarkably handsome. Socrates stretched out his staff so that the young man had to stop.

"Where can bread be found?" asked the philosopher.

The young man's manner was modest and pleasing as he told Socrates where to buy bread.

"And where can wine be found?" asked the philosopher.

With the same pleasant manner the young man told Socrates where to get wine.

"And where can the good and the noble be found?" asked the philosopher.

The young man was puzzled and unable to answer.

"Follow me and learn," said the philosopher. The young man obeyed and from that time forward was the pupil and friend of Socrates. He was called Xenophon, a name that afterward became famous among the Greeks.

The king of Persia at that time was Artaxerxes. He had a younger brother named Cyrus, who was the governor of some provinces of Asia Minor, which belonged to Persia. Cyrus thought that he had a better right to the throne than Artaxerxes and he determined to seize it.

The Persians had helped the Spartans in the Peloponnesian War, and Cyrus had found out what splendid fighters the Greeks were. He knew, also, that many of them had become so used to fighting that they did not like a life of peace and were willing to fight for any one who would pay them. He decided, therefore, to get the Greeks to help him to fight for the throne of Persia, and he sent to several Greek states to invite soldiers to join him, promising them great rewards if he succeeded.

Xenophon had a friend who was going with Cyrus and who advised Xenophon to go too. Xenophon talked the matter over with Socrates who told him to ask the oracle at Delphi what to do. So Xenophon went to Delphi, but as he had made up his mind to go on the expedition he did not ask the oracle whether he should go or not. He only asked to what gods he should sacrifice before he set out. After sacrificing as the oracle advised he started for Sardis, in Asia Minor, and reached that city just in time to join the expedition.

Eleven thousand Greeks from different states had entered the service of Cyrus; so that with his Persian forces, 100,000 strong, he had an army of 111,000 men. Xenophon was not a general, or even a soldier, in this army. He seems to have gone with his friend, hoping that some opening would be made for him.

There was a magnificent road from Sardis to Susa, Artaxerxes' capital. But even upon the best of roads an army of a hundred thousand men, most of whom were on foot, had to move slowly. Cyrus' troops went about fifteen miles a day, and it took them six months to reach a place called Cunaxa, about seventy miles from Babylon.

Here they found Artaxerxes at the head of an army of nearly a million men. The troops of the Persian king advanced with a great shout, thinking that the noise made by thousands of men shouting would terrify the Greeks. But the Greeks only raised their warcry—*"Victory!"*—and steadily advanced, overcoming everything that was opposed to them. Unfortunately, Cyrus went into the battle himself at the head of his Persian forces. Seeing his brother, he rushed forward, exclaiming, "I see the man," and wounded Artaxerxes with a javelin.

He himself, however, was quickly killed by the soldiers of Artaxerxes. As soon as their leader had fallen Cyrus' Persian soldiers lost heart and fled.

II

The Greeks were now in a terrible plight. They were six months' march from Sardis and opposed by an army a hundred times the size of their own.

In the battle of Cunaxa they had so thoroughly beaten the Persians that Artaxerxes and his men were afraid of them and decided to get rid of them by treachery. The Persian commander-in-chief, Tissaphernes, therefore invited the Greek generals to a friendly meeting and promised to furnish them guides and provisions, so that they might return safely to Greece. The generals, never suspecting foul play, went to the Persian camp. There they were all put to death.

The Greeks were now greatly alarmed. The night following the assassination of the generals was one of terror. Not a fire was lit, even for the cooking of the supper. All slept with arms at their sides while the sentries listened to catch the slightest sound.

Xenophon spent the night in thinking what was best to do. It was clear to him that some one must be chosen by the Greeks as their leader and that they all must stand by one another. He felt sure that if this were done there would be a good chance of getting home safely. In the morning he told his thoughts and hopes to others of the Greeks, who were greatly cheered by what he said. Although he had held no office in the army before, he was now made one of its generals.

The shortest way to get out of the kingdom of Persia was to go to the Euxine, now called the Black Sea, which lay many hundred miles to the north beyond rugged mountains. At one of the ports on the shore of that sea the Greeks hoped to find ships in which they might sail to Greece.

The march was at once begun. All sorts of hardships were met with. There were snow-storms and bitter north winds; it was sometimes hard to get enough food; the mountain tribes, through whose land the army had to march, were often unfriendly and rolled rocks down the mountain slopes upon the soldiers.

At last, however, the shores of the Euxine were reached. The Greeks, since the murder of their generals, had marched for five months in an enemy's territory. They had drawn supplies from the country and had lost but few of their men. The retreat was in fact a victory.

Xenophon returned to Greece, but he did not go back to Athens. During some of the time that he had followed a soldier's fortune he had fought with the Spartans against Athens and the Athenians had passed a sentence of exile against him.

He went to Sparta, and soon afterward settled on an estate in Elis. "Xenophon's farm" is still pointed out to visitors to Greece. He passed about twenty years quietly in hunting, writing, and entertaining his friends with stories of his life as a soldier on faraway battlefields.

From notes which he made he wrote a history called the Anabasis, or "March up," which is an account of Cyrus' march up to Babylon and of the retreat of the Greeks.

Owing to political troubles Xenophon finally had to leave his pleasant home in Elis. He went to Corinth, where it is supposed that he died.

EPAMINONDAS AND PELOPIDAS

I

In the city of Thebes not long after the Peloponnesian War lived two young men whose names were Pelopidas and Epaminondas. Pelopidas was rich; Epaminondas was poor. Both were fond of athletics and manly sports, but Epaminondas found his chief pleasure in books. Both were brave men and true and they loved each other like brothers.

Once, when their city was an ally of Sparta, they were sent by Thebes as soldiers to help the Spartans in a war with their neighbors, the Arcadians. The young men were fighting side by side when their comrades gave way and fled. Closing their shields together, they bravely held their ground and tried to drive back the Arcadians. Pelopidas was wounded and fell. Epaminondas would not desert his friend. Although badly wounded, he held the Arcadians in check until help came and he and Pelopidas were rescued.

In time Sparta became jealous of Thebes and tried to

take away the liberty of her people. A few rich Thebans were willing to help Sparta do this in order that they might be made the rulers. One day they led a band of Spartan soldiers, who happened to be passing, into the Cadmea. This was the rocky citadel of Thebes, which rose above the city as did the Acropolis at Athens. The Cadmea had never been captured. But on that day the garrison was taking a holiday, for the citadel had been given up to the women, who were celebrating a festival of Ceres in it. So the Spartans easily took possession of it, and having once got it they held it for four years.

During that time the men who had betrayed the citadel into the hands of the Spartans ruled Thebes as tyrants. They put some of the Thebans to death and banished others. Over three hundred were sent away. Among them was Pelopidas. Epaminondas was so poor that the tyrants did not think him of any consequence and he was allowed to stay in Thebes. He used his influence to get the young Thebans to drill in order to make themselves superior to the Spartans in skill and strength.

II

The exiles went to Athens. After living there for a few years Pelopidas determined to free his country, and he easily persuaded the other exiles and some Athenians to join in carrying out his plans.

When everything was ready the exiles left Athens. Twelve of them volunteered to get into Thebes and kill the tyrants. They disguised themselves as hunters, divided into four parties, and taking hounds with them, hunted through the fields around Thebes. As dusk came on they made their way into the city. It was a cold winter day, snow was beginning to fall and very few people were in the streets, so the exiles reached the house where all were to meet without being noticed. Twenty-six citizens joined them and all remained in the one house until near midnight.

A patriot who was in the plot had invited the tyrants to supper at his house. At the supper wine was served, and the tyrants drank freely. After the supper some of the patriots, dressed as women, were admitted to the banquet hall. As soon as they entered the room the guests greeted them warmly, but the supposed women at once threw off their veils, drew their swords and killed the tyrants.

Pelopidas, with another party, went to the houses of two of the tyrants who had refused the invitation to supper, and after a fight killed them. The patriots then went from house to house, calling on all the people to defend their homes. The Spartan soldiers in the Cadmea heard the noise and saw the lights, but were afraid to come out.

In the morning the other exiles with their friends from Athens came into the city, and all the citizens rose up in arms. The Spartan garrison gave up the Cadmea and Thebes was free.

II

Sparta waited eight years before a chance came to punish the Thebans. Then war was declared, and an army of ten thousand Spartans marched against Thebes.

The Thebans also raised an army, and through the influence of Pelopidas Epaminondas was elected one of the chief captains. Pelopidas himself was captain of a famous "sacred band" of three hundred young men who had taken an oath to give their lives in defense of liberty.

The two armies met near a town called Leuctra. There Epaminondas gained a great victory, although his army was less than half as large as that of the Spartans.

Epaminondas and Pelopidas drilled the men of Thebes so that they were the best soldiers in all Greece, and Thebes helped other Greek cities become independent.

Pelopidas went to Thessaly to aid the people of that state against a tyrant who was trying to rule all Thessaly. The army of Pelopidas was not nearly so large as that of the tyrant, but Pelopidas was victorious. Unfortunately, however, he was killed in the battle.

The Thessalians begged the Thebans to allow them to bury the hero, and their request was granted.

III

The death of Pelopidas was a sad blow to Epaminondas. However, he did not let his grief stand in the way of duty. Athens at this time had grown jealous of Thebes and had united with Sparta; so the armies of the two cities met the Thebans under Epaminondas in the year 362 B.C., near the town of Mantinea, where a long and fierce battle was fought. At length the Thebans were victorious and the Spartans were driven from the field.

The victory, however, was dearly bought. Just when the tide of battle was turning and the Spartan ranks were breaking Epaminondas received a wound in the breast from a spear. The shaft broke and the head remained fixed in the wound. Epaminondas was told by his physician that he would die as soon as the spearhead was removed. Those about him wept, and one lamented that he was dying without a child to keep his name alive.

"Leuctra and Mantinea," replied the hero, "are daughters who will keep my name alive."

When he was told that the victory was secure he cried, "I have lived long enough," and with his own hand drew the spear-head from his breast.

Thus passed away a man who stands out in Grecian history as a spotless hero—a soldier who never fought except for freedom, a man who lived only to do good.

PHILIP OF MACEDONIA

I

After the death of Epaminondas Thebes soon lost the high place she had gained among the states of Greece. For a while no state held that place. Sparta was never powerful after her defeats at Leuctra and Mantinea, and although Athens had rebuilt her Long Walls she was not the strong power that she had once been.

A state, partly Greek and partly barbarian, lying far to the north, suddenly took the lead in the affairs of Greece. It was Macedonia.

The king of Macedonia had a brother named Philip who had spent a part of his youth in Thebes. He had seen Thebes become the greatest of Grecian states through the bravery and military skill of Epaminondas, and he determined to make his own state great.

The chance came to carry out his determination. The king of Macedonia was assassinated, and the brother who succeeded him was slain in battle. Philip's infant nephew was heir to the throne, and Philip became the guardian of the little king. In a short time the claims of his nephew had been set aside and Philip was on the throne of Macedonia.

Not long after he became king Philip was married to Olympias, a proud and beautiful woman, daughter of the king of Epirus. Philip had seen her for the first time at a feast of the god of wine. She and her maidens were dancing among garlands of vines and flowers. On the head of Olympias was an ivy crown and in her hand a staff twined with a vine branch. As she danced her wild beauty won the heart of Philip. He asked her hand in marriage and she became his wife.

Philip soon showed that he was a wise ruler. He treated hs people with fairness, and they became very fond of him.

One day, after he had been drinking, he was acting as a judge and gave a decision against a woman. His sentence seemed so unfair to her that she thought he was under the influence of liquor. "I appeal," she cried.

"I am the king. To whom do you appeal?" asked Philip.

"I appeal from Philip drunk to Philip sober," she replied. The next day Philip considered her case again and decided in her favor.

II

It was, however, his skill as a soldier that most endeared Philip to his people. He knew that the Spartans had become the masters of Greece because every Spartan was a trained soldier, and he knew that Epaminondas had won his great battles because of the way in which he had arranged his men. Philip, therefore, had his army carefully drilled and in battle he arranged his soldiers in his famous "phalanx."

This phalanx consisted of a mass of men, sixteen deep. If there were 16,000 men the front rank had 1,000 standing side by side. Three feet behind these stood a second rank of 1,000. Behind the second rank stood a third line of 1,000 equally close, and so on until there was a solid body of men sixteen deep and a thousand wide. Every man bore a round shield, about two feet in diameter, and a spike or spear, twenty-one feet long. The shields were buckled to the left arm and were held close together. Before them bristled the spear-points like a hedge. Against these spear-points neither men nor horses could advance; and the charge of the phalanx broke down everything before it.

Athens and Thebes were finally aroused to action against Philip by the eloquence of Demosthenes, the great orator, who was constantly sounding a warning. An army was sent to oppose the Macedonian. Philip met this army at Chæronea, not far from Thebes, and there gained a great victory.

This put an end to the power of Athens and Thebes and made Philip master of all the states of Greece, except Sparta.

But Philip was wise and fair enough not to become a tyrant. He knew the history of Sparta. The military training of the Spartans had made them strong; their tyranny had made them weak, for no state of Greece was ever content to remain under Spartan rule. Philip, therefore, acted generously toward the conquered states. He let each manage its own affairs, while a General Council, like our Congress, managed matters in which all were concerned.

The first thing that Philip proposed to the Council of the States was that all Greece should make war against Persia. The members of the Council were delighted and Philip was invited to be the commander-in-chief of the expedition.

Preparations for the invasion of Persia had already begun when Philip's career was suddenly ended by an assassin who, at a wedding feast, plunged a sword into the body of the king and killed him.

ALEXANDER THE GREAT

I

Alexander, the son of Philip of Macedonia and Olympias, was born on the same night that the great temple of Diana at Ephesus, in Asia Minor, was burned. It is said that while the temple was burning sooth-sayers ran up and down the streets of Ephesus, crying out that the night had brought forth sad disaster to Asia. This was true of the birth of Alexander as well as of the burning of the temple.

Alexander was educated chiefly by the famous Greek philosopher, Aristotle. The young prince was an earnest pupil. It is said that he could recite the Iliad of Homer from beginning to end.

He excelled also in athletic sports. The horses of Thessaly, a state of Greece adjoining Macedonia, were famed for their speed and spirit. While Alexander was still a boy a fine Thessalian horse was offered to his father at a very high price. Philip wished to have the animal tried, but the horse was so wild that every one was afraid of him. Philip was about to send him away when

Alexander offered to ride him. The king gave him permission. Alexander had noticed that the animal was afraid of his own shadow. He therefore seized the plunging horse and turned his head toward the sun, so that his shadow fell behind him. Then patting his neck and speaking gently to him, he leaped upon his back and soon completely tamed him.

The head of the horse was supposed to have some likeness to that of an ox, so he was called Bucephalus, or Oxhead. He became Alexander's favorite horse and carried his master through many a march and many a battle.

Alexander's ambition was shown at an early age. While he was yet a mere boy he made up his mind to conquer the world, and when he learned from Aristotle that there were many other worlds in the universe, he was greatly saddened by the thought that he had not yet conquered one.

As Philip went on making one conquest after another Alexander became alarmed. "Why," he cried one day, "my father will leave nothing for me to do!"

However, when he became king, he found enough to do. First of all there were other claimants to the throne besides himself. Some of them Alexander put to death. Others fled the country. He learned that Thebes and other Greek states were thinking of throwing off the Macedonian yoke. He therefore gathered a large army and marched to Thebes at the head of it. The Thebans were over-awed and submitted to him without resistance. The Athenians, in spite of Demosthenes' advice, sent a messenger to him while he was at Thebes, offering their submission. A little later the Greeks met in general council at Corinth and gave him, as they had given Philip, the command of the expedition that was to be undertaken against Persia. Sparta alone refused to agree in the vote.

Alexander returned to Macedonia and marched

against some Thracian tribes in the northern part of his dominions. While he was subduing them a report of his death reached Greece, and Thebes again took up arms. Suddenly Alexander appeared in Greece with his victorious army. He took Thebes by assault and pulled to the ground every building in the city except the house once occupied by the famous poet Pindar. Six thousand of the inhabitants were put to death; a few escaped by flight and the rest were sold as slaves.

II

Alexander now began to prepare for the great expedition against Persia, which had so long been planned. Soon his army was ready to march. It consisted of less than 35,000 men, but with these he boldly crossed the Hellespont.

He landed on the Asiatic coast not far from the site of ancient Troy. From the plain of Troy he marched to the river Granicus, on the bank of which he fought his first battle with the Persians.

The Persian army was completely routed, and its commander killed himself rather than face the disgrace of his defeat. The great city of Sardis, the stronghold of the Persians in western Asia Minor, now opened its gates to the conqueror.

The following spring Alexander advanced into the province of Phrygia. In a temple in the city of Gordium was kept the chariot of Gordius, once a famous Phrygian king. The yoke of the chariot was fastened to the pole by a knot of tough fibre. The knot was said to have been tied by Gordius himself. It was very puzzling. An oracle had declared that whoever should untie it would become the master of Asia. Instead of trying to untie it Alexander cut it with one stroke of his sword. The people of Asia Minor took this as an omen that he was to be their master and offered him but little resistance.

Beyond the mountains in southeastern Asia Minor, the "Great King," Darius was waiting for the Greeks with an enormous army. He became impatient and crossed the mountains into Cilicia. A battle was fought at Issus, but the Persians were no match for the Greeks. The battle ended with overwhelming defeat to the army of Darius and he fled from the battle-field. He left not only his baggage and treasure, but his wife and mother and children, all of whom fell into Alexander's hands. These captives were treated with much respect and kindness by the conqueror.

Soon after the battle at Issus Damascus was captured. Alexander then moved against Tyre, a famous port of Syria, whose trade was with every land and whose merchants were princes. So great were the resources of the city that it withstood a siege of seven months; but at the end of that time it fell into Alexander's hand and thirty thousand of its citizens were captured and made slaves.

From Tyre Alexander marched toward Egypt. On the way he passed through the Holy Land. When he reached Jerusalem he was met by a friendly procession of priests and Levites, who came out from the gates of the city, with the high priest at their head, to bid the conqueror welcome.

Egypt, like the Holy Land, was won without a battle. The people were weary of Persian rule.

In Egypt Alexander did one of his wisest acts. He founded a city near the mouth of the Nile to be a great trading port. It is still called Alexandria after its founder. Another wise act on Alexander's part was to invite the Jews to settle in his new city. He saw that they were wonderful traders; and, as he expected, they made Alexandria a greater commercial city than Tyre.

In the spring of the year 331 B.C. Alexander again set out in pursuit of Darius, who had now collected another large army.

In October, not far from a place called Arbela, in Persia, the forces of Darius and Alexander met in their last great battle. Darius had done everything he could to insure the defeat of the Greeks. His army was said to number a million men. One division of it had two hundred chariots, to the wheels of which scythes were attached. The scythes went round with the wheels and were expected to mow down the Greeks like grass. In another division of the army were fifteen trained elephants that were intended to rush wildly among the Greeks and trample them down.

But the scythe-armed chariots, the elephants, and the million men were alike unsuccessful. The vast host was completely routed, and Darius turned his chariot and fled.

From Arbela Alexander pushed on to Babylon, whose brazen gates were thrown open to him. Susa, another great city of the Empire, surrendered without resistance. Then, to make his conquest complete he marched on to Persepolis, the magnificent capital of Persia proper. This city, with its immense treasure of silver and gold, fell into his hands. Five thousand camels and ten thousand mule-carts carried away the spoils, the value of which is said to have been $150,000,000.

Alexander pursued Darius, but before he overtook him the Great King was murdered by one of his own satraps. Alexander had the body buried with royal honors and punished the satrap with death.

The Empire of Persia now lay at Alexander's feet, and the work for which the expedition had set out was finished. The young king, however, had no desire to return to Macedonia. He had conquered the East, but the East had also conquered him. He had become a slave to its ways of living. His old simple Macedonian tastes had been laid aside and his life was given up to pleasure.

Soon, however, he undertook another conquest and at the head of his veteran soldiers advanced eastward into Bactria and added this province to his dominions. Among the Bactrian captives was a beautiful princess named Roxana, who became his bride.

Southeast of Persia lay India, a vast empire rich in gold and diamonds. Alexander desired to add it to his conquests.

Great mountain ranges enclose India on the north and northwest. Crossing these are passes, through which travelers from Central Asia must go to reach India.

Alexander went by the way of Khaiber Pass and marched steadily onward till he reached the river Hydaspes. Here an Indian king, named Porus, engaged him in battle. Porus proved to be the most desperate fighter Alexander had met with in all Asia. When the Indian was at length overpowered and captured and brought before the conqueror, Alexander asked him how he expected to be treated.

"Like a king," replied Porus.

"That you certainly shall be," said Alexander. And so he was, for it was the habit of Alexander to treat honorably all whom he conquered.

On the bank of the River Hydaspes Alexander had the misfortune to lose his horse Bucephalus. At the place where the animal died the conqueror founded a city which he named Bucephala in honor of his favorite.

The conqueror was not able to go on with his Indian campaign. His soldiers were worn out with marching and fighting and insisted that they would go no farther, and so, much against his will, Alexander was obliged to lead them back to Persia.

The return march was one of great hardship. At the mouth of the Indus Alexander sent the fleet to sail along the coast and up the Persian Gulf, while he led the land forces toward Susa and Babylon. The army had to march through a country which was hot, dry and barren. The men suffered dreadfully and Alexander shared their sufferings.

Shortly after reaching Babylon he was attacked by a fever, which he had not the strength to resist.

Around his death-bed were gathered his generals. They asked him whom he wished to succeed him. He drew his signet ring from his finger and handed it to Perdiccas with the words, "To the strongest." A little later he had ceased to breathe.

Thus passed away one of the greatest soldiers the world has ever known. At the time of his death, 323 B.C., he was only thirty-two years old. His victories had been won and his conquests had been made in the short space of twelve years.

DEMOSTHENES

I

In the city of Athens about twenty-five years after the Peloponnesian War there lived a delicate boy named Demosthenes. His father was a manufacturer of swords and made a great deal of money. But when Demosthenes was only seven years old his father died. Guardians had charge of his property for ten years. They robbed the boy of part of his fortune and managed the rest so badly that Demosthenes could not go to school to the best teachers in Athens because he had not money enough to pay them.

One day, when he was sixteen years old, a great trial was going on at Athens and he strolled into the court. There were fifteen hundred and one dicasts or, as we call them, jurymen in their seats, and the court was crowded with citizens who, like Demosthenes, had gone in from curiosity. A lawyer named Callistratus was speaking. He did not finish his speech for nearly four hours. But no one left the court until he ceased to speak. Then hundreds of people went out and hurried home.

Demosthenes waited to see the end. When each of the jurymen had thrown a voting pebble into a basket the clerk of the court counted the pebbles and told the result. Callistratus had won the case.

Demosthenes went home determined to become a lawyer and public speaker. In one year from that time he brought suit against his guardians, delivered four orations against them and won his case. He recovered a large part of the property which his father had left to his mother and himself.

After this he entered public life, but the first time he made a speech in the public assembly it was a complete failure. He stammered and could not speak loud enough, and in trying to do so he made odd faces.

People laughed at him, and even his friends told him that he never could be a speaker, so he went home greatly cast down.

Then an actor who was a great friend of his family went to see him and encouraged him. He asked Demosthenes to read to him some passages of poetry. Then the actor recited the same passages. The verses now seemed to have new meaning and beauty. The actor pronounced the words as if he felt them. The tones of his voice were clear and pleasant and his gestures were graceful. Demosthenes was charmed.

"You can learn to speak just as well as I do," said the actor, "if you are willing to work patiently. Do not be discouraged, but conquer your difficulties."

"I will," said Demosthenes. And he did.

It is said that to improve his voice he spoke with stones in his mouth, and to become accustomed to the noise and confusion of the public assembly he went to the seashore and recited there amid the roar of the waves. To overcome his habit of lifting one shoulder above the other he suspended a sword so that the point would prick his shoulder as he raised it.

He built an underground room in which he could

study without interruption and practice speaking without disturbing any one. He had one side of his head shaved so that he would be ashamed to leave this retreat. Then he remained there for months at a time engaged in study. One thing that he did while there was to copy eight times the speeches in the famous history of Thucydides. This was to teach him to use the most fitting language. Besides all this he took lessons of an excellent speaker named Isaeus who taught declamation. In this way the awkward boy who had been laughed out of the assembly became in time the greatest orator of Athens.

Not only was Demosthenes a graceful orator, but he was wise and patriotic. He soon acquired great influence in Athens and became one of the ten official orators.

At this time Philip of Macedon had organized a strong army and was beginning those conquests which in the end made him master of Greece. Demosthenes from the first regarded him with suspicion, but said nothing until convinced that Philip was threatening the liberty of Athens and of all Greece. Then he urged the Athenians to fight against Philip as their forefathers had fought against the Persians at Marathon, at Salamis and at Plataea. "Philip," he said, "is weak because he is selfish and unjust. He is strong only because he is energetic. Let us be equally energetic, and being unselfish and just, we shall triumph."

Philip's victory at Chaeronea completely disheartened the Athenians, and Demosthenes had to use all the power of his eloquence to rouse them. In his speeches he showed how the success of Philip and the failure of Athens were not due to the advisers of the people or to the generals who led their army, but to the Athenians themselves. "You idle away your time," said he, "going into barbers' shops and asking what news to-day, while

Philip is gathering forces with which to crush you and the rest of Greece with you."

Philip tried to bribe Demosthenes, but the orator was absolutely incorruptible, and to the end of his life he raised his voice and used his influence for the cause of freedom against both Philip and Alexander. He delivered twelve orations on this subject. Three of these orations were specially directed against Philip and are known as the Philippics. They are so bitter in their denunciation of Philip that to-day any speech which is very bitter and severe against a man or a party is called a "Philippic."

The most famous speech that Demosthenes ever made was in defence of himself and is known as the speech "On the Crown." He had advised the Athenians to unite with the Thebans against Philip. His advice was followed, and a victory was won. The Athenians were so much pleased that it was proposed to crown Demosthenes with a golden wreath at one of the great festivals. Now this proposal had to be voted on by the people, and some of Demosthenes' enemies objected. If the people refused to vote the crown it would have meant disgrace for Demosthenes and so he was obliged to go before the assembly to speak in defence of himself and to show that his advice to his countrymen had been correct. It was true that the Athenians had not been able to destroy Philip's power, or free the states of Greece from his control; but, said Demosthenes, "I insist that even if it had been known beforehand to all the world that Philip would succeed and that we should fail, not even then ought Athens to have taken any other course if she had any regard for her own glory or for her past or for the ages to come." By this he meant that it was the duty of her people to fight for what they believed to be right even if in the very beginning they had known that they could not succeed.

Grander words than these never fell from human

lips, and when the vote was taken the people decided that he should receive the crown.

II

When news reached Athens of the murder of Philip, Demosthenes rejoiced and placed a wreath upon his head, as if he were at a feast. He even persuaded the Athenians to make a thank-offering to their gods.

Alexander soon placed the Greek cities at his mercy. Then he demanded that Demosthenes and eight other Athenian orators should be delivered up to be punished for treason. Demosthenes told the people of Athens the story of the wolf and the sheep.

"Once on a time," he said, "the shepherds agreed with the wolf that henceforth they should be friends. The wolf promised faithfully never again to attack the sheep. But he said he thought it would be only fair that the shepherds should cease to keep dogs. The shepherds agreed and gave up their dogs. Then the wolf ate up the sheep."

The Athenians knew what Demosthenes meant, and heeded the lesson. They kept their watchdogs, Demosthenes and the other orators, safely at home.

Alexander at length withdrew his demand and treated the Athenians with kindness. However, this did not win the favor of Demosthenes, who continued to oppose the Macedonians at every step.

After some years one of Alexander's satraps stole a large treasure, fled to Athens and begged for protection. Demosthenes was unjustly accused of helping him and was condemned to pay a fine. He could not pay it and so went into exile.

When Alexander died the orator returned to Athens. The Athenians sent a man-of war to bring him to the Piraeus. The magistrates, the priests and all the citizens marched out to welcome him and escort him to the city.

Demosthenes now made a last effort to free Athens. But Macedonia was still strong, and Athens and those who loved her were weak. In a short time the demand was again made that the orators be given up to be punished and Demosthenes again had to flee for his life. He sought refuge in a temple of Poseidon on an island near the coast of Greece.

The sacredness of the temple ought to have protected him, but he was not allowed to escape. The captain of the soldiers who were sent to kill him told him that if he would come out of the temple he should be pardoned. Demosthenes knew well that this promise would be broken. He asked to be allowed a few moments in which to write a letter, and his request was granted. He wrote, and then placed the end of his writing-quill in his mouth. Those who were watching saw him grow pale. He tried to reach the door, but fell dead near the altar. He had taken poison which he had long carried in the end of his writing-quill, for he feared that if he ever fell into the hands of the Macedonians, he would die in prison, or by torture.

ARISTOTLE, ZENO, DIOGENES AND APELLES

I

While Alexander was conquering the world, there lived in Athens a man whose work survived hundreds of years after the conqueror's empire fell to pieces. Indeed, it exists to-day. This man was Aristotle, the great philosopher, at one time Alexander's tutor.

After Alexander became king Aristotle went to Athens and established a school of philosophy. His fame grew and he was called "the man of wisdom." He spent much of his time in writing, and wrote about almost everything that men thought of in his time. Some of his works are studied in our colleges to-day.

Like all other great men of Greece, Aristotle had enemies. Some of them accused him of not having respect for the gods. He, therefore, fled from Athens in order, as he said, to keep the Athenians from sinning against philosophy by banishing him. He died in exile.

It is said that for about two hundred years after his death people did not know what had become of his writings. The men to whom they were left had buried them in an underground chamber for fear the king of Pergamos, who was very proud of his library, would get hold of them. When the manuscripts were at last found they could still be read.

For hundreds of years after that Aristotle's writings were more widely studied in Europe than almost any other books.

II

Another great philosopher who lived during the time of Alexander was Zeno. He was born in Cyprus, but came to Athens in his youth.

He gave his lectures in a porch, called in Greek a Stoa, from which he and his followers are called Stoics. He taught that men should live simply, and learn to be neither fond of pleasure nor cast down by sorrow. To-day we call people *stoics* who endure pain and misfortune without complaining.

One of Zeno's rivals was a philosopher named Epicurus. He founded a school in Athens and taught there for thirty-six years. His enemies accused him of teaching that pleasure was the only thing to live for, and many people still have this idea. We call a man an "epicure" who is very fond of high living. Epicurus, however, really used the word *pleasure* to mean *peace of mind*, not the mere satisfaction of eating and drinking. Both he and his pupils lived in a very simple way.

One of the oddest of the Greek philosophers was Diogenes. He used to stand in the public places of the city and ridicule the follies of his fellow-citizens. Because of this habit he and his disciples were called *cynics*, or growlers, from a Greek word which means dog. It is said that he lived in a tub.

Many stories are told of the curious doings and sayings of Diogenes. Once in broad daylight he walked

311

through the streets of Athens carrying a lighted lantern.

"What are you about now, Diogenes?" asked one who met him.

"I am looking for a man," sneered Diogenes.

Once, when he was on a voyage, the ship in which he was sailing was captured by pirates. The passengers and crew were taken to Crete and sold as slaves. The auctioneer who was selling them asked Diogenes what he could do. "I can rule men," was the answer. "Sell me to some one who wishes a master."

When the great Council of the States of Greece honored Alexander by asking him to lead their forces against Persia, the young conqueror visited Diogenes. The philosopher was then living at Corinth, in the house of the man who had bought him as a slave. He was in the garden basking in the sun when Alexander visited him.

"Can I do anything to help you, Diogenes?" asked Alexander.

"Nothing, but get out of my sunshine," replied Diogenes.

As Alexander was leaving this man of few wants, he said, "If I were not Alexander, I should wish to be Diogenes." It was as though he had said, "If I were not going to conquer the world, I should like to have the power which Diogenes has to conquer self."

III

A number of celebrated painters lived during the reign of Alexander. The most famous was Apelles. Alexander would allow no one else to paint his portrait. Apelles had talent, but he became a great artist as much by his patient industry as by his talent. His motto was "Never a day without a line."

Once he painted a horse and exhibited it in a contest

with some of his rivals who also had painted pictures of
horses. He saw that the judges were not going to give
the prize to his picture, so he requested that all the pictures should be shown to some horses. This was done,
and the animals paid no more attention to the pictures
of Apelles' rivals than they would have paid to blank
boards, but when Apelles' horse was shown to them
they neighed as though they had seen a friend.

PTOLEMY

I

One of Alexander's favorite generals was Ptolemy. In the division of the Empire Egypt was placed in his charge. Other parts of the Empire were intrusted to other generals. One had Macedonia, another Thrace, another Syria. At first they ruled as governors for Alexander's young son, but after a while they became independent and were called kings.

Ptolemy and his descendants ruled Egypt for more than three hundred and fifty years. They were a great line of sovereigns and did much for the good of the country. We are accustomed to think of them as Egyptians, but really they were Greeks living in Egypt.

One of Ptolemy's first acts, and one which shows that he was a man of affectionate feeling, was to bring the body of Alexander from Babylon to Egypt. It was first buried in Memphis but afterward removed to Alexandria, because, as you remember, this city was founded by Alexander and named after him.

Ptolemy made Alexandria his capital and did a great

deal to beautify the city. He founded a museum and began collecting books for a library.

His son, Ptolemy Philadelphus, carried on this work and made the library the largest and best in the world. Most of the books were made of the pith of the papyrus or paper plant, of which you have read in the story of Pisistratus. They were written in Greek and Latin.

Ptolemy appreciated the intelligence and learning of the Jews and treated them with so much kindness and gave them so many liberties that great numbers of them settled in Egypt.

Two things that Ptolemy Philadelphus did are especially worth remembering. One was to cause the Bible of the Jews to be translated into Greek; the other was to open again a great canal which had been dug many centuries before from the Nile to the Red Sea, but had long been filled up by the drifting sand of the desert. This was something like the cutting of the Suez Canal.

Ptolemy's canal connected the Atlantic with the Indian Ocean. Ships could sail from the Atlantic across the Mediterranean, then through the canal and the Red Sea, and on to India.

At that time Egypt raised more wheat than any other country in the world, so she had a great commerce. In exchange for her wheat she bought the products of Europe and Asia, and Alexandria became the richest city of the world.

But, more than that, the Ptolemies, especially Philadelphus, invited learned men to their court and gave them support so that they might carry on their own studies and teach others.

At one time there were 14,000 students receiving instruction in the city. Thus Alexandria became the home of learning. It was there that pupils were first taught that the earth is round, and one of the great astronomers who lived there found out very nearly the length of the earth's circumference and diameter.

The people of Alexandria knew more about these things two hundred years before Christ than the people of Europe did a thousand years after. The science of today about which you hear so much is only the continuation of what was begun by the wonderful Greeks whom the Ptolemies gathered about them in Alexandria.

One of the Ptolemy line was the celebrated Cleopatra, an able ruler and the most fascinating woman of her time. You will read something of her history in "*Famous Men of Rome*," a companion volume to this book.

PYRRHUS

I

A prince named Pyrrhus lived in the state of Epirus not far from the home of the great Achilles. At twelve years of age he became king, but the government was carried on for him by guardians.

About that time he read the story of Alexander the Great, and determined to be like him, a great conqueror. While he was dreaming of victories in foreign lands war came to him in his own country, and he was driven from Epirus. Ptolemy of Egypt helped him to defeat his enemies and regain his throne. Then he resolved anew to conquer as Alexander had conquered, and he began with Alexander's own Macedonia. After a war that lasted several years he got possession of one-half the country. One of Alexander's generals took the other half. However, the people in Pyrrhus' half preferred the old general as a ruler, and in seven months Pyrrhus had to give up his Macedonian kingdom.

He reigned quietly in Epirus for a few years. Then a chance came to try and conquer the Romans who lived just across the Adriatic Sea. Pyrrhus was delighted. Ruling Epirus was a dull business. In the south of Italy a great many Greeks had settled. Greek was the language of the people who lived there and the region was called "Great Greece."

Rome wished to rule all Italy, but those Greeks were not willing to be under Roman rule; so they sent word to Pyrrhus that they were in trouble and would like him to help them.

Preparations for war were at once made and as soon as possible Pyrrhus landed on the shores of Italy with an army of about 30,000 men and twenty elephants.

A great battle was fought, and Pyrrhus won the victory, but the loss of life was dreadful. As he walked among the dead after the battle he said, "Another such victory and I shall have to go home alone." Half his men were slain.

However, the Greeks of South Italy furnished him with fresh soldiers and he gained a second victory.

The war came to an end in a very curious way. One of the servants of Pyrrhus deserted to the Romans and offered to poison his master for the consuls. The consuls sent back the deserter to Pyrrhus under guard and with a message that they scorned to gain a victory through treason.

Pyrrhus, to show his gratitude, then sent back to Rome all the prisoners whom he held, without asking any ransom. This made the enemies friends, and a truce was concluded. It was one of the terms of the truce that Pyrrhus should leave Italy.

A large number of Greeks lived in Sicily. They had built Syracuse and other large cities and towns. At that time Carthage in Africa was a powerful city and the Carthaginians were trying to conquer the Sicilian

Greeks. Pyrrhus crossed to Sicily to help his countrymen.

But his Italian friends got into trouble with the Romans again and begged him once more to help them. Accordingly he left Sicily and went back to Italy. Now, however, his good fortune forsook him. He was totally defeated by the Romans under Curius Dentatus and forced to leave Italy.

He now returned to Epirus, but as he was no lover of peace he soon went to war a second time with Macedonia. Again he conquered the land of Alexander, but again the king of Macedonia regained the kingdom.

Not content to rule Epirus, Pyrrhus next went into the Peloponnesus and fought against the Spartans, but they drove him from their territory.

Finally he went to Argos and took part in a civil war which was going on in that state.

A fight took place in one of the streets of Argos, and during it a woman threw a tile from the roof of her house. It struck Pyrrhus upon the head and stunned him, and some of the soldiers of the party against whom he was fighting ran up and killed him. (287 B.C.)

II

Sicily, about whose struggle with the Carthaginians you have just read, was the home of a famous mathematician named Archimedes. He was born at Syracuse in 287 B.C., and was only a boy when Pyrrhus was in Sicily helping the Carthaginians fight the Sicilians. Many years later Syracuse was besieged by another enemy, the Romans. Archimedes, then an old man, proved of great help to his countrymen. He invented engines for throwing stones at the enemy. By using these engines the Sicilians kept the Romans at bay for a long time.

It is said that Archimedes set fire to the Roman ships with powerful burning-glasses. At last, however, Syracuse fell, and Archimedes was put to death by a Roman soldier, contrary to the order of the Roman commander.

CLEOMENES III

I

About a hundred years after the death of Alexander the Great lived a young prince named Cleomenes. His father was one of the kings of Sparta and bore the name of one of the greatest of Greek heroes, Leonidas, the famous defender of Thermopylae. One day, when the prince was about eighteen years old, he started from home to go hunting. He had not gone far from the city gate when one of his father's slaves overtook him and handed to him a writing tablet. On its waxed surface Cleomenes read the words, "Leonidas the king to Cleomenes: Come back to the palace the moment you have read this note." Cleomemes turned and went back toward the city.

Late in the afternoon he reached the palace. The gateway was hung with a garland of flowers, and entering he found the women busily arranging roses and lilies in every room.

As soon as he saw his father, he asked, "Is anyone going to be married?"

"You are," replied his father. "This evening I wish you to marry Agiatis, the widow of King Agis. I am having the palace decorated for the wedding. She is beautiful and good and the heiress of one of the richest men in Sparta."

"But," said Cleomenes, "how can she ever be willing to marry your son?"

"I am the king," replied Leonidas, "and she is bound to obey me."

"Since you wish it, I will marry her," said Cleomenes, "but I never can hope that she will love me."

Cleomenes had good reason for saying this; for Leonidas had caused his fellow-king, Agis, the husband of Agiatis, to be murdered.

Agis had been one of the best and greatest of Sparta's kings. He had been distressed at the state of his country when he came to the throne. The old customs of Lycurgus had been set aside. Since the close of the Peloponnesian War, when Sparta had proved more than a match for Athens, a great change had come over the kingdom. Her men were no longer warriors. The hope of Agis was that he might persuade the people to live according to the old laws which no one now obeyed.

But Leonidas, his fellow-king, did not wish to return to the old ways of living, and the five ephors, or magistrates of Sparta, were friends of his. They determined to put Agis to death. The ephors seized him upon the street and carried him to prison, and—for no other reason than that he had tried to carry out the laws of Lycurgus and restore the glory of Sparta—he was put to death.

This had been done at the order of Leonidas. Cleomenes therefore had reason to think that Agiatis never would marry him. However, the marriage took place as Leonidas wished, and although Agiatis hated Leonidas, who had murdered her husband, she soon learned to love Cleomenes, who was manly and true, and who devoted his life to making her happy.

She talked to him of Agis and what he had wished to do for Sparta. As Cleomenes listened he made up his mind to do just what Agis had wished to do. He saw that luxurious ways of living had weakened Sparta and destroyed her influence. And he saw also that his father's friends were not the few good and brave men still left in Sparta, but rich men who cared for nothing but money and pleasure.

II

Leonidas died a few years after the murder of Agis, and then Cleomenes became king.

At this time a great general named Aratus was at the head of a league of Greek cities called the Achæan League. It seemed likely that it would soon control all the Peloponnesus. Cleomenes therefore persuaded the Spartans to go to war against the Achæans.

In several battles he defeated Aratus and won for himself great fame as a soldier. This made the Spartans very fond of him, and he thought that the time had arrived when he might persuade them to obey once more the old laws and customs.

But the ephors were opposed to the changes which he wished to make, and so he boldly put them to death.

Next day he banished eighty citizens who were opposed to his plans. He then explained to the people why he had done this and why he had put the ephors to death.

"If without bloodshed," he said, "I could have driven from Sparta luxury and extravagance, debts and usury —the riches of the few and the poverty of the many—I should have thought myself the happiest of kings."

He declared that the laws of Lycurgus must be enforced and the land be again divided among the citizens.

The people were delighted when they heard all this, and much more were they pleased when Cleomenes and his father-in-law were the first to give up their lands for division. The rest of the citizens did the same, and so, six hundred years after Lycurgus, there was a new division of property, and once more every Spartan had land enough to raise wheat and oil and wine for his family for a year.

Again the citizens dined at public tables on simple Spartan fare, and the youths were trained and drilled as Lycurgus had ordered. The Pyrrhic Dance, which trained soldiers in quick movements, was revived. Again the army was well disciplined, and the soldiers of Sparta became, as long ago, the best among the Greeks. The king himself set his people an example of simple living.

Some of the Greeks had laughed when Cleomenes said he would tread in the steps of Lycurgus and Solon; but when they saw Sparta victorious on the battlefield and the city prosperous and happy once more they could not help admiring the man who had brought the change about.

But in time a dreadful disaster befell Cleomenes and Sparta. The Achæan League invited the Macedonian king Antigonus to bring an army to help them against Cleomenes, and in a single battle the Spartans lost almost everything that they had gained.

The other king, who was Cleomenes' own brother, was killed, and out of six thousand men whom he commanded only two hundred survived.

Cleomenes made his way to Sparta and advised the citizens to submit to the Macedonians, which they did, and the independence of Sparta was gone forever.

Cleomenes had hopes of getting help from Ptolemy, king of Egypt. So he sailed to that country, and he was promised assistance. But, unfortunately, Ptolemy died, and the next king made Cleomenes a prisoner because an enemy of the great Spartan had said that he was plotting against the Egyptian king. Cleomenes saw no way of escape and so put an end to his life.

He was one of the greatest men of the last days of Greece.

THE FALL OF GREECE

The states of Greece tried again and again to throw off the Macedonian yoke. Unfortunately, however, they often quarreled with one another and were not united against Macedonia. For this reason the kings of that state kept their place as masters of Greece for another hundred years.

Then the Romans invaded the country, and in a battle fought near a town called Pydna the Macedonians were defeated and their king Perseus was taken prisoner. This brought the Macedonian kingdom to an end. Macedonia was made part of the Roman Empire and men were sent from Rome to rule it.

Epirus was next captured. A hundred and fifty thousand of its inhabitants were sold into slavery and the state was made a Roman province.

After the fall of Macedonia the other states of Greece still continued fighting with one another. So in about twenty years (B.C. 146) a Roman army was sent against them. A battle was fought near Corinth in which the Greeks were completely defeated.

Corinth at that time was one of the richest and most

beautiful cities in the world. After the battle the Roman general let his soldiers enter the houses and take what they pleased. Pictures, marble statues and jewelry were taken and shipped to Rome. It is said that two of the rough Roman soldiers played a game of dice on one of the finest pictures,—so little did they value works of art.

Two thousand of the men of Corinth were put to death by the Romans, and the women and children were made slaves. After the buildings of the city had been plundered they were set on fire.

And now Athens, Thebes, Sparta and the other Greek states became, like Macedonia, parts of the Empire of Rome.

From the rule of Rome Greece passed, in the Middle Ages, under the rule of Turkey, and it was only about seventy-five years ago that she revolted from Turkey and became once more an independent country.

If ever you go to Greece, as thousands of people do, to visit the places where her great men lived, you will see little but ruins. The columns of the temples are broken, the stones of their walls lie scattered on the ground.

And yet Greece, even amid ruin and decay, is still teaching the world. Many of the words that stand for branches of learning in our language to-day are Greek words. Such words are *arithmetic* and *mathematics*. They show plainly that the first teachers of mathematics in Europe were Greeks. *Gymnasium* and *athletics* are also Greek words. They show that the Greeks set us the example of running races, wrestling, jumping, throwing quoits and doing other such things to make our bodies strong. *Poet*, too, and *poem* are Greek, and remind us that the Greeks taught us how to write poetry. *Grammar*, *rhetoric* and *geography* are Greek words. So are *logic*, *astronomy* and *surgery*. These and hundreds of other words in daily use show how much we have inherited from the Greeks.

Although the old-time glory of Greece has waned,

the light of art and science which she kindled in the
world grows brighter as time rolls on.

The Babylonian Story of the Deluge
And
the Epic of Gilgamish

by

Ernest Alfred Thompson Wallis Budge

Reviewed, corrected, layout, foreword, designed
and covered by

J. O. P

A
X
EDITORIAL